Lecture Notes in Computer Science   12864

More information about this subseries at http://www.springer.com/series/7407

Alfons Laarman · Ana Sokolova (Eds.)

Model Checking Software

27th International Symposium, SPIN 2021
Virtual Event, July 12, 2021
Proceedings

 Springer

Editors
Alfons Laarman (ID)
Leiden University
Leiden, The Netherlands

Ana Sokolova (ID)
University of Salzburg
Salzburg, Austria

ISSN 0302-9743   ISSN 1611-3349 (electronic)
Lecture Notes in Computer Science
ISBN 978-3-030-84628-2   ISBN 978-3-030-84629-9 (eBook)
https://doi.org/10.1007/978-3-030-84629-9

LNCS Sublibrary: SL1 – Theoretical Computer Science and General Issues

This Springer imprint is published by the registered company Springer Nature Switzerland AG
The registered company address is: Gewerbestrasse 11, 6330 Cham, Switzerland

Preface

This volume contains the proceedings of the 27th International Symposium on Model Checking Software, SPIN 2021, held online from Leiden, the Netherlands, on July 12, 2021, with a record number of upwards of 250 registered participants. SPIN is a well-recognized periodic event started in 1995 around the model checking tool SPIN. Since 1995, the event has evolved and has been consolidated as a reference symposium in the area of formal methods related to model checking. The previous edition of the SPIN symposium took place in Beijing (China).

The SPIN 2021 edition requested regular papers, short papers, and tool demos in the following areas: Formal verification techniques for automated analysis of software; Formal analysis for modeling languages, such as UML/state charts; Formal specification languages, temporal logic, design-by-contract; Model checking; Automated theorem proving, including SAT and SMT; Verifying compilers; Abstraction and symbolic execution techniques; Static analysis and abstract interpretation; Combination of verification techniques; Modular and compositional verification techniques; Verification of timed and probabilistic systems; Automated testing using advanced analysis techniques; Combination of static and dynamic analyses; Derivation of specifications, test cases, or other useful material via formal analysis; Case studies of interesting systems or with interesting results; Engineering and implementation of software verification and analysis tools; Benchmark and comparative studies for formal verification and analysis tools; Formal methods of education and training; Insightful surveys or historical accounts on topics of relevance to the symposium; Relevant tools and algorithms for modern hardware, e.g. parallel, GPU, TPU, FPGA, cloud, and quantum.

The symposium attracted 20 submissions that were rigorously reviewed by three Program Committee (PC) members. The selection process included further online discussion open to all PC members. As a result, eight papers were selected for presentation at the symposium and publication in Springer's proceedings. The program consisted of eight regular papers and three invited talks. Two of the invited speakers submitted an invited paper on the topic of their talk.

We would like to thank all the authors who submitted papers, the Steering Committee, the PC, the additional reviewers, the invited speakers, the participants, and the organizers of the cohosted events for making SPIN 2021 a successful event. We also thank all the sponsors that provided online facilities and financial support to make the symposium possible.

June 2021

Alfons Laarman
Ana Sokolova

Organization

General Chairs

Alfons Laarman   Leiden University, The Netherlands
Ana Sokolova   University of Salzburg, Austria

Steering Committee

Dragan Bošnački (Chair)   Eindhoven University of Technology, The Netherlands
Susanne Graf   Verimag, France
Gerard Holzmann   Nimble Research, USA
Stefan Leue   University of Konstanz, Germany
Neha Rungta   Amazon Web Services, USA
Jaco van de Pol   Aarhus University, Denmark
Willem Visser   Stellenbosch University, South Africa

Program Committee

Jiří Barnat   Masaryk University, Czech Republic
Maurice H. ter Beek   ISTI-CNR, Italy
Tom van Dijk   University of Twente, The Netherlands
Vedran Dunjko   Leiden University, The Netherlands
Stefan Edelkamp   University of Koblenz, Germany
Grigory Fedyukovich   Florida State University, USA
Henri Hansen   Tampere University of Technology, Finland
Arnd Hartmanns   University of Twente, The Netherlands
Gerard Holzmann   Nimble Research, USA
Antti Hyvärinen   Università della Svizzera italiana, Italy
Nils Jansen   Radboud University Nijmegen, The Netherlands
Peter Gjøl Jensen   Aalborg University, Denmark
Sung-Shik Jongmans   Open University of the Netherlands and CWI, The Netherlands
Jeroen Keiren   Eindhoven University of Technology, The Netherlands
Igor Konnov   Inria, France
Alberto Lluch Lafuente   Technical University of Denmark, Denmark
Kuldeep S. Meel   National University of Singapore, Singapore
Alice Miller   University of Glasgow, UK
Sergio Mover   École Polytechnique, France
Rajagopal Nagarajan   Middlesex University, UK
Doron Peled   Bar Ilan University, Israel
Tatjana Petrov   University of Konstanz, Germany

Jaco van de Pol	Aarhus University, Denmark
Stephen F. Siegel	University of Delaware, USA
Carsten Sinz	Karlsruhe Institute of Technology, Germany
Jiří Srba	Aalborg University, Denmark
Michael Tautschnig	Amazon Web Services, USA
Yann Thierry-Mieg	Sorbonne University, France
Yakir Vizel	Technion, Israel
Georg Weissenbacher	Vienna University of Technology, Austria
Anton Wijs	Eindhoven University of Technology, The Netherlands

Additional Reviewers

Frederik M. Bønneland
Morten Konggaard Schou
Sebastian Junges
Bram Kohlen

Contents

Case Studies

Invited Talks

The Marriage Between Safety and Cybersecurity: Still Practicing

Marielle Stoelinga[1,2]([✉]) [iD], Christina Kolb[1], Stefano M. Nicoletti[1] [iD],
Carlos E. Budde[3] [iD], and Ernst Moritz Hahn[1] [iD]

[1] Formal Methods and Tools, University of Twente, Enschede, The Netherlands
{m.i.a.stoelinga,c.kolb,s.m.nicoletti,c.e.budde,e.m.hahn}@utwente.nl
[2] Department of Software Science, Radboud University, Nijmegen, The Netherlands
[3] Department of Information Engineering and Computer Science,
University of Trento, Trento, Italy
carlosesteban.budde@unitn.it

Abstract. Emerging technologies, like self-driving cars, drones, and the Internet-of-Things must not impose threats to people, neither due to accidental failures (safety), nor due to malicious attacks (security). As historically separated fields, safety and security are often analyzed in isolation. They are, however, heavily intertwined: measures that increase safety often decrease security and vice versa. Also, security vulnerabilities often cause safety hazards, e.g. in autonomous cars. Therefore, for effective decision-making, safety and security must be considered in combination.

This paper discusses three major challenges that a successful integration of safety and security faces: (1) The complex interaction between safety and security (2) The lack of efficient algorithms to compute system-level risk metrics (3) The lack of proper risk quantification methods. We will point out several research directions to tackle these challenges, exploiting novel combinations of mathematical game theory, stochastic model checking, as well as the Bayesian, fuzzy, and Dempster-Schafer frameworks for uncertainty reasoning. Finally, we report on early results in these directions.

Keywords: Safety · Security · Model-based · Interaction · Fault trees · Attack trees · Fault tree-attack tree integration

1 Introduction

New technology comes with new risks: drones may drop on to people, self-driving cars may get hacked, medical implants may leak in people's body. Such risks concern both accidental failures (safety) and malicious attacks (security). Here, *security* refers to the property that allows the system to perform its mission or critical functions despite risks posed by threats [25]. *Safety*, in contrast, is the absence of risk of harm due to malfunctioning behavior of technological systems [32].

This work was partially funded by ERC Consolidator Grant 864075 (*CAESAR*).

A. Laarman and A. Sokolova (Eds.): SPIN 2021, LNCS 12864, pp. 3–21, 2021.
https://doi.org/10.1007/978-3-030-84629-9_1

Safety and security are heavily intertwined. Measures that increase safety may decrease security and vice versa: the Internet-of-Things offers ample opportunities to monitor the safety of a power plant, but their many access points are notorious for enabling hackers to enter the system. Passwords secure patients' medical data, but are a hindrance during emergencies. It is therefore widely acknowledged, also by international risk standards [21,39], that safety and security must be analyzed in combination [3,36]. The overarching challenge in safety and security risk management is decision making: which risks are most threatening, and which countermeasures are most (cost-)effective? Such decisions are notoriously hard to take: it is well-known (e.g. from Nobel prize winner Daniel Kahneman [24]) that people, have very poor intuitions for risks and probability.

> **Vision.** To make effective decisions, *risk management should be accountable.*
> 1. *systematic*, so that no risks are overlooked;
> 2. *transparent*, so that experts can share and discuss their viewpoints;
> 3. *objective*, i.e. based on recorded facts and figures, rather than on (fallible) intuitions.

Hurdles. Tough hurdles that have hindered the effective integration of safety and security [1,32] are their opposite perspectives on:

H1. *User intention:* safety concerns unintended mishaps, while security is about malicious attacks.
H2. *Dynamics:* Whereas safety analysis is often static, developing design-time solutions; security demands constant defence against new vulnerabilities.
H3. Risk *quantification:* Whereas safety analysis can fruitfully exploit historic failure data, risk quantification for security is a major open problem. With hackers continuously changing their targets and strategies, historic data is of little value. Therefore, security decisions are often based on subjective estimates.

The demanding challenge in safety-security co-analysis is to overarch these diametrical viewpoints.

Challenges. To overcome these hurdles above and make decision making about safety and security less ad hoc, and more systematic, transparent, and quantitative, three challenges have to be solved.

– A systematic way to map safety and security risks, identifying how failures and vulnerabilities propagate through the system and lead to system level disruptions.
– Effective algorithms to compute system level risk safety and security metrics, together with diagnostic algorithms that explain how such metrics arise, and how one could improve these.
– Novel risk quantification methods. Reliable numbers are indispensable in decision making. Since objective data is often not available, we need algorithms that reason under uncertainty.

The ERC project CAESAR. The ERC-funded project CAESAR picks up the challenges above, exploring three novel directions:

1. *Game-theoretic methods* uniting the cooperative versus malicious user intention in safety versus security (H1). Our aim is to model the attacker versus defender as two players in a stochastic game. We will focus on a time dependent game (H2) that faithfully models the complex interaction between safety and security aspects.
2. *Stochastic model checking techniques* to compute safety-security risk metrics. Metrics are pivotal to prioritize risks and select effective countermeasures, as they clarify how failures and attacks affect system-level performance. Since risk is defined as a combination of likelihood and severity, metrics are stochastic by nature. Apart from computing numbers, we will also elucidate how these numbers arise.
3. *Risk quantification methods that handle data uncertainty.* Effective decision making requires insight in the most frequent failures and attacks. Since objective data is scarce, security decisions are often based on subjective estimates. We will combine objective and subjective probabilities, exploiting three prominent frameworks for data uncertainty: Bayesian reasoning, fuzzy logic and Dempster-Schafer theory. These explicate the underlying assumptions and (dis)agreements about risks.

Contributions. This paper outlines the first results and the approach taken in CAESAR: we present findings of a literature survey, where we compare existing formalisms for safety-security co-analysis and identify several gaps. An important outcome of our survey is that most of these formalisms are based on various combinations of the popular formalisms of attack trees for security analysis and fault trees for safety analysis. One important instance of a research gap is that in fault trees and attack trees OR-gates are interpreted in a different manner. This difference in interpretation is not considered in current analysis algorithms. To obtain a unified framework for safety and security building on these mechanisms, we thus have to unify the interpretation of such gates. Afterwards, we outline how CAESAR aims to solve such gaps. We discuss how recent results in attack tree analysis provides results for tree-shaped attack trees and fault trees as well as a formal semantics of DAG-shaped attack trees and fault trees. In these results, we exploit methods based on binary decision diagrams. Throughout the paper, we indicate current results as well a research gaps.

Organization of the Paper. Section 1 has provided an introduction to this paper. Section 2 provides some background on the interaction between safety and security and on the two formalisms attack trees and fault trees. Section 3 presents an overview of formalisms of safety-security co-analysis. Section 4 provides a comparison between attack trees and fault trees, highlighting similarities and differences and defining metrics. Section 5 discusses analysis algorithms for attack and fault trees. Section 6 concludes the paper.

2   Background

Attack Trees and Fault Trees. Attack trees and fault trees are popular models in dependability analysis, representing respectively how low-level attacks and failures propagate through the system and lead to system-level disruptions. As shown in Fig. 1, these are tree-like structures that culminate in a top level event (TLE), which models a system-level failure or attack. The TLE is thus refined via intermediate events, equipped with gates: the AND-gate indicates that all children must fail (be attacked) in order for the gate to fail (be attacked). For the OR-gate to fail (be attacked), at least one of its children need to fail (be attacked). The leaves in a FT are called *basic events (BEs)* and model atomic failures; the leaves in ATs model atomic attack steps, called *basic attack steps (BASs)*. Despite their names, FTs and ATs are directed acyclic graphs, since intermediate events can share children.

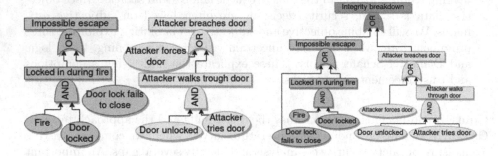

Fig. 1. Fault tree (left), attack tree (center) and their combination (right). These represent respectively safety, security, and combined risks. In the FT, for the intermediate event "locked in during fire" to happen, both a fire and the door being locked have to occur, modelled through an AND-gate. In the AT, for an attacker to breach the front door he/she needs to either walk through an unlocked door or to force a locked door, modeled as an OR. On the right, a possible combination of ATs and FTs in the attack fault trees formalism [46].

FTs and ATs enable numerous analysis methods [28]: *Cut set analysis* indicates which combinations of BEs or BASs lead to the TLE. The set {Fire, Locked} is a cut set in Fig. 1. Quantitative analyses compute *dependability metrics*, such as the system reliability, attack probabilities and costs. For example, by equipping the BEs and BASs with probabilities, one can compute the likelihood of a system level failure or attack to occur.

Both FTs and ATs are part of international standards [14] and have been used to analyse numerous case studies [11,19,48]. FTs and ATs also feature some differences: FTs often focus on probabilities, whereas ATs consider several other attributes, like cost, effort and required skills. Further, FTs have been extended with repairs [44], and dynamic gates [17,22]; ATs with defenses, and sequential AND (SAND) gates [19,27].

Section 4 presents a more formal treatment of fault trees and attack trees, and in particular their different quantitative interpretation of the OR-gate. Their comparison is summarized in Table 3.

Safety-Security Dependencies. One of the key challenges in safety-security co-analysis is to model their interaction. The paper [32] has identified four safety-security dependencies:

- *Conditional dependency* means that fulfillment of safety requirements conditions security or vice-versa.
- *Mutual reinforcement* means that fulfillment of safety requirements or safety measures contributes to security, or vice-versa, thereby enabling resource optimization and cost reduction.
- *Antagonism* arises when safety and security requirements or measures, considered jointly, lead to conflicting situations.
- *Independency* means that there is no interaction between safety and security properties.

Figure 1 shows a classical example of antagonism: the door needs to be locked in order to prevent an attacker from entering the house (security requirement), but it has to be unlocked to allow the owner to escape during a fire (safety requirement). In this scenario, mutual reinforcement can be achieved by introducing a fire door: this contributes to safety by limiting the spread of an eventual fire and to security by increasing the robustness of the door, thus making it harder to breach. Conditional dependency is, in our view, always present: for the lock to ensure security, it must function properly. E.g., it must not break when locking door. Similarly, safety solutions must be secure and not be hacked: it must not be possible to easily force the door open.

3 Formalisms for Safety-Security Co-analysis: An Overview

3.1 The Formalisms

As a first step in the CAESAR project, we carried out a literature survey [26], comparing the most prominent formalisms for safety-security co-analysis. Via a systematic literature search [8], which also considered earlier surveys on this topic [12,32,38], we have identified 10 important formalisms for model-based safety-security co-analysis. These are summarized in Table 1.

A first remarkable result of our survey is that the majority of safety-security formalisms combines attack trees (ATs) and fault trees (FTs). ATs and FTs are well established formalisms, extensively used in industry and academia. As previously mentioned, they are similar nature, and model respectively how failures and attacks propagate through a system. In that sense, combining attack trees and fault trees is a natural step. We further divided these approaches into two categories (plain combinations and extended combinations). A third category comprises architectural formalisms.

Table 1. Overview of safety-security formalisms. Citations from Google Scholar, April 2021.

Formalism	Ref.	Year	#Citations
Fault Tree/Attack Tree Integration (FT/AT)	[18]	2009	170
Component Fault Trees (CFTs)	[46]	2013	52
Attack-Fault Trees (AFTs)	[33]	2017	56
State/Event Fault Trees (SEFTs)	[42]	2013	25
Boolean Driven Markov Processes (BDMPs)	[31]	2014	36
Attack Tree Bow-ties (ATBTs)	[5]	2017	9
STAMP	[20]	2017	120
SysML	[40]	2011	72
Architectural Analysis and Design Language (AADL)	[16]	2020	0
Bayesian Networks (BNs)	[30]	2015	46

1. Plain combinations of attack trees and fault trees. These formalisms combine attack trees and fault trees without adding additional constructs: fault tree/attack trees (FT/AT) [18], which investigate how the a basic event of a FT can be triggered by an attacker, refining these with ATs with the event in question as goal, component fault trees (CFTs) [46] merge attack trees and fault trees without any restrictions, Attack-Fault Trees (AFTs) [33] merge dynamic attack trees and dynamic fault trees.

2. Extensions of attack trees-fault tree combinations. These merge attack trees, fault trees with additional constructs: State/Event Fault Trees (SEFTs) [42] exploit Petri nets to refine the basic attack steps in an attack tree and the basic component failures in a fault tree. The Petri nets can for instance model that the attack and failure behavior is different depending whether a door is open or closed. Boolean Driven Markov Processes (BDMPs) [31] extend attack trees and fault trees with both Petri nets and triggers. The latter model sequential behaviour, where one fault or attack triggers another one. Finally, Attack Tree Bow-ties (ATBTs) [5], extend bowties [37] with attack trees, where bowties themselves combine fault trees with event trees.

3. Architectural formalisms and bayesian networks. Apart from combinations of attack trees and fault trees, we identified a third category, containing formalisms that take as a starting point the system architecture: The Systems-Theoretic Accident Model and Processes (STAMP) [20], is an accident causality model, rooted in the observation that system risks do not come from component failures, but rather from inadequate control or enforcement of safety and security constraints. Systems-Theoretic Process Analysis then systematically identifies the consequences of incorrect control and feedback actions, e.g., when these happen too early, in the wrong order, or were maliciously inserted.

SysML-sec [43] extend the SysML modeling framework with safety and security requirements, which can be checked using model checkers. In particular, SysML-sec supports the modelling of communication channels between processes with the encryption methods and their complexity overhead.

The Architectural Analysis and Design Language (AADL) [16] enables safety analysis, via the AADL error model, and security analysis via the AADL LAMP extension. In this way the same AADL model can be separately analyzed to investigate safety and security properties.

Finally, albeit somewhat artificially, we also put Bayesian Networks (BNs) for safety-security analysis in this category [30]. This model allows to represent probabilistic dependencies between several variables via a directed acyclic graph. BNs are used to model safety and security dependencies. The two root nodes represent system safety and security. BNs can analyze which nodes influence other nodes and how (conditional independence analysis) calculate reliability metrics.

3.2 Findings

The analysis we performed highlighted some notable findings, summarized in Table 2. For each analyzed formalism we highlight the dependencies it captures, its modeling constructs, the analysis types it enables, case studies that were performed deploying this formalism and possible tools.

Table 2. Comparison of safety-security formalisms. A = Antagonism, CD = Conditional Dependency, MR = Mutual reinforcement, I = Independence. * = capable when NOT-gate is supported. → = capable but only directional from security to safety.

Formalism	Dependencies				Modelling	Analysis		Application	Tool
	A	CD	MR	I		QL	QT		
FT/AT	*	→		x	ATs refine FT leaves	x	x	Chemical plant	
CFTs	*	x	x	x	Merge ATs+FTs	x	x	Cruise control	
AFTs	x	x	x	x	Merge dynamic ATs+FTs	x	x	Pipeline, lock door	UPPAAL
SEFTs	x	→	x	x	FTs+Petri nets	x	x	Tyre pressure, lock door	ESSaRel
BDMPs	x	x	x	x	Triggers, Petri nets	x	x	Pipeline, lock door	KB3, Figaro
ATBTs	*	→		x	Bowties+FT/AT	x	x	Pipeline, Stuxnet	
STAMP			x		Process controller	x		Synchronous-islanding	
SysML					System components	x		Embedded systems	TTool
AADL			x		System components + ports	x		Lock door	Cheddar, Marzhin
BNs	x	x	x	x	Conditional prob	x	x	Pipeline	MSBNx

Finding #1: The majority of approaches combine attack trees and fault trees. As stated, six out of the ten formalisms combine attack trees and fault trees. This is not surprising, since FTs and ATs are well established model-based formalisms, extensively used both in industry and academia.

Finding #2: No novel modeling constructs are introduced. Despite the shown combinations and extensions, existing safety-security co-analysis do not introduce novel modeling constructs to capture safety-security interactions. They do merge existing safety and security formalisms, however they do not add new operators. As such, they are suited to represent safety and security features in one model, but do not seem to appropriately capture the interaction between them.

Finding #3: Safety-security interactions are still ill-understood. In spite of the definitions provided in [32], we are convinced that safety-security interactions can still be defined more thoroughly by adopting more rigour and by focusing on requirements and events. In particular, it is not so clear to which entities the safety-security interactions refer: do these concern safety-security requirements, measures, or something else? Clarifying their definitions is a prerequisite for properly modeling safety-security interactions in a mathematical formalism.

Finding #4: No novel metrics were proposed. Analyzed formalisms adopt classic metrics, such as mean time to failure and attacker success probabilities. However, none of them introduce new metrics to quantify safety-security dependencies or to analyze trade-offs, e.g., through Pareto analysis. New metrics and trade offs are paramount to understand the interaction between safety and security aspects.

Finding #5: No large case studies were carried out. To the best of our knowledge, no large case studies were carried out. The majority of analyzed papers present small examples used to showcase the formalism in question. Some notable exceptions are [31] and [33]: here, the medium-sized example of a pipeline is presented. However for safety and security, when considered separately, large case studies do exist [7].

Finding #6: Different formalisms model different safety-security interactions. As shown in Table 2, only AFTs, BDMPs and BNs can unconditionally model all four dependencies between safety and security. CFTs and SEFTs can model them provided with extensions/with some limitations.

> **Research gaps.**
> - Realistic *large-sized case studies* concerning safety-security interactions are still missing. Performing large-sized case study analysis would contribute to further address additional gaps:
> - It would clarify the nature of *safety-security interactions*, that are currently still ill-understood. Furthermore, it would help improve standard definitions for safety-security interdependencies;
> - From this understanding, *novel metrics* and *novel modeling constructs* for safety-security co-analysis - that are still missing - could be developed.

4 Attack Trees Versus Fault Trees

We saw that most safety-security formalisms combine attack trees and fault trees. This is a natural step, since attack trees and fault trees bear many similarities. What is less known, is that they also feature a number of remarkable differences, elaborated in [10]. In particular, the interpretation of the OR-gate is crucially different in attack trees than in fault trees, and therefore their analysis should not be mindlessly combined. Below, we present the most remarkable similarities and differences, summarized in Table 3.

Table 3. Differences between attack and fault trees

Syntax	Attack trees	Fault trees
Leaves	Basic attack steps (BAS)	Basic events (BEs)
Non-leaves	Subgoals	Intermediate events (IEs)
Static gates	AND, OR	AND, OR, VOT
Dynamic gates	SAND	SPARE, FDEP, PAND
Other extensions	Defenses	Repairs, maintenance
Analysis		
Qualitative	(Minimal) attack vectors/scenarios	(Minimal) cut sets
Attributes	probability, cost, time, skill, impact	probability
Metrics	Min cost, time, skill	Reliability, availability,
	Max impact, probability	MTTF, MTBF
Semantics		
Qualitative	Structure function	Structure function
Stochastic		
AND(a,b)	$p_a \cdot p_b$	$p_a \cdot p_b$
OR(a,b)	$\min(p_a, p_a)$	$p_a + p_b - p_a \cdot p_b$

4.1 Attack Trees Versus Fault Trees

It is no surprise that ATs and FTs are similar to each other, since ATs were inspired by FTs. FTs were introduced in 1961 at Bell Labs to study a ballistic missile [13,45,47]. Weiss introduced threat logic trees—the origin of ATs—in 1991, and its "similarity... to fault trees suggests that graph-based security modelling has its roots in safety modelling" [28].

Attack trees and fault trees come in various variants and extensions. Following [9], we categorize these along two axes. First, we distinguish between *static* and *dynamic* trees. Static attack and fault trees are equipped with Boolean gates. Dynamic trees come with additional gates to model time-dependent behavior.

Second, we distinguish between *tree-shaped* and *DAG-shaped* trees. Trees are relatively easy to analyse via a bottom up algorithm. This algorithms works for all quantitative attributes (cost, time, probability) as long as they constitute an attribute domain.

4.2 The Static Case

Syntax. The basic variants, called *static* or *standard* fault and attack trees, have the exact same syntax: trees or DAGs equipped with AND and OR gates. Fault trees often contain a (k, m) voting gate, which fails if k out of the n inputs fail; these can however be expressed in terms of AND and OR gates. We use the word *disruption tree* (DT) for either an attack tree or a fault tree.

Formally, DTs are rooted DAGs with typed nodes, for which we consider types $\mathbb{T} = \{\texttt{LEAF}, \texttt{OR}, \texttt{AND}\}$. For Booleans we use $\mathbb{B} = \{\texttt{1}, \texttt{0}\}$. The edges of a DT are given by a function ch that assigns to each node its (possibly empty) sequence of children. We use set notation for sequences, e.g. $e \in (e_1, \ldots, e_m)$ means $\exists i.\, e_i = e$, and we denote the empty sequence by ε.

Definition 1. *A disruption tree is a tuple $T = (N, t, ch)$ where:*

- *N is a finite set of nodes;*
- *$t\colon N \to \mathbb{T}$ gives the type of each node;*
- *$ch\colon N \to N^*$ gives the sequence of children of a node.*

Moreover, T satisfies the following constraints:

- *(N, E) is a connected DAG, where $E = \{(v, u) \in N^2 \mid u \in ch(v)\}$;*
- *T has a unique root, denoted R_T: $\exists!\, R_T \in N.\ \forall v \in N.\ R_T \notin ch(v)$;*
- *$\texttt{LEAF}_T$ nodes are the leaves of T: $\forall v \in N.\ t(v) = \texttt{LEAF} \Leftrightarrow ch(v) = \varepsilon$.*

4.3 Semantics

Semantics pin down the mathematical meaning for attack and fault trees. The semantics of both fault trees and attack trees is given in terms of their *structure function*, indicating which sets of leaves cause the top level events to happen.

Thus, the *structure function* of a disruption tree T is a function $f_T\colon \mathbb{B}^n \to \mathbb{B}$. Technically, a status vector $\boldsymbol{v} = \langle v_1, \ldots, v_n \rangle$ indicates for each leaf i whether it was disrupted, i.e., $v_i = 1$ if leaf i has failed or was attacked. Then $f_T(\boldsymbol{v}) \in \{0, 1\}$ indicates whether the whole system was disrupted. This function can be defined recursively in the nodes of T: $f_T(v, A)$ tells whether $A \subseteq \texttt{LEAF}$ suffices to disrupt node $v \in N$ of T, where A encodes $\boldsymbol{v}$ as usual.

Definition 2. *The structure function $f_T\colon N \times 2^{\texttt{LEAF}} \to \mathbb{B}$ of a disruption tree T is given by:*

$$f_T(v, A) = \begin{cases} 1 & \text{if } t(v) = \texttt{OR} \quad \text{and } \exists u \in ch(v).f_T(u, A) = 1, \\ 1 & \text{if } t(v) = \texttt{AND} \quad \text{and } \forall u \in ch(v).f_T(u, A) = 1, \\ 1 & \text{if } t(v) = \texttt{LEAF} \text{ and } v \in A, \\ 0 & \text{otherwise.} \end{cases}$$

The structure function can be used to asses suites: a *disruption suite* $\mathcal{S} \subseteq 2^{\text{LEAF}}$ represents all ways in which the system can be compromised. From those, one is interested in disruptions $A \in \mathcal{S}$ that actually represent a threat. These correspond to (minimal) cut sets in fault trees and attack scenarios in attack trees. To find them, we let $f_T(A) \doteq f_T(R_T, A)$ and call disruption A *successful* if $f_T(A) = 1$, i.e. it makes the top-level of T succeed (resp. be attacked or failed). If, moreover, no proper subset of A is successful then A is a *minimal disruption*.

It is well known that attack trees and fault trees are *coherent* [4], meaning that adding attack steps/basic events preserves success: if A is causes the TLE to happen, then so is $A \cup \{a\}$ for any $a \in \text{LEAF}$. Thus, the suite of successful disruptions of an DT is characterised by its minimal disruptions.

Definition 3. *The* semantics of a static DT T *is its suite of minimal disruptions:* $[\![T]\!] = \{A \subseteq 2^{\text{LEAF}} \mid f_T(A) \wedge A \text{ is minimal}\}$.

4.4 Metrics for Attack and Fault Trees

Dependability metrics quantify key performance indicators (KPIs), that quantify several dependability characteristics of a system. Such metrics serve several purposes, e.g. allowing to compare different design alternatives w.r.t. the desired dependability features; computing the effectiveness of measures; verifying whether a solution meets its dependability requirements; etc.

Metrics for attack trees focus on a wide variety of attributes, such as the cost of an attack, its time and, success probability. These can be conveniently summarized via an attribute domain [35]. Metrics for fault trees focus on probabilistic aspects, such as the system reliability (i.e. the probability that a system fails within its mission time T), the availability (i.e., the average percentage of time that the system is up), mean time to failure, etc.

Attribute Metrics. We define dependability metrics for DTs in three steps: first an attribution α enrich the leaves with attributes, assigning a value to each $a \in \text{LEAF}$, then a dependability metric $\widehat{\alpha}$ assigns a value to each disruption scenario A; and finally the metric $\widecheck{\alpha}$ assigns a value to each disruption suite.

Example 1. Consider the AT in Fig. 1b. The metric we study is the time required to execute a successful attack. Thus, the attribution α equips each AT leaf with its attack time, setting e.g. $\alpha(\text{Attacker forces door}) = 5$, $\alpha(\text{Door unlocked}) = 0$ and $\alpha(\text{Attacker tries door}) = 2$. If all attack steps are executed sequentially, then the time needed to execute an attack $A = \{a_1, \ldots a_n\}$ is sum of the attack times of the BASs:

$$\widehat{\alpha}(a_1, \ldots a_n) = \sum_{i=1}^{n} \alpha(a_i)$$

Both for attackers and defenders of the system, it is relevant to consider the shortest attack in an attack suite $\mathcal{S}$:

$$\widecheck{\alpha}(\{A_1, \ldots A_n\}) = \min\{\widehat{\alpha}(A_1), \ldots \widehat{\alpha}(A_n)\}$$

Other metrics give rise to other attribute definitions. For example, the success probability of an attack is the product of the success probabilities of the BAS. The probability of attack suite S is the probability of the most successful attack in S. The cost of an attack is the sum of the cost of the BASs, and the cost of an attack suite is the minimum cost of its attacks. A formal definition is as follows.

Definition 4. *Given a DT and a set V of values:*

1. *an attribution* α: LEAF $\rightarrow V$ *assigns an attribute value* $\alpha(a)$, *or shortly an attribute, to each leaf a;*
2. *a dependability metric over disruptions is a function* $\widehat{\alpha}$: $\mathscr{A}_T \rightarrow V$ *that assigns a value c to each disruption A;*
3. *a dependability metric over disruption suites is a function and to a function* $\breve{\alpha}$: $\mathscr{S}_T \rightarrow V$ *that assigns a value* $\breve{\alpha}(S)$ *to each disruption suite S.*

We write $\breve{\alpha}(T)$ *for* $\breve{\alpha}(\llbracket T \rrbracket)$, *setting the metric of a DT to the metric of its minimal disruption suites.*

Remark 1. We choose the notation $\widehat{\alpha}$ for metrics over disruptions, since ˆ resembles $\triangle$, and $\widehat{\alpha}(A)$ corresponds to the interpretation of the AND gate. Similarly, $\breve{\alpha}$ resembles $\triangledown$, and corresponds to the OR gate, since $\breve{\alpha}(S)$ often chooses the best disruption set among all $A \in S$.

Different Metric Interpretation of the OR-Gate. It is important to realize that the quantitative interpretation of the OR-gate is different in attack trees than in fault trees. Fault trees assume that all components work in parallel. Thus, component i fails with probability p_i, the fault tree $OR(C_1, C_2)$ fails with probability $p_1 + p_2 - p_1 \cdot p_2$. In attack trees, the OR-gate works in parallel. The interpretation of the attack tree $OR(C_1, C_2)$ is that the attacker executes either C_1 or C_2. Since the attacker maximizes their success probability, the probability on a successful attack in the tree $OR(C_1, C_2)$ equals $max(p_1, p_2)$.

This distinction is completely ignored in the analysis methods for all six attack-fault combinations/extensions [5, 18, 31, 33, 42, 46]. In particular, the analysis methods for computing probabilities may not account for the different interpretation of the OR-gates related to safety or security events. This could further lead to incorrect computations of dependability metrics e.g., probability values.

5   Analysis Algorithms for Attack and Fault Trees

Numerous analysis methods for quantitative analysis of attack trees and fault trees exist [2, 6, 15, 23, 29, 41, 45]. In this section, we give an overview of two common algorithms for fault trees and attack trees.

5.1 Algorithms for Tree-Shaped DTs

We first provide the algorithms for tree-structured DTs, where every node in the graph has a single parent. These can be analyzed via a bottom-up algorithm, propagating the values from the bottom to the root of the tree. In order for this procedure to work for all metrics, we combine the inputs of the AND-gate using an operator $\triangle$, and the inputs of the or gate via $\triangledown$. Then this procedure works whenever the algebraic structure $(V, \triangle, \triangledown)$ constitutes a semiring [35].

Next, we treat the computationally more complex DAG-structured DTs. These can be analyzed by converting the DT to a binary decision diagram (BDD). Again, this works if $(V, \triangle, \triangledown)$ is a semiring [9].

Input: Tree-structured DT T,
    node v from T,
    attribution $\alpha\colon \mathrm{BAS}_T \to V$,
    semiring attribute domain
    $D = (V, \triangledown, \triangle)$.
Output: Metric value $\breve{\alpha}(T) \in V$
    from node v downwards.

1 **if** $t(v) = \mathrm{OR}$ **then**
2   **return** $\triangledown_{u \in ch(v)}$ BU(T, u, α, D)
3 **else if** $t(v) = \mathrm{AND}$ **then**
4   **return** $\triangle_{u \in ch(v)}$ BU(T, u, α, D)
5 **else** // $t(v) = \mathrm{BAS}$
6   **return** $\alpha(v)$

Algorithm 1: BU for tree DTs

Input: BDD B_T from static DT T,
    node w from B_T,
    attribution $\alpha\colon \mathrm{BAS}_T \to V$, semiring
    attribute domain
    $D_* = (V, \triangledown, \triangle, 1_\triangledown, 1_\triangle)$.
Output: Metric value $\breve{\alpha}(T) \in V$ from node
    w downwards.

1 **if** $Lab(w) = 0$ **then**
2   **return** $1_\triangledown$
3 **else if** $Lab(w) = 1$ **then**
4   **return** $1_\triangle$
5 **else** // non-terminal $Lab(w) = v \in \mathrm{BAS}_T$
6   **return** BDD$(B_T, Low(w), \alpha, D_*)\ \triangledown$
      $\big(\mathrm{BDD}(B_T, High(w), \alpha, D_*) \triangle \alpha(v)\big)$

Algorithm 2: BDD for static DAG DTs

Example 2. We illustrate the (straightforward) bottom up algorithm via the attack tree in Fig. 2. We compute the time required to reach the top event, with the same attribute values as before: Abbreviating $f =$ Attacker forces door, $u =$ Door unlocked and $t =$ Attacker tries door, we have $\alpha(f) = 5$, $\alpha(u) = 0$ and $\alpha(t) = 2$. The bottom up computation first computes the time required to achieve the subgoal "Attacker walks through door", abbreviated as w. Since the attack time metric interprets the AND-gate as the sum, we take $\triangle = +$ and obtain the value for w as the sum of the metric values of its children "Attacker forces door" and "Door unlocked", abbreviated u and f respectively.

Fig. 2. Algorithm 1 for min. attack time.

$$\breve{\alpha}(w) = \breve{\alpha}(f) \triangle \breve{\alpha}(u) = \alpha(f) \triangle \alpha(u) = 0 + 2 = 2.$$

Similarly, we compute the time required for the TLA "Attacker breaches door", abbreviated b. Since the attack time metric interprets the OR-gate as the minimum, we take $\nabla = \min$ and obtain the value for b as the minimum of the metric values of its children f and w:

$$\breve{\alpha}(b) = \breve{\alpha}(f) \nabla \breve{\alpha}(u) = \min(\alpha(f), \alpha(u)) = \min(5, 2) = 2.$$

The above procedure, formalized in Algorithm 1, works whenever the structure $(V, \nabla, \triangle)$ constitute an attribute domain. Note that this algorithm is linear in the number of DT nodes.

Definition 5. *Let V be a set:*

1. *an* attribute domain *over V is a tuple $D = (V, \nabla, \triangle)$, whose disjunctive operator $\nabla \colon V^2 \to V$, and conjunctive operator $\triangle \colon V^2 \to V$, are associative and commutative;*
2. *the attribute domain is a semiring[1] if $\triangle$ distributes over ∇, i.e. $\forall x, y, z \in V$. $\triangle (y \nabla z) = (x \triangle y) \nabla (x \triangle z)$;*
3. *let T be a static DT and α an attribution on V. The* metric for T *associated to α and D is given by:*

$$\breve{\alpha}(T) = \underbrace{\bigvee_{A \in \llbracket T \rrbracket}}_{\breve{\alpha}} \underbrace{\bigwedge_{a \in A} \alpha(a)}_{\widehat{\alpha}}.$$

5.2   Algorithms for DAG-Shaped DTs

DTs with shared subtrees cannot be analysed via a bottom-up procedure on their DAG structure. This is a classical result from fault tree analysis [34]. Intuitively, the problem is that a visit to node v in any bottom-up procedure that operates on the DT structure can only aggregate information on its descendants.

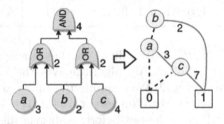

Fig. 3. DAG-shaped AT (left) and its BDD (right).

This is illustrated by the DAG-shaped AT in Fig. 3: We assign attack time to the leaves: $\alpha(a) = 3$, $\alpha(b) = 2$ and $\alpha(c) = 4$. Then the bottom up algorithm yields the following results: for the OR-gates, we take the minimum value between the children, which both equal 2, and for the AND-gate we sum the values of the children, resulting in 4. However, this computation does not take the sharing of b into account. In fact, the shortest attack is to take the BAS b, which takes time 2.

As a matter of fact, computing metrics in a DAG-structured DT T is an NP-complete problem. Various methods to analyse DAG-structured DTs have

---

[1] Since we require $\triangle$ to be commutative, D is in fact a commutative semiring. Further, rings often include a neutral element for disjunction and an absorbing element for conjunction, but these are not needed in Definition 5.

been proposed: contributions over the last 15 years include [2,6,15,23,29]. We now detail our recent work on binary decision diagrams (BDDs) [9].

BDD Algorithms. BDDs offer a very compact representation of Boolean functions, and can therefore represent the structure function of a DT T: Each BDD node v is labeled with a leaf a of T, and has two children: its left node v_L (reached via a dashed line) represents the structure function of T in case a has the value 0; its right child v_R (reached via a solid line) represents the structure function of T in case a evaluates to 1. The key insight in [9] is that the values of an attribute domain can be computed recursively over this BDD, thereby avoiding duplication of values as in Fig. 3. The idea is as follows. The value for the BDD terminal node labeled with 0 is set to the constant $1_\nabla \in V$; the BDD terminal node labeled with 1 is set to $1_\Delta \in V$. For an internal node v with children v_L and v_R, we proceed as follows: When choosing v_R, i.e. the basic event a occurs, we extend the value computed at v_R with the attribute value of a. We do so via the Δ operator, since taking the right child corresponds to executing both a and all leaves needed in $\alpha(v_R)$. If a is not executed, then we do not incur the value of $\alpha(a)$, and only take $\breve{\alpha}(v_L)$. Now, the best disruption (i.e. attack or cut set) is obtained by choosing the best option, by deploying the ∇ operator: either one does not execute a, incurring $\breve{\alpha}(v_L)$, or executes a and incurs $\alpha(a) \Delta \breve{\alpha}(v_R)$. This yields the value $\breve{\alpha}(v) = \breve{\alpha}(v_L) \nabla (\alpha(a) \Delta \breve{\alpha}(v_R))$. This is illustrated in (Fig. 3, in blue). As we can see, the TLE can fail either by the failure of b in 2 time units or by the failure of a and c but not of b, in 7 time units. Algorithm 2 shows the pseudocode of this algorithm. The algorithm is linear in the size of the BDD, but that the BDD size can be exponential in the size of the DT. In particular, the BDD heavily depends on the order for the variables. In practice good heuristics are available, making BDD-computations efficient in practice.

5.3 Research Gaps

Research gaps.
- *An overarching formalism* is still missing. Since attack trees and fault trees interpret the OR-gate in a different manner, proper combinations must feature two variants of the OR-gate: one that coincides with the AT-interpretation and for the FT-variant.
- Another research gap concerns *proper analysis of OR-gates*. Analysis algorithms must handle both the aforementioned variants of OR-gates. Section 5 partially solves this problem for the case of tree-structured attack-fault trees. Efficient analysis of DAG-structured attack-fault tree combinations remains an open problem.

6 Conclusions

Conclusion. Safety and security interactions have been identified as important topics in complex systems, and multiple modeling methods have been developed in an attempt to account for their interactions. Our preliminary results show that most of these methods are based on extending and/or combining existing safety and security modeling methods. No specific metrics or novel modeling constructs are introduced. The majority of considered formalisms combine/extend attack trees and fault trees. As a consequential next step, we performed a thorough analysis of similarities and differences between ATs and FTs. Their static variants - SATs and SFTs - share the same syntax: we group them under the label of disruption trees (DTs), for which we provide shared semantics. Furthermore, we show how to compute dependability metrics on DTs highlighting differences between ATs and FTs when needed, e.g., the different interpretation of the OR-gate. Finally, we propose analysis algorithms for ATs and FTs both for their tree-shaped and DAG-shaped variants.

Future Work. While addressing some of the research gaps, this work also highlights future challenges. With the growing need for safety-security co-analysis, the urge of a better understanding of safety-security interactions arises:

Open problems.
- To foster this understanding, realistic *large-sized case study analysis* concerning safety-security interactions should be performed.
- This would clarify the nature of *safety-security interactions* - that are still ill-understood - and help *improve standard definitions* for safety-security interdependencies.
- As mentioned, *novel metrics* and *novel modeling constructs* for safety-security co-analysis - that are still missing - could then be developed, alongisde an overarching formalism.
- This *overarching formalism* would need to account for two different OR-gates: one that coincides with the AT-variant and one for the FT-variant.
- Furthermore, *proper analysis of OR-gates* has to be performed, as analysis algorithms must handle both the aforementioned variants of OR-gates.

References

1. Amorim, T., Schneider, D., Nguyen, V.Y., Schmittner, C., Schoitsch, E.: Five major reasons why safety and security haven't married (yet). ERCIM News **102**, 16–17 (2015)
2. Arnold, F., Guck, D., Kumar, R., Stoelinga, M.: Sequential and parallel attack tree modelling. In: Koornneef, F., van Gulijk, C. (eds.) SAFECOMP 2015. LNCS, vol. 9338, pp. 291–299. Springer, Cham (2015). https://doi.org/10.1007/978-3-319-24249-1_25

3. Avizienis, A., Laprie, J.C., Randell, B., Landwehr, C.E.: Basic concepts and taxonomy of dependable and secure computing. IEEE Trans. Dependable Sec. Comput. **1**, 11–33 (2004)
4. Barlow, R.E., Proschan, F.: Statistical Theory of Reliability and Life Testing: Probability Models. International Series in Decision Processes. Holt, Rinehart and Winston, New York (1975)
5. Bernsmed, K., Frøystad, C., Meland, P.H., Nesheim, D.A., Rødseth, Ø.J.: Visualizing cyber security risks with bow-tie diagrams. In: Liu, P., Mauw, S., Stølen, K. (eds.) GraMSec 2017. LNCS, vol. 10744, pp. 38–56. Springer, Cham (2018). https://doi.org/10.1007/978-3-319-74860-3_3
6. Bobbio, A., Egidi, L., Terruggia, R.: A methodology for qualitative/quantitative analysis of weighted attack trees. IFAC **46**(22), 133–138 (2013)
7. Bozzano, M., et al.: A model checker for AADL. In: Touili, T., Cook, B., Jackson, P. (eds.) CAV 2010. LNCS, vol. 6174, pp. 562–565. Springer, Heidelberg (2010). https://doi.org/10.1007/978-3-642-14295-6_48
8. Brocke, J., Simons, A., Niehaves, B., Riemer, K., Plattfaut, R., Cleven, A.: Reconstructing the giant: on the importance of rigour in documenting the literature search process. In: ECIS (2009)
9. Budde, C.E., Stoelinga, M.: Efficient algorithms for quantitative attack tree analysis. In: CSF, pp. 501–515. IEEE Computer Society (2021). ISSN: 2374-8303. https://doi.org/10.1109/CSF51468.2021.00041
10. Budde, C.E., Kolb, C., Stoelinga, M.: Attack trees vs. fault trees: two sides of the same coin from different currencies. In: QEST (to appear)
11. Byres, E.J., Franz, M., Miller, D.: The use of attack trees in assessing vulnerabilities in SCADA systems. In: Proceedings of the International Infrastructure Survivability Workshop, pp. 3–10. Citeseer (2004)
12. Chockalingam, S., Hadžiosmanović, D., Pieters, W., Teixeira, A., van Gelder, P.: Integrated safety and security risk assessment methods: a survey of key characteristics and applications. In: Havarneanu, G., Setola, R., Nassopoulos, H., Wolthusen, S. (eds.) CRITIS 2016. LNCS, vol. 10242, pp. 50–62. Springer, Cham (2017). https://doi.org/10.1007/978-3-319-71368-7_5
13. Clifton, E., et al.: Fault tree analysis-a history. In: Proceedings of the 17th International Systems Safety Conference, pp. 1–9 (1999)
14. Commission, I.E., et al.: IEC 61025: Fault tree analysis. IEC Standards (2006)
15. Dalton, G.C., Mills, R.F., Colombi, Raines, R.A.: Analyzing attack trees using generalized stochastic Petri nets. In: 2006 IEEE Information Assurance Workshop, pp. 116–123 (2006)
16. Dissaux, P., Singhoff, F., Lemarchand, L., Tran, H., Atchadam, I.: Combined real-time, safety and security model analysis. In: ERTSS (2020)
17. Dugan, J.B., Bavuso, S.J., Boyd, M.A.: Dynamic fault-tree models for fault-tolerant computer systems. IEEE Trans. Reliab. **41**(3), 363–377 (1992)
18. Fovino, I.N., Masera, M., De Cian, A.: Integrating cyber attacks within fault trees. Reliab. Eng. Syst. Saf. **94**(9), 1394–1402 (2009)
19. Fraile, M., Ford, M., Gadyatskaya, O., Kumar, R., Stoelinga, M., Trujillo-Rasua, R.: Using attack-defense trees to analyze threats and countermeasures in an ATM: a case study. In: Horkoff, J., Jeusfeld, M.A., Persson, A. (eds.) PoEM 2016. LNBIP, vol. 267, pp. 326–334. Springer, Cham (2016). https://doi.org/10.1007/978-3-319-48393-1_24
20. Friedberg, I., McLaughlin, K., Smith, P., Laverty, D., Sezer, S.: STPA-SafeSec: Safety and security analysis for cyber-physical systems. J. Inf. Secur. Appl. **34**, 183–196 (2017)

21. ISO/IEC 25010:2011, S., software engineering: Systems and software quality requirements and evaluation (square). System and software quality models (2011)
22. Junges, S., Guck, D., Katoen, J., Stoelinga, M.: Uncovering dynamic fault trees. In: 2016 46th Annual IEEE/IFIP International Conference on Dependable Systems and Networks (DSN), pp. 299–310 (2016)
23. Jürgenson, A., Willemson, J.: Computing exact outcomes of multi-parameter attack trees. In: Meersman, R., Tari, Z. (eds.) OTM 2008. LNCS, vol. 5332, pp. 1036–1051. Springer, Heidelberg (2008). https://doi.org/10.1007/978-3-540-88873-4_8
24. Kahneman, D.: A perspective on judgment and choice: mapping bounded rationality. Am. Psychol. **58**(9), 697 (2003)
25. Kimelman, D., Kimelman, M., Mandelin, D., Yellin, D.M.: Bayesian approaches to matching architectural diagrams. Trans. Software Eng. **36**(2), 248–274 (2010)
26. Kolb, C., Nicoletti, S.M., Peppelman, M., Stoelinga, M.: Model-based safety and security co-analysis: a survey. In: arXiv (2021)
27. Kordy, B., Mauw, S., Radomirović, S., Schweitzer, P.: Attack-defense trees. J. Logic Comput. **24**(1), 55–87 (2012)
28. Kordy, B., Piètre-Cambacédès, L., Schweitzer, P.: DAG-based attack and defense modeling: don't miss the forest for the attack trees. Comput. Sci. Rev. **13–14**, 1–38 (2014)
29. Kordy, B., Wideł, W.: On quantitative analysis of attack–defense trees with repeated labels. In: Bauer, L., Küsters, R. (eds.) POST 2018. LNCS, vol. 10804, pp. 325–346. Springer, Cham (2018). https://doi.org/10.1007/978-3-319-89722-6_14
30. Kornecki, A.J., Subramanian, N., Zalewski, J.: Studying interrelationships of safety and security for software assurance in cyber-physical systems: approach based on Bayesian belief networks. In: 2013 FedCSIS, pp. 1393–1399. IEEE (2013)
31. Kriaa, S., Bouissou, M., Colin, F., Halgand, Y., Pietre-Cambacedes, L.: Safety and security interactions modeling using the BDMP Formalism: case study of a pipeline. In: Bondavalli, A., Di Giandomenico, F. (eds.) SAFECOMP 2014. LNCS, vol. 8666, pp. 326–341. Springer, Cham (2014). https://doi.org/10.1007/978-3-319-10506-2_22
32. Kriaa, S., Pietre-Cambacedes, L., Bouissou, M., Halgand, Y.: A survey of approaches combining safety and security for industrial control systems. Reliab. Eng. Syst. Saf. **139**, 156–178 (2015)
33. Kumar, R., Stoelinga, M.: Quantitative security and safety analysis with attack-fault trees. In: 2017 IEEE 18th International Symposium on High Assurance Systems Engineering (HASE), pp. 25–32 (2017)
34. Lee, W., Grosh, D., Tillman, F., Lie, C.: Fault tree analysis, methods, and applications: a review. IEEE Trans. Reliab. **R-34**(3), 194–203 (1985)
35. Mauw, S., Oostdijk, M.: Foundations of attack trees. In: Won, D.H., Kim, S. (eds.) ICISC 2005. LNCS, vol. 3935, pp. 186–198. Springer, Heidelberg (2006). https://doi.org/10.1007/11734727_17
36. Nicol, D.M., H.Sanders, W., Trivedi, K.S.: Model-based evaluation: From dependability to security. IEEE Trans. Dep. Sec. Comput. **1**(1), 48–65 (2004)
37. Nielsen, D.S.: The Cause/Consequence Diagram Method as a Basis for Quantitative Accident Analysis. Risø National Laboratory (1971)
38. Nigam, V., Pretschner, A., Ruess, H.: Model-based safety and security engineering (2019)
39. Organization, I.S.: ISO/dis 26262: Road vehicles, functional safety. Technical report (2009)

40. Pedroza, G., Apvrille, L., Knorreck, D.: AVATAR: A SysML environment for the formal verification of safety and security properties. In: 2011 NOTERE, pp. 1–10. IEEE (2011)
41. Rauzy, A.: New algorithms for fault trees analysis. Reliab. Eng. Syst. Saf. **40**(3), 203–211 (1993)
42. Roth, M., Liggesmeyer, P.: Modeling and analysis of safety-critical cyber physical systems using state/event fault trees. In: SAFECOMP 2013 (2013)
43. Roudier, Y., Apvrille, L.: SysML-Sec: A model driven approach for designing safe and secure systems. In: MODELSWARD
44. Ruijters, E., Guck, D., Drolenga, P., Stoelinga, M.: Fault maintenance trees: reliability centered maintenance via statistical model checking. In: 2016 Annual Reliability and Maintainability Symposium (RAMS), pp. 1–6 (2016)
45. Ruijters, E., Stoelinga, M.: Fault tree analysis: a survey of the state-of-the-art in modeling, analysis and tools. Comput. Sci. Rev. **15–16**, 29–62 (2015)
46. Steiner, M., Liggesmeyer, P.: Combination of safety and security analysis - finding security problems that threaten the safety of a system (2016)
47. Watson, H.: Launch control safety study. Technical Report, Section VII, Vol. 1. Bell Labs (1961)
48. Zampino, E.J.: Application of fault-tree analysis to troubleshooting the NASA GRC icing research tunnel. In: Annual Reliability and Maintainability Symposium, 2001 Proceedings, pp. 16–22 (2001)

A Hands-On Introduction to Spatial Model Checking Using VoxLogicA
– Invited Contribution

Vincenzo Ciancia[1]([⊠])[iD], Gina Belmonte[2][iD], Diego Latella[1][iD],
and Mieke Massink[1][iD]

[1] Istituto di Scienza e Tecnologie dell'Informazione "A. Faedo",
Consiglio Nazionale delle Ricerche, Pisa, Italy
{vincenzo.ciancia,diego.latella,mieke.massink}@isti.cnr.it
[2] Azienda Toscana Nord Ovest, S. C. Fisica Sanitaria Nord, Lucca, Italy
gina.belmonte@uslnordovest.toscana.it

Abstract. This paper provides a tutorial-style introduction, and a
guide, to the recent advancements in spatial model checking that have
made some relevant results possible. Among these, we mention fully automated segmentation of regions of interest in medical images by short,
unambiguous spatial-logical specifications. This tutorial is aimed both
at domain experts in medical imaging who would like to learn simple
(scripting-alike) techniques for image analysis, making use of a modern,
declarative language, and at experts in Formal Methods in Computer
Science and Model Checking who would like to grasp how the theory
of Spatial Logic and Model Checking has been turned into logic-based,
dataset-oriented imaging techniques.

Keywords: Spatial logic · Model checking · Tutorial

1 Introduction

The topological approach to spatial model checking was introduced in [16,17],
as a fully automated method to verify properties of points in a spatial structure,
such as a graph, or a digital image. The theory of spatial model checking has
its roots in the spatial interpretation of modal logics dating back to Tarski (see
[9] for a thorough introduction to the subject). Spatial properties of points are
related to topological aspects such as being *near* to points satisfying a given
property, or being able to *reach* a point satisfying a certain property, passing
only through points obeying to specific constraints. The *Spatial Logic of Closure
Spaces* defined in [16] is quite expressive, which has been demonstrated in case

Research partially supported by the MIUR PRIN 2017FTXR7S "IT-MaTTerS".
This tutorial is meant to complement the invited talk in the *27th International SPIN
Symposium on Model Checking of Software* by Vincenzo Ciancia, therefore listed as
the first author. All the authors equally contributed to developments of the presented
research line and are primary authors of this paper.

A. Laarman and A. Sokolova (Eds.): SPIN 2021, LNCS 12864, pp. 22–41, 2021.
https://doi.org/10.1007/978-3-030-84629-9_2

studies ranging from smart transportation [19] to bike sharing [18,23], to medical image analysis [3,6–8]. The arbitrary nesting of spatial properties is the key to obtain such strong capabilities.

In the tool VoxLogicA, presented in [8], and designed from scratch for image analysis, logical operators can be freely mixed with a few imaging operators, related to colour thresholding, texture analysis, or normalization. The tool is quite fast, de to various factors: most primitives are implemented using the state-of-the-art imaging library SimpleITK[1]; expressions are never recomputed (reduction of the syntax tree to a directed acyclic graph is used as a form of *memoization*); operations are implicitly parallelised on multi-core CPUs. Case studies such as brain tumour segmentation [3,8], labelling of white and grey matter [7], and contouring of nevi [6] have shown that simple, unambiguous and explainable logical specifications can compete in accuracy with state-of-the-art machine-learning based methods[2].

So far, however, even if the VoxLogicA approach is meant to be domain-expert-friendly and the tool itself is quite straightforward to use, applications of spatial model checking have been confined to a limited group of "initiated" collaborators. One reason for this is a conceptual gap between the theory of topological spatial logics for discrete structures, presented in [16,17], and the technicalities of a full case study such as that of [6], where the most relevant keywords are *dataset, overlay, ground truth, region of interest*, etc.

In this paper, we attempt to fill this gap by providing a gentle, hands-on introduction to the subject of spatial model checking for image analysis. The intended audience of this paper is two-fold: we aim at reaching both domain experts in image analysis (who could even be non-programmers, but are willing to get acquainted with the benefits of declarative analysis, and learn simple scripting-alike techniques to automatise imaging tasks, based on spatial features of points or regions) and experts in Formal Methods in Computer Science, and in particular in model checking, who are able to understand the technical aspects of VoxLogicA, but need some guidance to gather insights from the ideas behind its image analysis capabilities.

In Sect. 2, we introduce the spatial model checker VoxLogicA starting from the practicalities: how to invoke the tool, the format of input files, visualization of results, log files, and how to run the tool against a dataset. In Sect. 3, we illustrate by examples the core capabilities of spatial-logical reasoning, that is, the concepts of *nearness* and *reachability*. In Sect. 4, we introduce the use of Vox-LogicA as a method to obtain numbers or Boolean values from whole images, for instance in order to query datasets to find images satisfying given properties. In Sect. 5, we illustrate some slightly more advanced examples of spatial

---

[1] See https://simpleitk.org/.

[2] Indeed, it is not the intention of the research line around VoxLogicA to compete against machine-learning based approaches. Rather, we expect that the two can be complementary: VoxLogicA specifications can certainly be used to coordinate various machine-learning based steps in order to obtain procedures that have a degree of machine-learning based operation, but are still modifiable and explainable.

operators, including *distance transform* and *filtering*, via a background segmentation example. Therein, we also briefly discuss a *statistical texture similarity* operator. In Sect. 6, we provide a brief guide to the related literature, focusing on recent applications of Spatial Logics in Computer Science, both based on the Spatial Logics of Closure Spaces proposed in [16,17] and not depending upon it. In Sect. 7, we illustrate the more recent research lines that are being pursued by the VoxLogicA group, including the use of *GPU computing* to speed up spatial model checking, the study of a dataset oriented graphical user interface for the design of logical specifications, and a freshly designed spatial model checker for analysing *3D meshes* using the Spatial Logic of Closure Spaces.

2   Using VoxLogicA: Practicalities

In this tutorial, we will use the command line interface of VoxLogicA[3]. After unpacking/installing the tool, running the executable from its full path, with no arguments, will produce a help message listing the options. VoxLogicA specifications contain a description of the *model* to be analysed (essentially, a set of images of the same size), and a list of properties to be verified. For executing a specification, only one argument is needed, that is, the specification name, so the model checker can be run as follows:

```
/path/to/VoxLogicA input.imgql
```

In our first examples, we will use the following image of a maze, with green exit, white corridors, black walls, four coloured square placeholders (cyan, orange, magenta, blue), and a pink trapdoor.

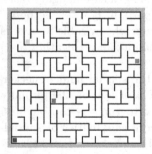

It is very important to remark that although for simplicity, in this tutorial we encode all properties of interest as colours (and doing so can be useful in several situations), real-world examples may require more precise annotation of properties of pixels. In medical images, for instance, it is quite common that a dataset contains, for each case, several separated, possibly overlapping images of the same size, either Boolean valued, or divided into regions by the use of integer

---

[3] We use VoxLogicA version 1.0. It can be downloaded from https://github.com/ vincenzoml/VoxLogicA. The example images and files of this paper are available at the same web site.

labels. Such annotations are called *regions of interest* (ROIs). Indeed, VoxLogicA can load more than one image by using several **load** instructions, and thus easily work with multiple ROIs. Similarly, a dataset may contain more than one "base" image. For example, a dataset related to brain tumours could contain acquisitions made with different MRI modalities, which emphasize different aspects of a patient situation. Analysis methods that can make use of multiple modalities are called *multi-modal*. Again, since VoxLogicA can load multiple images in the same specification, it can be readily used for multi-modal analysis.

2.1   The Declarative Language ImgQL

The input language of VoxLogicA, namely the *Image Query Language* ImgQL, has only five commands:

- **load** x ="filename.{png,nii,nii.gz,jpg,bmp,...}"
  loads an image in one of the supported file formats, and binds its to the (constant) name x. Note that ImgQL is a "pure" language, with no side effects. Therefore all names are constant, not variables (there is no assignment).
- **save**"filename.{png,nii,nii.gz,jpg,bmp,...}" expression
  saves the result of an expression returning an image[4] to a file;
- **print** "label" expression
  prints the result of an expression returning a number, or a boolean value, to the log file, accompanied by a given label to be easily recognisable;
- **let** name = expression
  where name starts with a lowercase letter, declares a constant; the **let** construct has two more variants, described below;
- **let** fname(x1,...,xn) = expression
  where fname starts with a lowercase letter, declares a function;
- **let** OP(x1,...,xn) = expression
  where OP consists of uppercase letters and symbols, declares an *operator*, which is different from a function only by the syntax used to invoke it. Unary operators are prefix (e.g. the *not/complement* operator !x); binary operators are infix (e.g. the or/union operator x & y); if more than two arguments are supplied, these are added in square brackets; for instance, **let** OP(x,y,z,t) = ... defines the operator OP invoked as x OP[z,t] y;
- **import** "filename.imgql"
  imports a library of **let** declarations; no other command than **let** can appear in an imported file. The file stdlib.imgql located in the same directory as the VoxLogicA executable is automatically imported. Files are first searched in the same directory as the executable. If the file name contains no extension and the file is not found, VoxLogicA also attempts to load a file with the same name and .imgql extension.

---

[4] A VoxLogicA expression may return either an image – which can be Boolean-valued, number-valued, or have multiple number-valued channels – or a single value, which can be either a number or a Boolean value. No distinction is made between integer and floating point numbers; all numbers are treated as floating point internally.

2.2 Loading and Saving Models

We shall first demonstrate **load** and **save** constructs. We will load our maze image, and save an output image only containing its routes, that is, the white area. Below, the specification is shown on the left, and the result on the right. In white, the pixels satisfying the whole specification, which as we shall see (and purely coincidentally, in this example) are the white pixels of the input image.

```
load img = "maze01.png"
let corridor = (red(img) =. 255) &
    (green(img) =. 255) & (blue(img) =. 255)

save "output/example01.png" corridor
```

The **load** instruction binds to name img the image contained in the input file. The **save** instruction saves to the output file the result of an expression (we have bound the expression to the name corridor, but that would not be necessary in principle; the expression could have directly appeared as an argument of the **save** instruction). Throughout this tutorial, we save all our output files in a directory named "output". This is convenient, but indeed not mandatory; the file would be saved in the *current working directory* if no path was supplied. If output directories are specified, these are automatically created if not existing.

Let us analyse the definition of corridor, aimed at selecting only the white pixels in the image. First let us look at the sub-expression **red**(img) =. 255. The expression **red**(img) takes as parameter the image img, and returns an image consisting in only the red component of the image (similarly, there are functions **green** and **blue** for the other two components of the RGB colour space). Since the input file is a 8-bits-per-channel image, the result of **red**(img) is a number-valued image, having the same width and height of the original one, containing a numeric value between 0 and 255 in each pixel. Note that the Vox-LogicA type system does not distinguish between integers and floating points. Internally, all numbers are 32-bits floating point in order to guarantee precision of the analysis. The infix operator =. takes on its left a number-valued image i, and on its right a number n. As in some scientific computation languages, the dot in an operator is on the side of numbers, whereas "matrices" (in our case, images) do not have a dot. The result is a Boolean-valued image, containing in each pixel at coordinates (x, y) the value true if the value of i at the pixel (x, y) is equal to n. Similarly, there are operators >. (greater than a value), >=. (greater or equal than a value) and so on. The infix operator & is logical conjunction ("and") (similarly, there is a disjunction operator | ("or"), and negation ! ("not")). The operator & takes as input two Boolean-valued images, and returns a Boolean-valued images which, pixel by pixel, contains the conjunction of the corresponding values. Therefore the meaning of the whole expression (**red**(img) =. 255) & (**green**(img) =. 255) & (**blue**(img) =. 255) is to return a Boolean image that has value true only on the *white* pixels (all the three components have maximum value).

Since the **save** instruction requires a Boolean valued image to be saved in the png format, which only allows integer values, the truth values are encoded as 0 for the value false and 255 for the value true. This is to ease visualisation of the verification results, as it corresponds to using the colour black for false and white for true, as it is clearly visible in the resulting image.

Finally, sometimes it is easier to visualise results by super-imposing them on the original image. For this, the overlayColor function of the standard library can be of help. It takes as arguments an "overlay" Boolean-valued image (to be super-imposed in a colour), a "background" image (which will be rendered "below" the super-imposed layer), and three colour components, red, green and blue. It returns an image having the pixels coloured in the same way as "background" on the pixels where "overlay" is false, and in the colour specified by the three colour components on the pixels where "overlay" is true. In the example below, we super-impose in red the expression denoting corridors, on top of our base maze image. In order to do so, we define a single-argument function named view that shows its only argument in red, and will be reused later.

```
let view(x) = overlayColor(x,img,255,0,0)

save "output/example02.png" view(corridor)
```

2.3 Anatomy of VoxLogicA Logs

The log of our first analysis is reported below (path names have been edited).

```
[ 84ms] [info] Parsing input...
[127ms] [info] Preparing computation...
[157ms] [info] Importing file "/path/to/stdlib.imgql"
[167ms] [info] Loading file "/path/to/maze01.png"
[205ms] [warn] image maze01.png has 4 color components per voxel.
               Assuming RGBA color space (CMYK is not supported).
[241ms] [info] Starting computation...
[242ms] [info] Running 10 tasks
[292ms] [warn] saving boolean image to example01.png;
               value 'true' is 255, not 1
[296ms] [info] Saving file "/path/to/output/example01.png"
[334ms] [info] ... done.
```

The log has three columns. The first one contains the time at which each message has been printed (relative to the start of the program). The second column contains the severity level of the message, which can be "**informative**", "**warning**", "**failure**", or "**user**" for messages issued using the `print` instruction. The third column contains the message itself. Among the many possible messages, the number of tasks (in this case, 10) can be useful to estimate the complexity of a formula. It is however worth emphasizing that the number of tasks that will be executed is not directly proportional to the number of subformulas, but rather to the number of *unique* subformulas. The model checking engine of VoxLogicA never computes expressions twice, so the same number of tasks are obtained e.g., by writing `f(expression1,expression1)` or `let x = expression1` and then `f(x,x)`. The number of unique expressions depends on reduction of the given formulas to the core primitives of VoxLogicA (which can be listed using the `--ops` command line option).

2.4   Working with Datasets

One of the major issues related to image analysis using declarative languages is how much *ad-hoc* is resulting specification is. On the other hand, the work in [3,6–8] has been successful in carrying out complex imaging tasks, such as brain tumour or nevus segmentation, because "success" is measured against a reasonably large dataset, proving generality of the proposed specification. To the best of our knowledge so far, declarative specifications work best against *homogeneous* datasets[5]. So are, for instance, 3D Magnetic Resonance Images (MRI) obtained using specific MRI modalities, such as the MRI-FLAIR[6] used in [8]. Among many common features, all MRI-FLAIR brain images have a dark background, the cerebrospinal fluid is dark, and the tumour area is always hyper-intense. Indeed such constraint may be relaxed, and effective analysis methodologies can be developed on datasets that are *partitioned* into a number of different, but homogeneous classes, as it happens in [6].

Currently, there is no built-in facility in VoxLogicA to work with datasets, and extract useful information (such as, for instance, performance scores that ought to be optimized). Specifications are meant to be run against single cases. This could be the subject of future improvements to the tool, but currently, it is just easier to resort to an external tool orchestrating several runs of the model checker by replacing file names according to patterns that are defined based on the dataset. For instance, a script for datasets of the Brain Tumour Segmentation challenge [30] is provided in the VoxLogicA repository, and can be readily adapted to datasets with different naming conventions.

---

[5] In this respect, we consider our work still as the beginning of a research line, and we cannot predict if, for instance, novel logical operators will enable the development of very general specifications that operate on inhomogeneous domains.

[6] Fluid-attenuated Inversion Recovery. See e.g. Wikipedia contributors, "Fluid-attenuated inversion recovery," Wikipedia, The Free Encyclopedia, https://en.wikipedia.org/w/index.php?title=Fluid-attenuated_inversion_recovery.

3   Topological Properties and Reachability

We shall now expand our specification in order to illustrate the use of reachability formulas. First of all, we declare a bunch of constants, to simplify the specification by identifying the various coloured squares (which could be thought of as points of interest, or as actors willing to move in the maze), the corridors, the walls, and the exit.

```
let rgbcol(r,g,b) =
    (red(img) =. r) & (green(img) =. g) & (blue(img) =. b)

let corridor = rgbcol(255,255,255)
let exit = rgbcol(0,255,0)
let trapdoor = rgbcol(255,128,128)

let cyan = rgbcol(0,255,255)
let orange = rgbcol(255,128,0)
let magenta = rgbcol(255,0,255)
let blueSq = rgbcol(0,0,255)

let all = cyan | orange | magenta | blueSq
```

For reachability properties, we will employ the operator $\leadsto$. A pixel p satisfies a $\leadsto$ b if there is a path starting in p and ending in a point satisfying b, such that all points of the path satisfy a[7]. Let us now find the pixels belonging to the corridors from which the exit can be reached. These are the pixels from which a path can be drawn traversing the corridors, until a pixel which is **adjacent** to the exit is found. The property of being adjacent to the exit can be expressed using the *near* operator, denoted by **N** in ImgQL. Thus, the points from which an exit can be reached are represented by the expression freeCorridor below.

```
let freeCorridor = corridor ~> (N exit)

save "output/example04.png"
    view(freeCorridor)
```

Additionally, we can identify the points of interest from which an exit can be reached passing through corridors, by chaining two reachability properties[8]. Indeed, only the cyan and blue squares are coloured in red.

---

[7] This is a variant of the ρ operator used in [8], the difference being that with ρ, the extremes of the path do not need to satisfy a.

[8] The reader should now pause, and understand (even by experimenting) why actually, two reachability properties *are* needed.

```
let freeSquares = all ~> N freeCorridor

save "output/example05.png"
    view(freeSquares)
```

Now consider our maze as if it was an abstract model of an emergency scenario. A person, who could be in one of the cyan, blue, or orange spots holds the key to the pink trapdoor, and ought to go there, open the trapdoor and rescue a person in the magenta spot, then reach the exit. Let us try to express it using the ~> operator. There could be more than one way of doing so. Our proposal is a chain of nested reachability properties. Indeed, only the cyan square satisfies the specification.

```
let rescuer =  (cyan | blueSq | orange)
    ~> N (corridor ~>
        (N (trapdoor ~>
            N (corridor ~>
                N (magenta ~>
                    N ((corridor | trapdoor) ~>
                        N exit ))))))

save "output/example06.png" view(rescuer)
```

4   Global Properties and Region Calculi

VoxLogicA has a number of *global* operators, among which those that can compute the maximum and minimum of the values where a specific Boolean-value image is true, or that can compute the volume (number of pixels) of a Boolean-valued image. The results of such operators can be inspected using the **print** instruction, having a syntax similar to that of the **save** instruction.

For instance, the volume of the corridors (if useful for any purpose), the number of pixels of the whole image, and the ratio between the two, can be computed and displayed in the log as follows (below, tt is the Boolean operator "true", which holds at any pixel):

```
print "corridors volume" volume(corridor)
print "image volume" volume(tt)
print "corridors / total volume" volume(corridor) ./. volume(tt)

[258ms] [user] image volume=1048576.0
[274ms] [user] corridors volume=786307.0
[275ms] [user] corridors/total volume=0.7498807907
```

Typically, such values are then collected by a script – for instance, when running VoxLogicA against a dataset as explained in Sect. 2.4 – and eventually used for statistical purposes. A simple application of the volume operator is to check whether, in a given image, there exists a point having a given property, by checking whether the volume of the pixels satisfying that property is greater than 0. For instance, in order to check whether there are any "rescuers" in an image of a maze, we can do as follows:

```
let exists(x) = volume(x) .>. 0
print "existsRescuer" exists(rescuer)
```

```
[545ms] [user] existsRescuer=true
```

By the above, VoxLogicA can also be used as a method to *query* datasets of images in order to identify those that satisfy specific requirements. For instance, a real-world scenario could be that of using the procedure for brain tumour segmentation described in [8] in a dataset of patients, in order to identify cases with particularly large brain tumours, or e.g., where the tumour is very close to the cerebellum. Similarly, the nevus segmentation procedure of [6] could be turned into a method to identify patients with nevi having specific characteristics (e.g. ratio between border and surface, etc.). The position paper [5] further elaborates on this idea.

Expanding on global operators, the paper [20] demonstrated that the classical binary operators of the family of *Region Calculi* can be defined in ImgQL. More precisely, given two regions, it is possible to check whether such regions are *disconnected, externally connected, equal, partially overlapping*, or if one is a *tangential* or *non-tangential proper part* of the other.

The operators of the region calculus have been implemented in a VoxLogicA library, consisting in the file RegionCalculus.imgql residing in the same directory as the VoxLogicA executable. Users can load such library by writing:

```
import "RegionCalculus.imgql"
```

Recall that also the standard library "stdlib.imgql", which is automatically imported, resides in the same directory. It can be useful for the reader to inspect these two files, in order to learn about the pre-defined derived operators, and how they can be defined using the basic primitives of VoxLogicA.

5   Advanced Topics: Background Removal, Distance, Filtering, Texture Similarity

In this section, we illustrate a slightly more advanced example, making use of reachability and the built-in *border* predicate to remove the background from a coloured image. Such method is actually used in [8] to remove the background from the dataset of brain images employed therein and identify the area containing the brain. In passing, we will illustrate a kind of "filter" pattern used to *smoothen* images in order to remove non-essential details, using the built-in *distance transform* operator.

We will use the image on the left below, depicting three coloured plastic discs laying on a grey surface; note that although the background is quite uniform, it is not just made of a single colour, due to illumination. Our example will be aimed at "masking" the background from the image, by colouring it in green, in order to obtain the image on the right. Note that the exercise does *not* require to colour in black the parts of the background that are inside the smaller holes of the three coloured discs, which therefore remain grey.

As a first step, the most obvious thing to do is to apply a threshold on the red, green and blue components of the image, in order to separate the grey areas, in which all the three components have a high value at the same time, from the coloured areas, where some components are predominant.

```
load i = "three_coloured_items.png"

let greyish =
    (red(i) >. 120) & (green(i) >. 120) &
    (blue(i) >. 120)

let view(x) = overlayColor(x,i,0,255,0)
save "output/greyish.png" view(greyish)
```

We have again defined a `view` function, this time showing our results in green in order to maximise contrast. Note that the threshold we have used works quite well, but still leaves some fuzzy margin near to the lower-right corner of the image (where the background is darker). Moreover, quite obviously, also the inner part of the holes in the coloured discs has been selected by the threshold. Finally, we note that there are small areas that are not captured by the threshold, mostly, close to the border of the discs, and the purple disc also contains some noise, due to some grey shadows in the picture. Such issues are clearly visible, for instance, by zooming in on the relevant areas, as done below.

In order to exclude the "inner" points from our selection (inner parts of the holes and green points in the purple disc), the built-in predicate `border` of VoxLogicA can be of help. Such predicate is true only at the borders of an image.

This means the area where `border` is true is only 1 pixel wide, and would not be clearly visible in a picture. So we have an excuse to illustrate the *distance transform* operator, since it can be use to thicken the border and visualise it more clearly. Later, we will use the same operator for *smoothening*.

The distance transform `pdt(x)` is an imaging primitive that, given a Boolean-valued image x, returns a number-valued image where each pixel p contains the numeric value of the *Euclidean distance* of p from the points where x is true. This is defined as the minimum of the distance of p from *any* point where x is true. To be more precise, below we use the so-called "positive" distance transform, which is zero on the points where x is true (hence the "p" in `pdt`). In image formats that have a notion of physical dimension of pixels, the distance is expressed in millimetres; otherwise, the distance unit corresponds to the width of a pixel.

```
let normalise(x,v) =
   (x /. max(x)) *. v

save "output/pdt.png"
   normalise(pdt(border),255)
```

To ease visualization of the result, we defined the function `normalise(x,v)`, dividing the value of the image x in each pixel by the maximum value, so that the maximum in the result is 1; then by multiplying it by v, the maximum becomes v. When saving, we let v take the value 255 which is the maximum representable value in an 8-bit grayscale image[9]. Visually, the resulting image is dark in areas very close to the border, whereas pixels that are far from the border are coloured in more intense shades of white. By applying a threshold on the distance transform, we can visualize the border by "thickening it" as follows.

```
let thickBorder = pdt(border) <. 30

save "output/thickBorder.png"
   view(thickBorder)
```

---

[9] In order to avoid issues related to overflow and low precision of 8-bit integers altogether, VoxLogicA can save images in the `nifti` format. Such format can use floating point values in pixels (and can also represent multi-dimensional images, for instance 3D MRI or CAT medical images). See https://nifti.nimh.nih.gov/.

Now that it is clear what the `border` predicate does, we can return to our background segmentation specification, and identify those greyish areas that touch the border, in order to separate them from the inside of holes and the noisy result of the threshold operation on the purple disc-

```
let greyishTouchBorder =
    greyish ~> border

save "output/greyishTouchBorder.png"
    view(greyishTouchBorder)
```

The resulting image is quite close to the result we have in mind, but not there yet. There is noise in the result, both on the lower-right corner of the image, and close to the border of the discs, as we already noted. In order to remove noise, very often in imaging some form of *smoothening* is used, as illustrated below.

```
let distgeq(x,y) = x .<= pdt(y)
let distleq(x,y) = x .>= pdt(y)
let flt(x,a) = distleq(x,distgeq(x,!a))
let dualSmoothen(x,a) =
    flt(x,a) | (!flt(x,!a))

let smooth =
    dualSmoothen(10,greyishTouchBorder)

save "output/filtered.png" view(smooth)
```

We define the `flt(x,a)` function with two arguments, a number x and a Boolean-valued image a. The idea is that the area where a is true is first shrunk, by only keeping the points that lay at a distance greater or equal than x from its *complement* `!a`, and then enlarged by taking the points that lay at a distance less or equal than x from the "shrunk" image. The initial shrinking eliminates areas that are smaller in radius than x, whereas enlarging the result "fills" the resulting holes.

In previous work, the `flt` function is usually applied to a Boolean-valued image, in order to remove noise in the area where the image is *true*. In this example, however, both the part of `greyishTouchBorder` which has value *true* and that having value *false* may be noisy. Therefore, we define the `dualSmoothen` function that applies the `flt` function both to an image and to its complement, and combines the two results. To aid the intuition, the reader may think that the `dualSmoothen` function enlarges `flt(x,a)` by *adding* to it whatever point p that is *removed* from its complement `!a` in the expression `flt(x,!a)`. Technically, this is done by adding to it *any* point in `!flt(x,!a)` (which includes both the points p in the above situation, and the points that are *already* in flt(x,a)). Zooming in demonstrates the combined effect of selecting only the part of greyish that touches the border, and of the dual smoothening. The result is shown on the right, against the image greyish, reported on the left, for comparison.

Finally, the remaining "holes" near to the border can be filled as follows.

```
let final = smooth | ((!smooth) ~> border)

save "output/final.png" view(final)
```

A very similar method has been successfully employed for 3D MRI-FLAIR dataset in the brain tumour case study of [8]. More advanced techniques can be used, involving, for instance, the *statistical texture similarity* operator, presented in [3,8]. The texture similarity operator associates to each pixel p a *similarity score* between -1 and 1, relating an area with a given radius r around p to a target region, denoted by a Boolean-valued image, by comparing the k-bins histograms of the area around p, and of the target region, using a method called *cross-correlation*. For instance, the background segmentation method employed in [6] finds the areas of the image that have a texture similar to the area close to the border. We refer the reader to the cited papers, and only show a similarity map obtained using such method, where darker areas are less similar to the area near to the border.

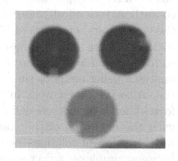

```
let similar(x,r,k) =
    crossCorrelation(r,
        intensity(i),intensity(i),
            x,min(intensity(i)),
                max(intensity(i)),k)

let simMap =
    similar((pdt(border) <. 3),30,4)

save "output/texture.png"
    normalise(simMap +. 1,200)
```

The function similar(x,r,k) computes the similarity score with respect to a target region (Boolean valued image) x, with radius r and number of bins k.

We report the full definition of `similar` for the reader to return to it, after studying the topic in more detail. We just note that we use a very low number of bins ($k = 4$) and a high radius ($r = 30$) in order to obtain a quite coarse-grained analysis, which yields a good similarity map for background segmentation purposes (the similarity map is meant to be thresholded just like we did with the red, green and blue components of the image in the beginning). Finally, observe that we normalise values between -1 and 1, therefore we add the value 1 to each pixel[10].

6   Related Work

As we already mentioned, the VoxLogicA approach stems from topological spatial logics. The reader interested in the theoretical developments behind this fascinating topic should consult the Handbook of Spatial Logics [1], containing several monographic chapters on selected topics in the field.

The development of SLCS in [16] has spawned a few research lines. The work in [4,31–33] proposes the *Signal Spatio-temporal Logic* (SSTL) that combines the analysis of continuous signals through the *Signal Temporal Logic* with the topological spatial operators of SLCS. In [34], SSTL has been used for specifying spatio-temporal patters in the context of particle-based simulation, as part of a statistical spatio-temporal model-checking approach, following the method described in [18]. The results presented in [35] introduce a spatio-temporal logic for bigraphs, inspired by [24], and use the tool `topochecker` presented in [15] for verification. The recent work in [2] demonstrated that SLCS formulas can be interpreted in a fully distributed way, for monitoring purposes across a network. The research line started in [14] aims at providing a categorical generalisation of modal logics with reachability, based on *hyperdoctrines*, covering many examples such as fuzzy sets, algebraic structures, coalgebras, and also known cases such as Kripke frames and probabilistic frames. The study of model-based equivalences (such as bisimulation) and minimisation algorithms that are correct and complete with respect to logical equivalence of the Spatial Logic of Closure Spaces has been recently pursued in [21,22,27]. In [10], some of the authors of this paper co-authored an effort towards model checking of continuous space, by re-using the continuous semantics of SLCS given in [17] in the restricted, computation-friendly setting of models based on polyhedral valuations, which are *triangulated* to form *simplicial complexes*. As an application, *3D meshes* can be loaded and analysed using methods similar to those that have been illustrated in this tutorial. Also the recent work in [28] interprets SLCS on simplicial complexes; the focus therein is not on defining a notion of reachability which is compatible with the definition of [17]; rather, the authors exploit simplicial complexes as a description of relations between data, and the chosen accessibility relations between simplexes reflect such choice.

---

[10] We do not normalise the result to the maximum representable value 255, but just to 200, to make the lighter areas grey, which is more prominent on white paper.

Furthermore, without claiming to be exhaustive, we cite a few approaches to logic-based spatio-temporal analysis that are not directly related to SLCS. In [25] spiral electric waves—a precursor to atrial and ventricular fibrillation—are detected and specified using a spatial logic and model-checking tools. The formulas of the logic are learned from the spatial patterns under investigation and the onset of spiral waves is detected using bounded model checking. In the logical language SpaTeL [26], space is hierarchically divided in quadrants, and complex logic formulas, in the form of *quad-trees*, are built using machine learning methods. In [29], the authors define a logic language grounded on a chemical-based coordination model. Logic formulas are evaluated in a distributed manner by using an inference procedure which verifies them against the current global state of the system, checking whether the emergent global behaviour obeys to the required properties.

7 Outlook

We hope that reading this tutorial up-to here has not only initiated the reader to the basics of Spatial Model Checking and VoxLogicA, but has also raised some interest in the ongoing developments that will soon become relevant additions to the landscape of instruments devoted to spatial model checking. Currently, the VoxLogicA group is pursuing a few major research lines.

First and foremost, the immediate interest of the group is in advancing the healthcare related applications of Formal Methods and Spatial Model Checking in particular. Besides identifying new promising case studies, and improving the existing results, the integration, to some degree, of Machine Learning methods into logical specifications is an interesting scientific challenge. This could be used, for instance, to calibrate numeric parameters, or to accomplish some basic imaging tasks using Machine Learning, and coordinate them using explainable logical specifications to obtain more refined, complex results.

Very relevant for, but not limited to, the healthcare applications is the development of a dataset-oriented user interface that can leverage studies on the cognitive load on users (see e.g. [11]) in order to make logic-based analysis simpler to develop and more effective.

The natural setting in which such a user interface can be used is that of *interactive* development of logical specifications against training datasets. Currently, even if VoxLogicA is quite fast (often requiring no more than a few seconds to complete the analysis of a single case), running an analysis against a whole dataset is a *batch* (non-interactive) process. The progress on the implementation of spatial model checking on GPUs [12,13] may lead to a dramatic improvement in this respect.

Another way to reduce the computational cost of analysis is by making the models to be analysed *smaller*. The study of *minimization* algorithms up-to logical equivalence may be a key advancement in this direction [21,22].

Also relevant in so called "future healthcare" is the study of novel imaging modalities based on 3D meshes (instead of pixels/voxels); in the same vein, artificial vision and augmented reality applications are already starting to appear, especially in surgery. The work in [10] is the starting point of an effort in the direction of bringing the spatial analysis capabilities of VoxLogicA to the realm of 3D meshes. We note in passing that the applications of such methods are definitely not limited to the domain of healthcare, as 3D modelling is pervasive in several fields of modern Computer Science and its applications.

It is not difficult to imagine that a language such as ImgQL (dubbed a "query language" from its inception) could be useful as a true query language for datasets of images (think e.g. of the large radiological "Picture Archiving and Communication Systems (PACS)" that are nowadays in use in hospitals). One may be interested, for instance, in finding all the patients having a brain tumour of a particularly large size, or where the tumour may be too close to a specific organ at risk. In a recent position paper [5] some preliminary ideas are sketched in more detail.

Finally, we mention that, even though everything that was described in this paper is based on purely spatial analysis, the VoxLogicA group already has expertise in spatio-temporal modelling and logical specifications, through the tool topochecker, which was in a sense a predecessor to VoxLogicA but still has unique spatio-temporal verification capabilities (see [15,18,19,23,24]). Indeed, it is a planned future development to add such capabilities to VoxLogicA.

Acknowledgements. The authors wish to explicitly thank the current collaborators Nick Bezhanisvili, Giovanna Broccia, Laura Bussi, David Gabelaia, Fabio Gadducci, Gianluca Grilletti, Erik de Vink, and the coordinator of the *Formal Methods and Tools laboratory of ISTI-CNR* Maurice ter Beek, for their continuative support in turning the early developments of Spatial Model Checking, and the more recent work on VoxLogicA, into a solid research line, with several promising ongoing developments. The authors gratefully thank the Program Committee members of the *27th International SPIN Symposium on Model Checking of Software* (PC chairs Alfons Laarman and Ana Sokolova) for giving us the opportunity to disseminate our results to such an amazing audience.

References

1. Aiello, M., Pratt-Hartmann, I., Benthem, van, J.: Handbook of Spatial Logics. Springer (2007). https://doi.org/10.1007/978-1-4020-5587-4
2. Audrito, G., Casadei, R., Damiani, F., Stolz, V., Viroli, M.: Adaptive distributed monitors of spatial properties for cyber–physical systems. J. Syst. Softw. **175**, 110908 (2021). https://doi.org/10.1016/j.jss.2021.110908
3. Banci Buonamici, F., Belmonte, G., Ciancia, V., Latella, D., Massink, M.: Spatial logics and model checking for medical imaging. Int. J. Softw. Tools Technol. Transfer **22**(2), 195–217 (2019). https://doi.org/10.1007/s10009-019-00511-9
4. Bartocci, E., Bortolussi, L., Loreti, M., Nenzi, L.: Monitoring mobile and spatially distributed cyber-physical systems. In: 15th ACM-IEEE International Conference on Formal Methods and Models for System Design, MEMOCODE, pp. 146–155. ACM (2017). https://doi.org/10.1145/3127041.3127050

5. Belmonte, G., Broccia, G., Bussi, L., Ciancia, V., Latella, D., Massink, M.: Querying medical imaging datasets using spatial logics (position paper). In: HEDA2021: The International Health Data Workshop 2021 in conjunction with 10th International Conference on Model and Data Engineering (MEDI 2021). Communications in Computer and Information Science. Springer (2021, to Appear)
6. Belmonte, G., Broccia, G., Vincenzo, C., Latella, D., Massink, M.: Feasibility of spatial model checking for nevus segmentation. In: Proceedings of the 9th International Conference on Formal Methods in Software Engineering (FormaliSE'21), pp. 1–12. IEEE (2021). https://doi.org/10.1109/FormaliSE52586.2021.00007
7. Belmonte, G., Ciancia, V., Latella, D., Massink, M.: Innovating medical image analysis via spatial logics. In: ter Beek, M.H., Fantechi, A., Semini, L. (eds.) From Software Engineering to Formal Methods and Tools, and Back. LNCS, vol. 11865, pp. 85–109. Springer, Cham (2019). https://doi.org/10.1007/978-3-030-30985-5_7
8. Belmonte, G., Ciancia, V., Latella, D., Massink, M.: VoxLogicA: a spatial model checker for declarative image analysis. In: Vojnar, T., Zhang, L. (eds.) TACAS 2019. LNCS, vol. 11427, pp. 281–298. Springer, Cham (2019). https://doi.org/10.1007/978-3-030-17462-0_16
9. van Benthem, J., Bezhanishvili, G.: Modal logics of space. In: Handbook of Spatial Logics [1], pp. 217–298. https://doi.org/10.1007/978-1-4020-5587-4_5
10. Bezhanishvili, N., Ciancia, V., Gabelaia, D., Grilletti, G., Latella, D., Massink, M.: Geometric model checking of continuous space (2021). https://arxiv.org/abs/2105.06194
11. Broccia, G., Milazzo, P., Ölveczky, P.C.: Formal modeling and analysis of safety-critical human multitasking. Innov. Syst. Softw. Eng. 15(3-4), 169–190 (2019). https://doi.org/10.1007/s11334-019-00333-7
12. Bussi, L., Ciancia, V., Gadducci, F.: A spatial model checker in GPU (extended version). CoRR abs/2010.07284 (2020). https://arxiv.org/abs/2010.07284
13. Bussi, L., Ciancia, V., Gadducci, F.: Towards a spatial model checker on GPU. In: Peters, K., Willemse, T.A.C. (eds.) Formal Techniques for Distributed Objects, Components, and Systems FORTE 2021. LNCS, vol. 12719, pp. 188–196. Springer, Cham (2021). https://doi.org/10.1007/978-3-030-78089-0_12
14. Castelnovo, D., Miculan, M.: Closure hyperdoctrines, with paths. CoRR abs/2007.04213 (2020). https://arxiv.org/abs/2007.04213
15. Ciancia, V., Grilletti, G., Latella, D., Loreti, M., Massink, M.: An experimental spatio-temporal model checker. In: Bianculli, D., Calinescu, R., Rumpe, B. (eds.) SEFM 2015. LNCS, vol. 9509, pp. 297–311. Springer, Heidelberg (2015). https://doi.org/10.1007/978-3-662-49224-6_24
16. Ciancia, V., Latella, D., Loreti, M., Massink, M.: Specifying and verifying properties of space. In: Diaz, J., Lanese, I., Sangiorgi, D. (eds.) TCS 2014. LNCS, vol. 8705, pp. 222–235. Springer, Heidelberg (2014). https://doi.org/10.1007/978-3-662-44602-7_18
17. Ciancia, V., Latella, D., Loreti, M., Massink, M.: Model checking spatial logics for closure spaces. Logical Methods Comput. Sci. 12(4) (2016). https://doi.org/10.2168/LMCS-12(4:2)2016
18. Ciancia, V., Latella, D., Massink, M., Paškauskas, R., Vandin, A.: A tool-chain for statistical spatio-temporal model checking of bike sharing systems. In: Margaria, T., Steffen, B. (eds.) ISoLA 2016. LNCS, vol. 9952, pp. 657–673. Springer, Cham (2016). https://doi.org/10.1007/978-3-319-47166-2_46

19. Ciancia, V., Gilmore, S., Grilletti, G., Latella, D., Loreti, M., Massink, M.: Spatio-temporal model checking of vehicular movement in public transport systems. Int. J. Softw. Tools Technol. Transfer **20**(3), 289–311 (2018). https://doi.org/10.1007/s10009-018-0483-8

20. Ciancia, V., Latella, D., Massink, M.: Embedding RCC8D in the collective spatial logic CSLCS. In: Boreale, M., Corradini, F., Loreti, M., Pugliese, R. (eds.) Models, Languages, and Tools for Concurrent and Distributed Programming. LNCS, vol. 11665, pp. 260–277. Springer, Cham (2019). https://doi.org/10.1007/978-3-030-21485-2_15

21. Ciancia, V., Latella, D., Massink, M., de Vink, E.: Towards spatial bisimilarity for closure models: Logical and coalgebraic characterisations. CoRR abs/2005.05578 (2020). https://arxiv.org/abs/2005.05578

22. Ciancia, V., Latella, D., Massink, M., de Vink, E.: On bisimilarities for closure spaces - preliminary version (2021). https://arxiv.org/abs/2105.06690

23. Ciancia, V., Latella, D., Massink, M., Paškauskas, R.: Exploring spatio-temporal properties of bike-sharing systems. In: 2015 IEEE International Conference on Self-Adaptive and Self-Organizing Systems Workshops, SASO Workshops, pp. 74–79. IEEE Computer Society (2015). https://doi.org/10.1109/SASOW.2015.17

24. Grilletti, G.: Spatio-temporal model checking: explicit and abstraction-based methods. Master's thesis, University of Pisa (2016). https://etd.adm.unipi.it/t/etd-06282016-191103/

25. Grosu, R., Smolka, S., Corradini, F., Wasilewska, A., Entcheva, E., Bartocci, E.: Learning and detecting emergent behavior in networks of cardiac myocytes. Commun. ACM **52**(3), 97–105 (2009). https://doi.org/http://doi.acm.org/10.1145/1467247.1467271

26. Haghighi, I., Jones, A., Kong, Z., Bartocci, E., Grosu, R., Belta, C.: Spatel: A novel spatial-temporal logic and its applications to networked systems. In: Proceedings of the 18th International Conference on Hybrid Systems: Computation and Control, HSCC '15, pp. 189–198. ACM (2015). https://doi.org/10.1145/2728606.2728633

27. Linker, S., Papacchini, F., Sevegnani, M.: Analysing spatial properties on neighbourhood spaces. In: 45th International Symposium on Mathematical Foundations of Computer Science, MFCS, LIPIcs, vol. 170, pp. 66:1–66:14. Schloss Dagstuhl - Leibniz-Zentrum für Informatik (2020). https://doi.org/10.4230/LIPIcs.MFCS.2020.66

28. Loreti, M., Quadrini, M.: A spatial logic for a simplicial complex model (2021). https://arxiv.org/abs/2105.08708

29. Luca De Angelis, F., Di Marzo Serugendo, G.: A logic language for run time assessment of spatial properties in self-organizing systems. In: 2015 IEEE International Conference on Self-Adaptive and Self-Organizing Systems Workshops, pp. 86–91 (2015). https://doi.org/10.1109/SASOW.2015.19

30. Menze, B.H., et al.: The multimodal brain tumor image segmentation benchmark (brats). IEEE Trans. Med. Imag. **34**(10), 1993–2024 (2015). https://doi.org/10.1109/TMI.2014.2377694

31. Ciancia, V., Gilmore, S., Grilletti, G., Latella, D., Loreti, M., Massink, M.: Spatio-temporal model checking of vehicular movement in public transport systems. STTT **20**(3), 289–311 (2018). https://doi.org/10.1007/s10009-018-0483-8

32. Nenzi, L., Bortolussi, L.: Specifying and monitoring properties of stochastic spatio-temporal systems in signal temporal logic. In: Haviv, M., Knottenbelt, W.J., Maggi, L., Miorandi, D. (eds.) 8th International Conference on Performance Evaluation Methodologies and Tools, VALUETOOLS. ICST (2014). https://doi.org/10.4108/icst.valuetools.2014.258183

33. Nenzi, L., Bortolussi, L., Ciancia, V., Loreti, M., Massink, M.: Qualitative and quantitative monitoring of spatio-temporal properties. In: Bartocci, E., Majumdar, R. (eds.) RV 2015. LNCS, vol. 9333, pp. 21–37. Springer, Cham (2015). https://doi.org/10.1007/978-3-319-23820-3_2

34. Ruscheinski, A., Wolpers, A., Henning, P., Warnke, T., Haack, F., Uhrmacher, A.M.: Pragmatic logic-based spatio-temporal pattern checking in particle-based models. In: Winter Simulation Conference, WSC 2020, pp. 2245–2256. IEEE (2020). https://doi.org/10.1109/WSC48552.2020.9383908

35. Tsigkanos, C., Kehrer, T., Ghezzi, C.: Modeling and verification of evolving cyber-physical spaces. In: Proceedings of the 11th Joint Meeting on Foundations of Software Engineering, ESEC/FSE 2017, pp. 38–48. ACM (2017). https://doi.org/10.1145/3106237.3106299

Model Checking

Accelerating the Computation of Dead and Concurrent Places Using Reductions

Nicolas Amat$^{(\boxtimes)}$ [iD], Silvano Dal Zilio [iD], and Didier Le Botlan [iD]

LAAS-CNRS, Université de Toulouse, CNRS, INSA, Toulouse, France
namat@laas.fr

Abstract. We propose a new method for accelerating the computation of a concurrency relation, that is all pairs of places in a Petri net that can be marked together. Our approach relies on a state space abstraction, that involves a mix between structural reductions and linear algebra, and a new data-structure that is specifically designed for our task. Our algorithms are implemented in a tool, called Kong, that we test on a large collection of models used during the 2020 edition of the Model Checking Contest. Our experiments show that the approach works well, even when a moderate amount of reductions applies.

1 Introduction

We propose a new approach for computing the *concurrency relation* of a Petri net, that is all pairs of places that can be marked together in some reachable states. This problem has practical applications, for instance because of its use for decomposing a Petri net into the product of concurrent processes [9,10]. It also provides an interesting example of safety property that nicely extends the notion of *dead places*. These problems raise difficult technical challenges and provide an opportunity to test and improve new model checking techniques [11].

Naturally, it is possible to compute the concurrency relation by first computing the complete state space of a system and then checking, individually, the reachability of each pair of places. But this amounts to solving a quadratic number of reachability properties—where the parameter is the number of places in the net—and one would expect to find smarter solutions, even if it is only for some specific cases. We are also interested in partial solutions, where computing the whole state space is not feasible.

We recently became interested in this problem because we see it as a good testbed for a new model checking technique that we are actively developing [1,5,6]. It is an abstraction technique, based on the use of structural reductions [3], that we successfully implemented into a symbolic model checker called Tedd. The idea is to compute reductions of the form $N_1 \rhd_E N_2$, where: N_1 is an initial Petri net (that we want to analyse); N_2 is a residual net (hopefully simpler than N_1); and E is a system of linear equations. The goal is to preserve enough information in E so that we can rebuild the reachable markings of N_1 knowing only those of N_2. While there are many examples of the benefits of

© Springer Nature Switzerland AG 2021
A. Laarman and A. Sokolova (Eds.): SPIN 2021, LNCS 12864, pp. 45–62, 2021.
https://doi.org/10.1007/978-3-030-84629-9_3

structural reductions when model checking Petri nets, the use of an equation system (E) for tracing back the effect of reductions is new, and we are hopeful that this approach can be applied to other problems. For example, we proved recently [1] that this approach also works well when combined with SMT.

In this paper, we confirm that the same holds true when we tackle the concurrent places problem. In practice, we can often reduce a net N_1 into another net N_2 with far fewer places. We show that we can reconstruct the concurrency relation of N_1 from the one of N_2, using a surprising and very efficient "inverse transform" that depends only on E and does not involve computing reachable markings. (This is a model checking paper where no transitions are fired!) This is useful since the number of places is a predominant parameter when computing the concurrency relation. Note that we are not concerned with how to compute the relation on N_2, but only by how we can *accelerate* its calculation on N_1.

Related Work. Several works address the problem of finding or characterizing the concurrent places of a Petri net. This notion is mentioned under various names, such as *coexistency defined by markings* [18], *concurrency graph* [27] or *concurrency relation* [12,19,20,24,28]. The main motivation is that the concurrency relation characterizes the sub-parts, in a net, that can be simultaneously active. Therefore it plays a useful role when decomposing a net into a collection of independent components. This is the case in [28], where the authors draw a connection between concurrent places and the presence of "sequential modules (state machines)". Another example is the decomposition of nets into unit-safe NUPNs (Nested-Unit Petri Nets) [9,10], for which the computation of the concurrency relation is one of the main bottlenecks.

We know only a couple of tools that support the computation of the concurrency relation. A recent tool is part of the Hippo platform [28], available online. Our reference tool is CÆSAR.BDD, from the CADP toolbox [8,17], that uses BDD techniques to explore the state space of a net and find concurrent places. It supports the computation of a partial relation and can output the "concurrency matrix" of a net using a specific textual format [11]. We adopt the same format since we use CÆSAR.BDD to compute the concurrency relation on the residual net, N_2, and as a yardstick in our benchmarks.

Concerning our use of structural reductions, our main result can be interpreted as an example of *reduction theorem* [22], that allows to deduce properties of an initial model (N_1) from properties of a simpler, coarser-grained version (N_2). But our notion of reduction is more complex and corresponds to the one pioneered by Berthelot [3] (with the equations added). Several tools use reductions for checking reachability properties but none specializes in computing the concurrency relation. We can mention TAPAAL [7], an explicit-state model checker that combines partial-order reduction techniques and structural reductions or, more recently, ITS Tools [26], which combines several techniques, including structural reductions and the use of SAT and SMT solvers.

Outline and Contributions. We define the semantics of Petri nets and the notion of concurrent places in Sect. 2. This section also introduces a simplified notion of "reachability equivalence", called *polyhedral abstraction*, that gives a formal definition to the relation $N_1 \rhd_E N_2$. Section 3 contains our main contributions. We describe a new data-structure, called Token Flow Graph (TFG), that captures the particular structure of the equation system generated with our approach. We prove several results on TFGs that allow us to reason about the reachable places of a net by playing a token game on this graph. We use TFGs (Sect. 4) to define an algorithm that implements our "inverse transform" and show how to adapt it to situations where we only have partial knowledge of the residual concurrency relation. Our approach has been implemented and computing experiments (Sect. 5) show that reductions are effective on a large set of models. We perform our experiments on an independently managed collection of Petri nets (588 instances) corresponding to the safe nets used during the 2020 edition of the Model Checking Contest [2]. We observe that, even with a moderate amount of reductions (say we can remove 25% of the places), we can compute complete results much faster with reductions than without (often with speed-ups greater than $\times 100$). We also show that we perform well with incomplete relations, where we are both faster and more accurate.

2   Petri Nets and Polyhedral Abstraction

A *Petri net* N is a tuple $(P, T, \mathbf{pre}, \mathbf{post})$ where $P = \{p_1, \ldots, p_n\}$ is a finite set of places, $T = \{t_1, \ldots, t_k\}$ is a finite set of transitions (disjoint from P), and $\mathbf{pre} : T \to (P \to \mathbb{N})$ and $\mathbf{post} : T \to (P \to \mathbb{N})$ are the pre- and post-condition functions (also called the *flow functions* of N). We often simply write that p is a place of N when $p \in P$. A state m of a net, also called a *marking*, is a total mapping $m : P \to \mathbb{N}$ which assigns a number of *tokens*, $m(p)$, to each place of N. A marked net (N, m_0) is a pair composed of a net and its initial marking m_0.

A transition $t \in T$ is *enabled* at marking $m \in \mathbb{N}^P$ when $m(p) \geqslant \mathbf{pre}(t, p)$ for all places p in P. (We can also simply write $m \geqslant \mathbf{pre}(t)$, where $\geqslant$ stands for the component-wise comparison of markings.) A marking m' is reachable from a marking m by firing transition t, denoted $m \xrightarrow{t} m'$, if: (1) transition t is enabled at m; and (2) $m' = m - \mathbf{pre}(t) + \mathbf{post}(t)$. When the identity of the transition is unimportant, we simply write this relation $m \to m'$. More generally, marking m' is reachable from m in N, denoted $m \to^* m'$ if there is a (possibly empty) sequence of reductions such that $m \to \ldots \to m'$. We denote $R(N, m_0)$ the set of markings reachable from m_0 in N.

A marking m is k-bounded when each place has at most k tokens and a marked Petri net (N, m_0) is bounded when there is a constant k such that all reachable markings are k-bounded. While most of our results are valid in the general case—with nets that are not necessarily bounded and without any restrictions on the flow functions (the weights of the arcs)—our tool and our experiments focus on the class of 1-bounded nets, also called *safe* nets.

Given a marked net (N, m_0), we say that places p, q of N are concurrent when there exists a reachable marking m with both p and q marked. The *Concurrent Places* problem consists in enumerating all such pairs of places.

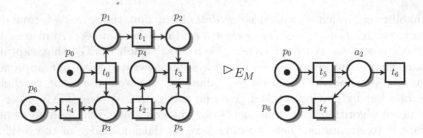

Fig. 1. An example of Petri net, M_1 (left), and one of its polyhedral abstraction, M_2 (right), with $E_M \triangleq (p_5 = p_4), (a_1 = p_1 + p_2), (a_2 = p_3 + p_4), (a_1 = a_2)$.

Definition 1 (Dead and Concurrent places). *We say that a place p of (N, m_0) is* not-dead *if there is m in $R(N, m_0)$ such that $m(p) > 0$. In a similar way, we say that places p, q are* concurrent, *denoted $p \parallel q$, if there is m in $R(N, m_0)$ such that both $m(p) > 0$ and $m(q) > 0$. By extension, we use the notation $p \parallel p$ when p is not-dead. We say that p, q are* nonconcurrent, *denoted $p \# q$, when they are not concurrent.*

Relation with Linear Arithmetic Constraints. Many results in Petri net theory are based on a relation with linear algebra and linear programming techniques [23, 25]. A celebrated example is that the potentially reachable markings of a net (N, m_0) are non-negative, integer solutions to the *state equation* problem, $m = I \cdot \sigma + m_0$, with I an integer matrix defined from the flow functions of N and σ a vector in $\mathbb{N}^k$. It is known that solutions to the system of linear equations $\sigma^T \cdot I = \mathbf{0}$ lead to *place invariants*, $\sigma^T \cdot m = \sigma^T \cdot m_0$, that can provide some information on the decomposition of a net into blocks of nonconcurrent places, and therefore information on the concurrency relation.

For example, for net M_1 (Fig. 1), we can compute invariant $p_4 - p_5 = 0$. This is enough to prove that places p_4 and p_5 are concurrent, if we can prove that at least one of them is not-dead. Likewise, an invariant of the form $p + q = 1$ is enough to prove that p and q are 1-bounded and cannot be concurrent. Unfortunately, invariants provide only an over-approximation of the set of reachable markings, and it may be difficult to find whether a net is part of the few known classes where the set of reachable markings equals the set of potentially reachable ones [16].

Our approach shares some similarities with this kind of reasoning. A main difference is that we will use equation systems to draw a relation between the reachable markings of two nets; not to express constraints about (potentially) reachable markings inside one net. Like with invariants, this will allow us, in many cases, to retrieve information about the concurrency relation without "firing any transition", that is without exploring the state space.

In the following, we will often use place names as variables, and markings $m : P \to \mathbb{N}$ as partial solutions to a set of linear equations. For the sake of simplicity, all our equations will be of the form $x = y_1 + \cdots + y_l$ or $y_1 + \cdots + y_l = k$ (with k a constant in $\mathbb{N}$).

Given a system of linear equations E, we denote $fv(E)$ the set of all its variables. We are only interested in the non-negative integer solutions of E. Hence, in our case, a *solution* to E is a total mapping from variables in $fv(E)$ to $\mathbb{N}$ such that all the equations in E are satisfied. We say that E is *consistent* when there is at least one such solution. Given these definitions, we say that the mapping $m : \{p_1, \ldots, p_n\} \to \mathbb{N}$ is a (partial) solution of E if the system $E, \lfloor m \rfloor$ is consistent, with $\lfloor m \rfloor$ the sequence of equations $p_1 = m(p_1), \ldots, p_n = m(p_n)$. (In some sense, we use $\lfloor m \rfloor$ as a substitution.) For instance, places p, q are concurrent if the system $p = 1 + x$, $q = 1 + y$, $\lfloor m \rfloor$ is consistent, where m is a reachable marking and x, y are some fresh (slack) variables.

Given two markings $m_1 : P_1 \to \mathbb{N}$ and $m_2 : P_2 \to \mathbb{N}$, from possibly different nets, we say that m_1 and m_2 are *compatible*, denoted $m_1 \equiv m_2$, if they have equal marking on their shared places: $m_1(p) = m_2(p)$ for all p in $P_1 \cap P_2$. This is a necessary and sufficient condition for the system $\lfloor m_1 \rfloor$, $\lfloor m_2 \rfloor$ to be consistent.

Polyhedral Abstraction. We recently defined a notion of *polyhedral abstraction* based on our previous work applying structural reductions to model counting [1,6]. We only need a simplified version of this notion here, which entails an equivalence between the state space of two nets, (N_1, m_1) and (N_2, m_2), "up-to" a system E of linear equations.

Definition 2 (E-equivalence). *We say that (N_1, m_1) is E-equivalent to (N_2, m_2), denoted $(N_1, m_1) \rhd_E (N_2, m_2)$, if and only if:*

(A1) E, $\lfloor m \rfloor$ *is consistent for all markings m in $R(N_1, m_1)$ and $R(N_2, m_2)$;*
(A2) *initial markings are* compatible, *meaning E, $\lfloor m_1 \rfloor$, $\lfloor m_2 \rfloor$ is consistent;*
(A3) *assume m'_1, m'_2 are markings of N_1, N_2, respectively, such that E, $\lfloor m'_1 \rfloor$, $\lfloor m'_2 \rfloor$ is consistent, then m'_1 is reachable if and only if m'_2 is reachable:*
$m'_1 \in R(N_1, m_1) \iff m'_2 \in R(N_2, m_2)$.

By definition, relation $\rhd_E$ is symmetric. We deliberately use a symbol oriented from left to right to stress the fact that N_2 should be a reduced version of N_1. In particular, we expect to have less places in N_2 than in N_1.

Given a relation $(N_1, m_1) \rhd_E (N_2, m_2)$, each marking m'_2 reachable in N_2 can be associated to a unique subset of markings in N_1, defined from the solutions to $E, \lfloor m'_2 \rfloor$ (by condition A1 and A3). We can show that this gives a partition of the reachable markings of (N_1, m_1) into "convex sets"—hence the name polyhedral abstraction—each associated to a reachable marking in N_2. Our approach is particularly useful when the state space of N_2 is very small compared to the one of N_1. In the extreme case, we can even find examples where N_2 is the "empty" net (a net with zero places, and therefore a unique marking), but this condition is not a requisite in our approach.

We can illustrate this result using the two marked nets M_1, M_2 in Fig. 1, for which we can prove that $M_1 \rhd_{E_M} M_2$. We have that $m'_2 \triangleq a_2 = 1$, $p_6 = 1$ is reachable in M_2, which means that every solution to the system $p_0 = 0$, $p_1 + p_2 = 1$, $p_3 + p_4 = 1$, $p_4 = p_5$, $p_6 = 1$ gives a reachable marking of M_1. Moreover, every solution such that $p_i \geqslant 1$ and $p_j \geqslant 1$ gives a witness that $p_i \parallel p_j$. For instance,

p_1, p_4, p_5 and p_6 are certainly concurrent together. We should exploit the fact that, under some assumptions about E, we can find all such "pairs of variables" without the need to explicitly solve systems of the form E, $\lfloor m \rfloor$; just by looking at the structure of E.

For this current work, we do not need to explain how to derive or check that an equivalence statement is correct in order to describe our method. In practice, we start from an initial net, (N_1, m_1), and derive (N_2, m_2) and E using a combination of several structural reduction rules. You can find a precise description of our set of rules in [6] and a proof that the result of these reductions always leads to a valid E-equivalence in [1]. In most cases, the system of linear equations obtained using this process exhibits a graph-like structure. In the next section, we describe a set of constraints that formalizes this observation. This is one of the contributions of this paper, since we never defined something equivalent in our previous works. We show with our benchmarks (Sect. 5) that these constraints are general enough to give good results on a large set of models.

3   Token Flow Graphs

We introduce a set of structural constraints on the equations occurring in an equivalence statement $(N_1, m_1) \rhd_E (N_2, m_2)$. The goal is to define an algorithm that is able to easily compute information on the concurrency relation of N_1, given the concurrency relation on N_2, by taking advantage of the structure of the equations in E.

We define the *Token Flow Graph* (TFG) of a system E of linear equations as a Directed Acyclic Graph (DAG) with one vertex for each variable occurring in E. Arcs in the TFG are used to depict the relation induced by equations in E. We consider two kinds of arcs. Arcs for *redundancy equations*, $q \rightarrow\!\!\bullet\, p$, to represent equations of the form $p = q$ (or $p = q + r + \ldots$), expressing that the marking of place p can be reconstructed from the marking of $q, r, \ldots$ In this case, we say that place p is *removed* by arc $q \rightarrow\!\!\bullet\, p$, because the marking of q may influence the marking of p, but not necessarily the other way round.

The second kind of arcs, $a \circ\!\!\rightarrow p$, is for *agglomeration equations*. It represents equations of the form $a = p + q$, generated when we agglomerate several places into a new one. In this case, we expect that if we can reach a marking with k tokens in a, then we can certainly reach a marking with k_1 tokens in p and k_2 tokens in q when $k = k_1 + k_2$ (see property Agglomeration in Lemma 2). Hence information flows in reverse order compared to the case of redundancy equations. This is why, in this case, we say that places/nodes p and q are removed. We also say that node a is *inserted*; it does not appear in N_1 but may appear as a new place in N_2. We can have more than two places in an agglomeration.

A TFG can also include nodes for *constants*, used to express invariant statements on the markings of the form $p + q = k$. To this end, we assume that we have a family of disjoint sets $K(n)$ (also disjoint from place and variable names), for each n in $\mathbb{N}$, such that the "valuation" of a node $v \in K(n)$ will always be n. We use K to denote the set of all constants.

Definition 3 (Token Flow Graph). *A TFG with set of places P is a directed (bi)graph* (V, R, A) *such that:* $V = P \cup S$ *is a set of vertices (or nodes) with* $S \subset K$ *a finite set of constants;* $R \in V \times V$ *is a set of* redundancy *arcs,* $v \rightarrowtail v'$; *and* $A \in V \times V$ *is a set of* agglomeration *arcs,* $v \circ\!\!\rightarrow v'$, *disjoint from R.*

The main source of complexity in our approach arises from the need to manage interdependencies between A and R nodes, that is situations where redundancies and agglomerations alternate. This is not something that can be easily achieved by looking only at the equations in E and what motivates the need to define a specific data-structure.

We define several notations that will be useful in the following. We use the notation $v \rightarrow v'$ when we have $(v \rightarrowtail v')$ in R or $(v \circ\!\!\rightarrow v')$ in A. We say that a node v is a *root* if it is never the target of an arc. A sequence of nodes $(v_1, \ldots, v_n)$ in V^n is a *path* if we have $v_i \rightarrow v_{i+1}$ for all $i < n$. We use the notation $v \rightarrow^\star v'$ when there is a path from v to v' in the graph, or when $v = v'$. We write $v \circ\!\!\rightarrow X$ when X is the largest subset $\{v_1, \ldots, v_k\}$ of V such that $X \neq \emptyset$ and $v \circ\!\!\rightarrow v_i \in A$ for all $i \in 1..k$. Similarly, we write $X \rightarrowtail v$ when X is the largest, non-empty set of nodes $\{v_1, \ldots, v_k\}$ such that $v_i \rightarrowtail v \in R$ for all $i \in 1..k$.

We display an example of Token Flow Graphs in Fig. 2, where "black dot" arcs model edges in R and "white dot" arcs model edges in A. The idea is that each relation $X \rightarrowtail v$ or $v \circ\!\!\rightarrow X$ corresponds to one equation $v = \sum_{v_i \in X} v_i$ in E, and that all the equations in E should be reflected in the TFG. We want to avoid situations where the same place is removed more than once, or where some place occurs in the TFG but is never mentioned in N_1, N_2 or E. All these constraints can be expressed using a suitable notion of well-formed graph.

Definition 4 (Well-Formed TFG). *A TFG* $G = (V, R, A)$ *for the equivalence statement* $(N_1, m_1) \rhd_E (N_2, m_2)$ *is* well-formed *when all the following constraints are met, where* P_1 *and* P_2 *stand for the set of places in* N_1 *and* N_2:

(T1) no unused names: $V \setminus K = P_1 \cup P_2 \cup fv(E)$,
(T2) nodes in K are roots: *if* $v \in V \cap K$ *then* v *is a root of* G,
(T3) nodes can be removed only once: *it is not possible to have* $p \circ\!\!\rightarrow q$ *and* $p' \rightarrow q$ *with* $p \neq p'$, *or to have both* $p \rightarrowtail q$ *and* $p \circ\!\!\rightarrow q$,
(T4) we have all and only the equations in E: *we have* $v \circ\!\!\rightarrow X$ *or* $X \rightarrowtail v$ *if and only if the equation* $v = \sum_{v_i \in X} v_i$ *is in* E.

Given a relation $(N_1, m_1) \rhd_E (N_2, m_2)$, the well-formedness conditions are enough to ensure the unicity of a TFG (up-to the choice of constant nodes) when we set each equation to be either in A or in R. In this case, we denote this TFG $[\![E]\!]$. In practice, we use a tool called Reduce to generate the E-equivalence from the initial net (N_1, m_1). This tool outputs a sequence of equations suitable to build a TFG and, for each equation, it adds a tag indicating if it is a Redundancy or an Agglomeration. We display in Fig. 2 the equations generated by Reduce for the net M_1 given in Fig. 1.

A consequence of condition (T3) is that a well-formed TFG is necessarily acyclic; once a place has been removed, it cannot be used to remove a place later.

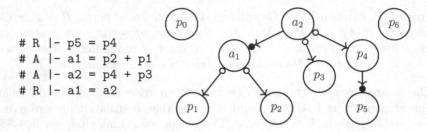

```
# R |- p5 = p4
# A |- a1 = p2 + p1
# A |- a2 = p4 + p3
# R |- a1 = a2
```

Fig. 2. Equations generated from net M_1, in Fig. 1, and associated TFG $[\![E_M]\!]$

Moreover, in the case of reductions generated from structural reductions, the roots of the graph are exactly the constant nodes and the places that occur in N_2 (since they are not removed by any equation). The constraints (T1)–(T4) are not artificial or arbitrary. In practice, we compute E-equivalences using multiple steps of structural reductions, and a TFG exactly records the constraints and information generated during these reductions. In some sense, equations E abstract a relation between the semantics of two nets, whereas a TFG records the structure of reductions between places during reductions.

Configurations of a Token Flow Graph. By construction, there is a strong connection between "systems of reduction equations", E, and their associated graph, $[\![E]\!]$. We show that a similar relation exists between solutions of E and "valuations" of the graph (what we call *configurations* thereafter).

A *configuration* c of a TFG (V, R, A) is a partial function from V to $\mathbb{N}$. We use the notation $c(v) = \bot$ when c is not defined on v and we always assume that $c(v) = n$ when v is a constant node in $K(n)$.

Configuration c is *total* when $c(v)$ is defined for all nodes v in V; otherwise it is said *partial*. We use the notation $c_{|N}$ for the configuration obtained from c by restricting its support to the set of places in the net N. We remark that when c is defined over all places of N then $c_{|N}$ can be viewed as a marking. By association with markings, we say that two configurations c and c' are *compatible*, denoted $c \equiv c'$, if they have same value on the nodes where they are both defined: $c(p) = c'(p)$ when $c(v) \neq \bot$ and $c'(v) \neq \bot$. We also use $\lfloor c \rfloor$ to represent the system $v_1 = c(v_1), \dots, v_k = c(v_k)$ where the $(v_i)_{i \in 1..k}$ are the nodes such that $c(v_i) \neq \bot$. We say that a configuration c is *well-defined* when the valuation of the nodes agrees with the equations associated with the A and R arcs of $[\![E]\!]$.

Definition 5 (Well-Defined Configurations). *Configuration c is well-defined when for all nodes p the following two conditions hold:* **(CBot)** *if $v \to w$ then $c(v) = \bot$ if and only if $c(w) = \bot$; and* **(CEq)** *if $c(v) \neq \bot$ and $v \circ\!\!\rightarrow X$ or $X \rightarrow\!\!\bullet\, v$ then $c(v) = \sum_{v_i \in X} c(v_i)$.*

We prove that the well-defined configurations of a TFG $[\![E]\!]$ are partial solutions of E, and reciprocally. Therefore, because all the variables in E are nodes in the TFG (condition T1) we have an equivalence between solutions of E and total, well-defined configurations of $[\![E]\!]$.

Lemma 1 (Well-defined Configurations are Solutions). *Assume $\llbracket E \rrbracket$ is a well-formed TFG for the equivalence $(N_1, m_1) \rhd_E (N_2, m_2)$. If c is a well-defined configuration of $\llbracket E \rrbracket$ then E , $\lfloor c \rfloor$ is consistent. Conversely, if c is a total configuration of $\llbracket E \rrbracket$ such that E , $\lfloor c \rfloor$ is consistent then c is also well-defined.*

We can prove several properties related to how the structure of a TFG constrains possible values in well-formed configurations. These results can be thought of as the equivalent of a "token game", which explains how tokens can propagate along the arcs of a TFG. This is useful in our context since we can assess that two nodes are concurrent when we can mark them in the same configuration. (A similar result holds for finding pairs of nonconcurrent nodes.)

Our first result shows that we can always propagate tokens from a node to its children, meaning that if a node has a token, we can find one in its *successors* (possibly in a different well-defined configuration). In the following, we use the notation $\downarrow v$ for the set of successors of v, meaning: $\downarrow p \triangleq \bigcup \{q \in V \mid p \to^* q\}$. Property (Backward) states a dual result; if a child node is marked then one of its parents must be marked.

Lemma 2 (Token Propagation). *Assume $\llbracket E \rrbracket$ is a well-formed TFG for the equivalence $(N_1, m_1) \rhd_E (N_2, m_2)$ and c a well-defined configuration of $\llbracket E \rrbracket$.*

(Forward) *if p, q are nodes such that $c(p) \neq \perp$ and $p \to^* q$ then we can find a well-defined configuration c' such that $c'(q) \geqslant c'(p) = c(p)$ and $c'(v) = c(v)$ for every node v not in $\downarrow p$.*

(Backward) *if $c(p) > 0$ then there is a root v such that $v \to^* p$ and $c(v) > 0$.*

(Agglomeration) *if $p \multimap \{q_1, \ldots, q_k\}$ and $c(p) \neq \perp$ then for every sequence $(l_i)_{i \in 1..k}$ of $\mathbb{N}^k$, if $c(p) = \sum_{i \in 1..k} l_i$ then we can find a well-defined configuration c' such that $c'(p) = c(p)$, and $c'(q_i) = l_i$ for all $i \in 1..k$, and $c'(v) = c(v)$ for every node v not in $\downarrow p$.*

Until this point, none of our results rely on the properties of E-equivalence. We now prove that there is an equivalence between reachable markings and configurations of $\llbracket E \rrbracket$. More precisely, we prove (Theorem 1) that every reachable marking in N_1 or N_2 can be extended into a well-defined configuration of $\llbracket E \rrbracket$. This entails that we can reconstruct all the reachable markings of N_1 by looking at well-defined configurations obtained from the reachable markings of N_2. Our algorithm (see next section) will be a bit smarter since we do not need to enumerate exhaustively all the markings of N_2. Instead, we only need to know which roots can be marked together.

Theorem 1 (Configuration Reachability). *Assume $\llbracket E \rrbracket$ is a well-formed TFG for the equivalence $(N_1, m_1) \rhd_E (N_2, m_2)$. If m is a marking in $R(N_1, m_1)$ or $R(N_2, m_2)$ then there exists a total, well-defined configuration c of $\llbracket E \rrbracket$ such that $c \equiv m$. Conversely, given a total, well-defined configuration c of $\llbracket E \rrbracket$, if marking $c_{|N_1}$ is reachable in (N_1, m_1) then $c_{|N_2}$ is reachable in (N_2, m_2).*

Proof (sketch). Take m a marking in $R(N_1, m_1)$. By property of E-abstraction, there is a reachable marking m_2' in $R(N_2, m_2)$ such that E , $\lfloor m \rfloor$, $\lfloor m_2' \rfloor$ is consistent. Therefore we can find a non-negative integer solution c to the system

E, $\lfloor m \rfloor$, $\lfloor m'_2 \rfloor$. And c is total because of condition (T1). For the converse property, we assume that c is a total and well-defined configuration of $[\![E]\!]$ and that $c_{|N_1}$ is a marking of $R(N_1, m_1)$. By Lemma 1, since c is well-defined, we have that E, $\lfloor c \rfloor$ is consistent, and therefore so is E, $\lfloor c_{|N_1} \rfloor$, $\lfloor c_{|N_2} \rfloor$. This entails $c_{|N_2}$ in $R(N_2, m_2)$ by condition (A3), as needed. $\square$

In the following, we will often consider that nets are safe. This is not a problem in practice since our reduction rules preserve safeness. Hence we do not need to check if (N_2, m_2) is safe when (N_1, m_1) is. The fact that the nets are safe has consequences. In particular, as a direct corollary of Theorem 1, we can assume that, for any well-defined configuration c, if $c_{|N_2}$ is reachable in (N_2, m_2) then $c(v) \in \{0, 1\}$.

By Theorem 1, if we take reachable markings in N_2—meaning we fix the values of roots in $[\![E]\!]$—we can find places of N_1 that are marked together by propagating tokens from the roots to the leaves (Lemma 2). In our algorithm, next, we show that we can compute the concurrency relation of N_1 by looking at just two cases: (1) we start with a token in a single root p, with p not dead, and propagate this token forward until we find a configuration with two places of N_1 marked together; or (2) we do the same but placing a token in two separate roots, p_1, p_2, such that $p_1 \parallel p_2$. We base our approach on the fact that we can extend the notion of concurrent places (in a marked net), to the notion of concurrent nodes in a TFG, meaning nodes that can be marked together in a "reachable configuration".

4   Dimensionality Reduction Algorithm

We define an algorithm that takes as inputs a well-formed TFG $[\![E]\!]$ plus the concurrency relation for the net (N_2, m_2), say $\parallel_2$, and outputs the concurrency relation for (N_1, m_1), say $\parallel_1$. Actually, our algorithm computes a *concurrency matrix*, C, that is a matrix such that $\mathrm{C}[v, w] = 1$ when the nodes v, w can be marked together in a "reachable configuration", and 0 otherwise. We prove (Theorem 2) that the relation induced by C matches with $\parallel_1$ on N_1. For the case of "partial relations", we use $\mathrm{C}[v, w] = \bullet$ to mean that the relation is undecided. In this case we say that matrix C is *incomplete*.

The complexity of computing the concurrency relation is highly dependent on the number of places in the net. For this reason, we say that our algorithm performs some sort of a "dimensionality reduction", because it allows us to solve a problem in a high-dimension space (the number of places in N_1) by solving it first on a lower dimension space (since N_2 may have far fewer places) and then transporting back the result to the original net. In practice, we compute the concurrency relation on (N_2, m_2) using the tool CÆSAR.BDD from the CADP toolbox; but we can rely on any kind of "oracle" to compute this relation for us. This step is not necessary when the initial net is fully reducible, in which case the concurrency relation for N_2 is trivial and all the roots in $[\![E]\!]$ are constants.

Function Matrix($\llbracket E \rrbracket$: TFG, $\|_2$: concurrency relation on (N_2, m_2))

Result: the concurrency matrix C

```
1  C ← 0                           /* the matrix is initialized with zeros */
2  foreach root v in ⟦E⟧ do
3  |   if v ∥₂ v then
4  |   |   succs[v] ← Propagate(⟦E⟧, C, v)
5  foreach pair of roots (v, w) in ⟦E⟧ do
6  |   if v ∥₂ w then
7  |   |   foreach (v′, w′) ∈ succs[v] × succs[w] do C[v′, w′] ← 1
8  return C
```

Function Propagate($\llbracket E \rrbracket$: TFG, C : concurrency matrix, v : node)

Result: the successors of v in $\llbracket E \rrbracket$. As a side-effect, we add to C all the relations that stem from knowing v not-dead.

```
1  C[v, v] ← 1
2  succs ← {v}                     /* succs collects the nodes in ↓v */
3  succr ← {}         /* auxiliary variable used to store ↓w when v —•→ w */
4  foreach w such that v ○→ w do succs ← succs ∪ Propagate(⟦E⟧, C, w)
5  foreach w such that v —•→ w do
6  |   succr ← Propagate(⟦E⟧, C, w)
7  |   foreach (v′, w′) ∈ succs × succr do C[v′, w′] ← 1
8  |   succs ← succs ∪ succr
9  return succs
```

We assume that $\llbracket E \rrbracket$ is a well-formed TFG for the relation $(N_1, m_1) \rhd_E (N_2, m_2)$; that both nets are safe; and that all the roots in $\llbracket E \rrbracket$ are either constants (in $K(0) \cup K(1)$) or places in N_2. We use symbol $\|_2$ for the concurrency relation on (N_2, m_2) and $\|_1$ on (N_1, m_1). To simplify our notations, we assume that $v \|_2 w$ when v is a constant node in $K(1)$ and w is not-dead. On the opposite, $v \#_2 w$ when $v \in K(0)$ or w is dead.

Our algorithm is divided into two main functions, Matrix and Propagate. In the main function, Matrix, we iterate over the non-dead roots of $\llbracket E \rrbracket$ and recursively propagates a "token" to its successors (the call to Propagate in line 4). After this step, we know all the live nodes in C. The call to Propagate has two effects. First, we retrieve the list of successors of the live roots. Second, as a side-effect, we update the concurrency matrix C by finding all the concurrent nodes that arise from a unique root. We can prove all such cases arise from redundancy arcs that are "under node v". Actually, we can prove that if $v \to w_1$ and $v \mathrel{-\!\!\bullet\!\!\to} w_2$ (with $w_1 \neq w_2$) then the nodes in the set $\downarrow v \setminus \downarrow w_2$ are concurrent to all the nodes in $\downarrow w_2$. Next, in the second **foreach** loop of Matrix, we compute the concurrent nodes that arise from two distinct live roots (v, w). In this case, we can prove that all the successors of v are concurrent with successors of w: all the pairs in $\downarrow v \times \downarrow w$ are concurrent.

We can prove that our algorithm is sound and complete using the theory that we developed on TFGs and configurations.

Theorem 2. *If C is the matrix returned by a call to* $\mathtt{Matrix}(\llbracket E \rrbracket, \Vert_2)$ *then for all places* p, q *in* N_1 *we have* $p \Vert_1 q$ *if and only if either* $\mathrm{C}[p,q] = 1$ *or* $\mathrm{C}[q,p] = 1$.

We can perform a cursory analysis of the complexity of our algorithm. By construction, we update the matrix by following the edges of $\llbracket E \rrbracket$, starting from the roots. Since a TFG is a DAG, it means that we could call function $\mathtt{Propagate}$ several times on the same node. However, a call to $\mathtt{Propagate}(\llbracket E \rrbracket, \mathrm{C}, v)$ can only update C by adding a 1 between nodes that are successors of v (information only flows in the direction of $\rightarrow$). It means that $\mathtt{Propagate}$ is idempotent; a subsequent call to $\mathtt{Propagate}(\llbracket E \rrbracket, \mathrm{C}, v)$ will never change the values in C. As a consequence, we can safely memoize the result of this call and we only need to go through a node at most once. More precisely, we need to call $\mathtt{Propagate}$ only on the nodes that are not-dead in $\llbracket E \rrbracket$. During each call to $\mathtt{Propagate}$, we may update at most $O(N^2)$ values in C, where N is the number of nodes in $\llbracket E \rrbracket$, which is also $O(|\mathrm{C}|)$, the size of our output. In conclusion, our algorithm has a linear time complexity (in the number of live nodes) if we count the numbers of function calls and a linear complexity, in the size of the output, if we count the number of updates to C. This has to be compared with the complexity of building then checking the state space of the net, which is PSPACE.

In practice, our algorithm is very efficient, highly parallelizable, and its execution time is often negligible when compared to the other tasks involved when computing the concurrency relation. We give some results on our performances in the next section.

Extensions to Incomplete Concurrency relations. With our approach, we only ever writes 1s into the concurrency matrix C. This is enough since we know relation $\Vert_2$ exactly and, in this case, relation $\Vert_1$ must also be complete (we can have only 0s or 1s in C). This is made clear by the fact that C is initialized with 0s everywhere. We can extend our algorithm to support the case where we only have a partial knowledge of $\Vert_2$. This is achieved by initializing C with the special value $\bullet$ (undefined) and adding rules that let us "propagate 0s" on the TFG, in the same way that our total algorithm only propagates 1s. For example, we know that if $\mathrm{C}[v, w] = 0$ (v, w are nonconcurrent) and $v \circ\!\!\rightarrow w'$ (we know that always $c(v) \geqslant c(w')$ on reachable configurations) then certainly $\mathrm{C}[w', w] = 0$. Likewise, we can prove that following rule for propagating "dead nodes" is sound: if $X \rightarrow\!\bullet\, v$ and $\mathrm{C}[w, w] = 0$ (node w is dead) for all $w \in X$ then $\mathrm{C}[v, v] = 0$.

Partial knowledge on the concurrency relation can be useful. Indeed, many use cases can deal with partial knowledge or only rely on the nonconcurrency relation (a 0 on the concurrency matrix). This is the case, for instance, when computing NUPN partitions, where it is always safe to replace a $\bullet$ with a 1. It also means that knowing that two places are nonconcurrent is often more valuable than knowing that they are concurrent; 0s are better than 1s.

We have implemented an extension of our algorithm for the case of incomplete matrices using this idea and we report some results obtained with it in the next section. Unfortunately, we do not have enough space to describe the full algorithm here. It is slightly more involved than for the complete case and is based on a collection of six additional axioms:

- If $C[v, v] = 0$ then $C[v, w] = 0$ for all node w in $[\![E]\!]$.
- If $v \circ\!\!\rightarrow X$ or $X \rightarrow\!\!\bullet v$ and $C[w, w] = 0$ for all nodes $w \in X$ then $C[v, v] = 0$.
- If $v \circ\!\!\rightarrow X$ or $X \rightarrow\!\!\bullet v$ and $C[v, v] = 0$ then $C[w, w] = 0$ for all nodes $w \in X$.
- If $v \circ\!\!\rightarrow X$ or $X \rightarrow\!\!\bullet v$ then $C[w, w'] = 0$ for all pairs of nodes $w, w' \in X$ such that $w \neq w'$.
- If $v \circ\!\!\rightarrow X$ or $X \rightarrow\!\!\bullet v$ and $C[w, v'] = 0$ for all nodes $w \in X$ then $C[v, v'] = 0$.
- If $v \circ\!\!\rightarrow X$ or $X \rightarrow\!\!\bullet v$ and $C[v, v'] = 0$ then $C[w, v'] = 0$ for all nodes w in X.

While we can show that the algorithm is sound, completeness takes a different meaning: we show that when nodes p and q are successors of roots v_1 and v_2 such that $C[v_i, v_i] \neq \bullet$ for all $i \in 1..2$ then necessarily $C[p, q] \neq \bullet$.

5   Experimental Results

We have implemented our algorithm in a new tool, called Kong (for Koncurrent places Grinder). The tool is open-source, under the GPLv3 license, and is freely available on GitHub (https://github.com/nicolasAmat/Kong). We have used the extensive database of models provided by the Model Checking Contest (MCC) [2,14] to experiment with our approach. Kong takes as inputs safe Petri nets defined using the Petri Net Markup Language (PNML) [15]. The tool does not compute net reductions directly but relies on another tool, called Reduce, that is developed inside the Tina toolbox [4,21]. For our experiments, we also need to compute the concurrency matrix of reduced nets. This is done using the tool CÆSAR.BDD (version 3.4, published in August 2020), that is part of the CADP toolbox [8,17], but we could adopt any other technology here.

Our benchmark is built from a collection of 588 instances of safe Petri nets used in the MCC 2020 competition. Since we rely on how much reduction we can find in nets, we computed the reduction ratio (r), obtained using Reduce, on all the instances (see Fig. 3). The ratio is calculated as the quotient between how many places can be removed and the number of places in the initial net. A ratio of 100% $(r = 1)$ means that the net is *fully reduced*; the residual net has no places and all the roots are constants. We see that there is a surprisingly high number of models whose size is more than halved with our approach (about 25% of the instances have a ratio $r \geqslant 0.5$), with approximately half of the instances that can be reduced by a ratio of 30% or more. We consider two values for the reduction ratio: one for reductions leading to a well-formed TFG (in dark blue), the other for the best possible reduction with Reduce (in light orange).

We observe that we lose few opportunities to reduce a net due to our wellformedness constraint. Actually, we mostly lose the ability to simplify some instances of "partial" marking graphs that could be reduced using inhibitor arcs (a feature not supported by CÆSAR.BDD). We evaluated the performance of Kong on the 424 instances of safe Petri nets with a reduction ratio greater than 1%.

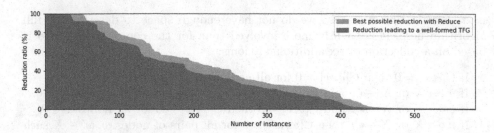

Fig. 3. Distribution of reduction ratios over the safe instances in the MCC

We ran Kong and CÆSAR.BDD on each of those instances, in two main modes: first with a time limit of 1 h to compare the number of totally solved instances (when the tool compute a complete concurrency matrix); next with a timeout of 60 s to compare the number of values (the filling ratios) computed in the partial matrices. Computation of a partial concurrency matrix with CÆSAR.BDD is done in two phases: first a "BDD exploration" phase that can be stopped by the user; then a post-processing phase that cannot be stopped. In practice this means that the execution time is often longer (because of the post-processing phase) when we do not use Kong: the mean computation time for CÆSAR.BDD alone is about 62 s, while it is less than 21 s when we use Kong and CÆSAR.BDD together. In each test, we compared the output of Kong with the values obtained on the initial net with CÆSAR.BDD and achieved 100% reliability.

Results for Totally Computed Matrices. We report our results on the computation of complete matrices and a timeout of 1 h in the table below. We report the number of computed matrices for three different categories of instances, *Low/Fair/High*, associated with different ratio ranges. We observe that we can compute more results with reductions than without (+25%). As could be expected, the gain is greater on category *High* (+53%), but it is still significant with the *Fair* instances (+32%).

REDUCTION RATIO (r)	# TEST CASES	# COMPUTED MATRICES KONG	CÆSAR.BDD	
Low $r \in {]}0, 0.25[$	160	90	88	×1.02
Fair $r \in [0.25, 0.5[$	112	53	40	×1.32
High $r \in [0.5, 1]$	152	97	63	×1.53
Total $r \in {]}0, 1]$	424	240	191	×1.25

To understand the impact of reductions on the computation time, we compare CÆSAR.BDD alone, on the initial net, and Kong+Reduce+CÆSAR.BDD on the reduced net. We display the result in a scatter plot, using a logarithmic scale (Fig. 4, left), with one point for each instance: time using reductions on the

y-axis, and without on the x-axis. We use colours to differentiate between *Fair* instances (light orange) and *High* ones (dark blue), and fix a value of 3600 s when one of the computation timeout. Hence the cluster of points on the right part of the plots are when CÆSAR.BDD alone timeouts. We observe that the reduction ratio has a clear impact on the speed-up and that almost all the data points are below the diagonal, meaning reductions accelerate the computation in almost all cases, with many test cases exhibiting speeds-up larger than ×10 or ×100 (materialized by dashed lines under the diagonal).

Results with Partial Matrices. We can also compare the "accuracy" of our approach when we have incomplete results. To this end, we compute the concurrency relation with a timeout of 60 s on CÆSAR.BDD. We compare the *filling ratio* obtained with and without reductions. For a net with n places, this ratio is given by the formula $2\,|C|/(n^2 + n)$, where $|C|$ is the number of 0s and 1s in the matrix. We display our results using a scatter plot with linear scale, see Fig. 4 (right). Again, we observe that almost all the data points are on one side of the diagonal, meaning in this case that reductions increase the number of computed values, with many examples (top line of the plot) where we can compute the complete relation in 60 s only using reductions. The graphic does not discriminate between the number of 1s and 0s, but we obtain similar good results when we consider the filling ratio for only the concurrent places (the 1 s) or only the nonconcurrent places (the 0 s).

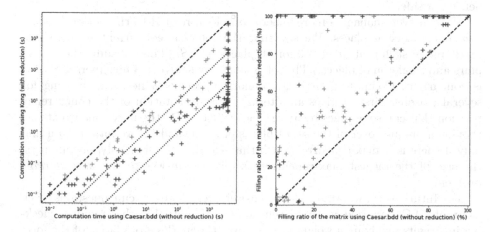

Fig. 4. Comparing Kong (y-axis) and CÆSAR.BDD (x-axis) for instances with $r \in [0.25, 0.5[$ (light orange) and $r \in [0.5, 1]$ (dark blue). One diagram (left) compares the computation time for complete matrices; the other (right) compares the filling ratio for partial matrices with a timeout of 60 s.

6 Conclusion and Further Work

The concurrency problem is difficult, especially when we cannot compute the complete state space of a net. We propose a method for transporting this problem from an initial "high-dimensionality" domain (the set of places in the net) into a smaller one (the set of places in the residual net). Our experiments confirm our intuition that the concurrency relation is much easier to compute after reductions (if the net can be reduced) and we provide an easy way to map back the result into the original net.

Our approach is based on a combination of structural reductions with linear equations first proposed in [5,6]. Our main contribution, in the current work, is the definition of a new data-structure that precisely captures the structure of these linear equations, what we call the Token Flow Graph (TFG). We use the TFGs to accelerate the computation of the concurrency relation, both in the complete and partial cases. We have many ideas on how to apply TFGs to other problems and how to extend them. A natural application would be for model counting (our original goal in [5]), where the TFG could lead to new algorithms for counting the number of (integer) solutions in the systems of linear equations that we manage. Another possible application is the *max-marking* problem, which means finding the maximum of the expression $\sum_{p \in P} m(p)$ over all reachable markings. On safe nets, this amounts to finding the maximal number of places that can be marked together. We can easily adapt our algorithm to compute this value and could even adapt it to compute the result when the net is not safe.

We can even manage a more general problem, related to the notion of *max-concurrent* sets of places. We say that the set S is concurrent if there is a reachable m such that $m(p) > 0$ for all places p in S. (This subsume the case of pairs and singleton of places.) The set S is *max-concurrent* if no superset $S' \supsetneq S$ is concurrent. Computing the max-concurrent sets of a net is interesting for several reasons. First, it gives an alternative representation of the concurrency relation that can sometimes be more space efficient: (1) the max-concurrent sets provide a unique cover of the set of places of a net, and (2) we have $p \parallel q$ if and only if there is S max-concurrent such that $\{p, q\} \subset S$. Obviously, on safe nets, the size of the biggest max-concurrent set is the answer to the *max-marking* problem.

For future work, we would like to answer even more difficult questions, such as proofs of Generalized Mutual Exclusion Constraints [13], that requires checking invariants involving a weighted sums over the marking of places, of the form $\sum_{p \in P} w_p.m(p)$. Another possible extension will be to support non-ordinary nets (which would require adding weights on the arcs of the TFG) and nets that are not safe (which can already be done with our current approach, but require changing some of the "axioms" used in our algorithm). Finally, another interesting direction for works would be to find reductions that preserve the concurrency relation (but not necessarily reachable states). As you can see, there is a lot to be done, which underlines the interest of studying TFGs.

Acknowledgements. We would like to thank Pierre Bouvier and Hubert Garavel for their insightful suggestions that helped improve the quality of this paper.

References

1. Amat, N., Berthomieu, B., Dal Zilio, S.: On the combination of polyhedral abstraction and SMT-based model checking for Petri Nets. In: Buchs, D., Carmona, J. (eds.) PETRI NETS 2021. LNCS, vol. 12734, pp. 164–185. Springer, Cham (2021). https://doi.org/10.1007/978-3-030-76983-3_9

2. Amparore, E., et al.: Presentation of the 9th edition of the model checking contest. In: Beyer, D., Huisman, M., Kordon, F., Steffen, B. (eds.) TACAS 2019. LNCS, vol. 11429, pp. 50–68. Springer, Cham (2019). https://doi.org/10.1007/978-3-030-17502-3_4

3. Berthelot, G.: Transformations and decompositions of nets. In: Brauer, W., Reisig, W., Rozenberg, G. (eds.) ACPN 1986. LNCS, vol. 254, pp. 359–376. Springer, Heidelberg (1987). https://doi.org/10.1007/978-3-540-47919-2_13

4. Berthomieu, B., Ribet, P.O., Vernadat, F.: The tool TINA - Construction of abstract state spaces for petri nets and time petri nets. Int. J. Prod. Res. **42**(14), 2741–2756 (2004). https://doi.org/10.1080/00207540412331312688; https://doi.org/10.1080/00207540412331312688

5. Berthomieu, B., Le Botlan, D., Dal Zilio, S.: Petri net reductions for counting markings. In: Gallardo, M.M., Merino, P. (eds.) SPIN 2018. LNCS, vol. 10869, pp. 65–84. Springer, Cham (2018). https://doi.org/10.1007/978-3-319-94111-0_4

6. Berthomieu, B., Le Botlan, D., Dal Zilio, S.: Counting Petri net markings from reduction equations. Int. J. Softw. Tools Technol. Transf. **22**(2), 163–181 (2019). https://doi.org/10.1007/s10009-019-00519-1

7. Bønneland, F.M., Dyhr, J., Jensen, P.G., Johannsen, M., Srba, J.: Stubborn versus structural reductions for Petri nets. J. Logical Algebraic Methods Program. **102**, 46–63 (2019). https://doi.org/10.1016/j.jlamp.2018.09.002

8. Bouvier, P., Garavel, H.: Efficient algorithms for three reachability problems in Safe Petri nets. In: Buchs, D., Carmona, J. (eds.) PETRI NETS 2021. LNCS, vol. 12734, pp. 339–359. Springer, Cham (2021). https://doi.org/10.1007/978-3-030-76983-3_17

9. Bouvier, P., Garavel, H., Ponce-de-León, H.: Automatic decomposition of Petri nets into automata networks – a synthetic account. In: Janicki, R., Sidorova, N., Chatain, T. (eds.) PETRI NETS 2020. LNCS, vol. 12152, pp. 3–23. Springer, Cham (2020). https://doi.org/10.1007/978-3-030-51831-8_1

10. Garavel, H.: Nested-unit Petri nets. J. Logical Algebraic Methods Program. **104**, 60–85 (2019). https://doi.org/10.1016/j.jlamp.2018.11.005

11. Garavel, H.: Proposal for adding useful features to Petri-net model checkers. Research Report 03087421, Inria Grenoble - Rhône-Alpes (2020). https://hal.inria.fr/hal-03087421

12. Garavel, H., Serwe, W.: State space reduction for process algebra specifications. In: Rattray, C., Maharaj, S., Shankland, C. (eds.) AMAST 2004. LNCS, vol. 3116, pp. 164–180. Springer, Heidelberg (2004). https://doi.org/10.1007/978-3-540-27815-3_16

13. Giua, A., DiCesare, F., Silva, M.: Generalized mutual exclusion contraints on nets with uncontrollable transitions. In: IEEE International Conference on Systems, Man, and Cybernetics. IEEE (1992). https://doi.org/10.1109/ICSMC.1992.271666

14. Hillah, L.M., Kordon, F.: Petri nets repository: a tool to benchmark and debug Petri net tools. In: van der Aalst, W., Best, E. (eds.) PETRI NETS 2017. LNCS, vol. 10258, pp. 125–135. Springer, Cham (2017). https://doi.org/10.1007/978-3-319-57861-3_9

15. Hillah, L.M., Kordon, F., Petrucci, L., Trèves, N.: PNML framework: an extendable reference implementation of the Petri net markup language. In: Lilius, J., Penczek, W. (eds.) PETRI NETS 2010. LNCS, vol. 6128, pp. 318–327. Springer, Heidelberg (2010). https://doi.org/10.1007/978-3-642-13675-7_20

16. Hujsa, T., Berthomieu, B., Dal Zilio, S., Le Botlan, D.: Checking marking reachability with the state equation in Petri net subclasses, 44 p (2020). https://hal.laas.fr/hal-02992521

17. INRIA: CADP (2020). https://cadp.inria.fr/

18. Janicki, R.: Nets, sequential components and concurrency relations. Theor. Comput. Sci. **29**(1–2) (1984). https://doi.org/10.1016/0304-3975(84)90014-8

19. Kovalyov, A.V.: Concurrency relations and the safety problem for Petri nets. In: Jensen, K. (ed.) ICATPN 1992. LNCS, vol. 616, pp. 299–309. Springer, Heidelberg (1992). https://doi.org/10.1007/3-540-55676-1_17

20. Kovalyov, A.: A polynomial algorithm to compute the concurrency relation of a regular STG. In: Hardware Design and Petri Nets. Springer, Boston (2000). https://doi.org/10.1007/978-1-4757-3143-9_6

21. LAAS-CNRS: Tina Toolbox (2020). http://projects.laas.fr/tina

22. Lipton, R.J.: Reduction: a method of proving properties of parallel programs. Commun. ACM **18**(12) (1975). https://doi.org/10.1145/361227.361234

23. Murata, T.: Petri nets: properties, analysis and applications. Proc. IEEE **77**(4), 541–580 (1989). https://doi.org/10.1109/5.24143

24. Semenov, A., Yakovlev, A.: Combining partial orders and symbolic traversal for efficient verification of asynchronous circuits. In: Proceedings of ASP-DAC'95/CHDL'95/VLSI'95 with EDA Technofair (1995). https://doi.org/10.1109/ASPDAC.1995.486371

25. Silva, M., Terue, E., Colom, J.M.: Linear algebraic and linear programming techniques for the analysis of place/transition net systems. In: Reisig, W., Rozenberg, G. (eds.) ACPN 1996. LNCS, vol. 1491, pp. 309–373. Springer, Heidelberg (1998). https://doi.org/10.1007/3-540-65306-6_19

26. Thierry-Mieg, Y.: Structural reductions revisited. In: Janicki, R., Sidorova, N., Chatain, T. (eds.) PETRI NETS 2020. LNCS, vol. 12152, pp. 303–323. Springer, Cham (2020). https://doi.org/10.1007/978-3-030-51831-8_15

27. Wisniewski, R., Karatkevich, A., Adamski, M., Costa, A., Gomes, L.: Prototyping of concurrent control systems with application of Petri Nets and comparability graphs. IEEE Trans. Control Syst. Technol. **26**(2) (2018). https://doi.org/10.1109/TCST.2017.2692204

28. Wiśniewski, R., Wiśniewska, M., Jarnut, M.: C-exact hypergraphs in concurrency and sequentiality analyses of cyber-physical systems specified by safe Petri nets. IEEE Access **7** (2019). https://doi.org/10.1109/ACCESS.2019.2893284

Spotlight Abstraction in Model Checking Real-Time Task Schedulability

Madoda Nxumalo[1,2(✉)], Nils Timm[1], and Stefan Gruner[1]

[1] Department of Computer Science, University of Pretoria, Pretoria, South Africa
{mnxumalo,ntimm,sg}@cs.up.ac.za
[2] Department of Computer Science, University of Eswatini, Kwaluseni, Eswatini
manxumalo@uniswa.sz

Abstract. In this paper we present a new abstraction technique for the model-checking of real-time systems with multiple tasks. Our technique enables the automatic and efficient analysis of the schedulability of real-time tasks for both preemptive and non-preemptive scheduling policies. It is based on the spotlight abstraction principle, which is applied to a queue that contains the tasks of the real-time system to be analyzed. This task-queue is partitioned into a so-called 'spotlight' and a 'shade'. Initially the spotlight contains only a small number of tasks which appear at the front of the queue and will be executed in the near future. The initial shade contains the remaining tasks which will be executed only after the spotlight tasks have been processed. On the basis of these assumptions an abstract state space model is generated. In this model the spotlight is considered in detail, whereas the behavior of the shade is almost entirely abstracted away. Such an abstract model is checked iteratively as follows: first the schedulability of the spotlight tasks is analyzed, and the result is saved for later re-use. If this result is still inconclusive, more tasks are brought from the shade into a now "broader" spotlight, with which the model checker can proceed. These steps are repeated until a decisive schedulability result is reached. In this manner we divide the entire model checking problem into smaller sub-problems such that, in the average case, the model checker's run-time is still acceptably short.

Keywords: Timed automata · Model checking · Three-valued abstraction · Schedulability · Queues

1 Introduction

Model checking is an efficient procedure for automatic software verification and analysis of temporal logic properties of finite or infinite state systems [14]. A model checker explores a finite state automaton which models the system under study and then decides whether a property is satisfied or not. A major challenge in model checking is the so-called state explosion problem: The model checker may run out of computational resources before a conclusive result can be obtained.

© Springer Nature Switzerland AG 2021
A. Laarman and A. Sokolova (Eds.): SPIN 2021, LNCS 12864, pp. 63–80, 2021.
https://doi.org/10.1007/978-3-030-84629-9_4

Abstraction is a useful technique for mitigating the state explosion problem by hiding some system details which are irrelevant for the checked property. Thus, abstraction can help with obtaining conclusive results even for a large state space model. Thus, typical software model checkers explore the state space of an *abstract* model instead of the concrete system. Research on software model checking focuses on the development of abstraction techniques that allow to reduce the state space complexity without losing the details that are necessary for a definite verification result.

Three-valued abstraction (3VA) [20] is a technique that replaces concrete program variables by three-valued predicates with three possible truth values, {*true, false, unknown*}, in short *(t,f,u)*. Concrete program states are mapped to abstract states according to their evaluations under a finite set of predicates. The third value, u is used to model the loss of details due to abstraction. 3VA is a generalization of Boolean predicate abstraction [5] based on three-valued Kleene logic [12]. Under 3VA, both t and f model checking results can be transferred to the concrete system, whereas an u result indicates that further predicates need to be added to the abstract model.

In this paper, we present a novel abstraction technique that enables efficient model checking of schedulability properties of real-time operating systems (RTOS). Schedulability analysis determines whether or not a given set of real-time tasks under a particular scheduling discipline can meet all of its timing constraints. In schedulability analysis, multiple parameters such as task priority, computation times and deadlines, synchronization, communication and precedence constraints cause high complexity. Our approach can model check the schedulability on systems that use different types of scheduling disciplines such as the non-preemptive First In First Out (FIFO), the preemptive Round Robin, and the priority-based and dynamic Earliest Deadline First (EDF). It is based on three-valued spotlight abstraction which is applied to a queue data structure that contains the real-time tasks to be executed by the RTOS.

Three-valued spotlight abstraction [20] is an extension of 3VA that allows to reduce the state space complexity of model checking discrete-time properties of concurrent software systems with integer variables. It divides the processes of a system into a so-called *spotlight* and *shade*. 3VA is applied to all processes in the spotlight while processes in the shade are collapsed and combined into a single component that coarsely approximates their behavior by making use of the truth value u. A verification run may return a definite result in {t, f} that can be transferred to the concrete system. Whereas an u verification result does not allow us to conclude whether the property holds or not, and it informs that the current level of abstraction is too coarse. In this case, iterative abstraction refinement is applied [22]. Under spotlight abstraction, refinement either adds new predicates to the abstract model, or it moves processes from the shade to the spotlight. The application of spotlight abstraction to real-time systems with continuous variables for the purpose of schedulability analysis has not been investigated so far.

In our new model checking approach for tasks in real-time operating systems, we verify schedulability properties formalized in timed computational tree logic, and we adapt the spotlight abstraction principle as follows: The queue of tasks is partitioned into a spotlight and a shade. The initial spotlight contains a small number of tasks which are at the front of the queue and will be executed by the processor in the near future. The maximum number of tasks in the spotlight is defined by a constant integer. The initial shade contains the remaining tasks to be executed at a later stage. The tasks belonging to the shade are combined to form a single abstract task. Each task in the spotlight, each processor, and the abstract task is modeled as a timed automaton. Timed automata are state models of real-timed systems [2]. Timed automata use dense models of time which are represented by a finite set of real number variables called clocks [10]. Clocks progress synchronously. The timed automata for tasks in the spotlight, an abstract task and each processor, are then combined to generate an abstract state space which is a parallel composition of timed automata. Based on this abstract model, the schedulability property is checked for the tasks in the spotlight.

Given a set of tasks in the spotlight queue, the schedulability property asks whether all tasks in the scheduler system will eventually execute within their deadlines. If the outcome is *true (false)*, then the property holds (is violated) for the entire set of tasks. If the shade is not empty, then we obtain a partial schedulability result, that is used as a condition in the next spotlight iteration. A partial schedulability result is obtained when a portion of tasks were scheduled within their deadlines while the schedulability of the processes in the shade is not determined yet.

In the next iteration a number of shade tasks is moved to the spotlight, and a new abstract state space is generated and the schedulability property is checked again. The tasks for which a schedulability result have already been obtained are removed from the spotlight and and they are placed in the shade as they need not to be considered again. These steps are repeated until all tasks in the queue have been in the spotlight and the partial schedulability results can be combined to an overall result. In this manner, our approach divides a model checking problem into smaller sub-problems and therefore reduces the state space complexity of model checking.

We defined a new approach to model check the schedulability of real-time tasks. Our approach applies spotlight abstraction to reduce the state space of the model under verification. For example, handling multiple clocks and clock constraints is complex, and by dividing the scheduler systems into a spotlight and shade, our approach can handle fewer clocks at each iteration. We developed algorithms for abstraction and model checking the schedulability of real-time tasks. Moreover, we implemented the approach. In an experimental evaluation we demonstrated that our new approach enables significant state space reductions.

2   Related Work

Our approach is motivated by several existing approaches to solve the schedulability analysis problem of real-time systems using timed automata. Each approach introduced a framework that extend timed automata with additional properties. Firstly, *stopwatch automata* [15] have been applied in [1] for over-approximative schedulability analyses on the basis of seeking and finding shortest paths in an underlying graph model and allow some clocks to pause when task preemption occurs. Similarly, our approach invokes a clock pause command to clocks. In our case clocks are paused in model checking to allow a refinement step. Secondly, [11] extended timed automata with a task queue data structure to model check asynchronous processes. In this way, the model becomes fully expressive as the automata always have complete information about all tasks in the queue, but that information does not include clocks because they are expensive to manipulate. Our approach attempts to keep each task in its original form together with its own clocks. This model was implemented in TIME-tool software [3] which uses the Uppaal model checker at the back-end. TIMES-tool solves schedulability analysis problem using a single clock. Thirdly, parametric timed automata (PTA) [9] is another framework that extends timed automata by allowing some configurations to be unknown parameters on clock constraints in order to reduce the state space complexity problem. IMITATOR [4] is a software for modeling and verifying systems modeled as PTA. Analogous to PTA our approach allows unknown clock valuations to represent tasks in a shade.

Abstraction of timed automata is mainly focused on restricting the clock constraints into zones. Zones are convex polyhedra that represent clock constraints. Herbreteau et al. [16] proved the soundness and completeness for reachability based on a parameterized abstraction approach that considers the lower and upper bounds of clock constraints in timed automata. Another abstraction approach is through aggregating the union of different zones into a single zone [13]. Roussanaly et al. [19] applied abstraction-refinement approaches for model checking safety properties on an abstract transition system encoded with Boolean formulas. They achieved abstraction on zones by restricting the set of clock constraints. In their refinement step the set of clock constraints that must be considered in the abstraction are evaluated and they excluded any found spurious counterexample. The above two approaches focused on forming abstract zones by weakening or strengthening the set of clock constraints into zones. Our approach defines aggregated abstract clocks and abstract clock constraints over tasks in the shade. Our approach allows for the interpretation of clock constraints for the abstract task into zones.

Bauer et al. [6] provided a framework for parametrized three-valued interpretation to hybrid automata for μ-calculus, to analyze hybrid dynamical systems that contain continuous variables on highly expressive logic. Their model preserved both true and false formulas from the abstract model to the concrete model. Their framework was based on discrete bounded bi-simulation abstractions and may/must-abstractions while our approach focuses on spotlight abstraction.

3   Encoding RTOS Scheduler Models as Timed Automata

We describe an encoding of a RTOS scheduler model as a timed automata. First, we provide the definitions, syntax and semantics of timed automata.

Definition 1. *A timed automaton is a tuple* $A = (L, l_0, F, C, \Sigma, I, E)$ *where;* L *is a non-empty, finite set of locations,* $l_0 \in L$ *is an initial location,* $F \subseteq L$ *is a subset of final locations,* C *is a finite set of clocks,* Σ *is a finite alphabet of actions,* $I : L \to \phi(C)$ *is a clock invariant mapping to each location where* $\phi(C)$ *is a set of clock constraints over* C. $\phi(C)$ *is a defined by the grammar* $g = x \sim d | x - y \sim d | g \wedge g$, *where* $x, y \in C, d \in \mathbb{N}$ *and* $\sim \in \{<, \leq\}$. $E \in L \times \phi(C) \times \Sigma \times 2^C \times L$ *is a finite set of edges between locations.*

Definition 2. *An edge* $(l, g, a, r, l') \in E$ *is denoted by* $l \xrightarrow{g,a,r} l'$ *where;* $g \in \phi$ *is a guard,* $a \in \Sigma$ *is an action and* r *is a reset function.*

A clock valuation is a mapping $v : C \to \mathbb{R}_{\geq 0}$. A reset function r on a clock valuation v sets the clocks in r to zero and leaves the others unchanged.

The semantics of timed automata is given as follows. A configuration of the automaton is a pair (l, v) consisting of a location and a clock valuation. A discrete transition is $(l, v) \xrightarrow{a} (l', v')$, for some $(l, g, a, r, l') \in E$ such that v satisfies g and $v' = r(v)$. A time transition is $(l, v) \xrightarrow{d} (l, v + d)$ for some $d \in \mathbb{R}_{\geq 0}$ such that $v + d$ satisfies $I(l)$. A compound transition is a time transition followed by a discrete transition: $(l, v) \xrightarrow{d,a} (l', v') \equiv (l, v) \xrightarrow{d} (l, v + d) \xrightarrow{a} (l', v')$. A *run* of a timed automaton starting from a configuration (l_0, v_0) is a finite or infinite path $\rho = (l_0, v_0) \xrightarrow{d_1, a_1} (l_1, v_1) \xrightarrow{d_2, a_2} (l_2, v_2) \ldots$ in the transition system.

Definition 3. *A parallel composition of timed automata* $A_1 || A_2 || \ldots || A_n$ *is the timed automaton* $A = (L, l_0, F, C, \Sigma, I, E)$ *where* $A_i = (L_i, l_0^i, F_i, C_i, \Sigma_i, I_i, E_i)$ *with all* L_i's, Σ_i's *and* C_i's *are disjoint, where;* $L = \prod_{i=1}^n L_i$, $\mathbf{l_0} = (l_0^1, \ldots, l_0^n)$, $\mathbf{F} = \prod_{i=1}^n F_i$, $C = \bigcup_{i=1}^n C_i$. $\Sigma = \bigcup_{i=1}^n (\Sigma_i \cup \{\bot\})$, $\bot$ *is an empty symbol. A location of* A *is* $\mathbf{l} = (l_1, \ldots, l_n) \in L$ *and clock valuation over* C *are* $\mathbf{v} = (v_1, \ldots, v_n)$. $I(\mathbf{l}) = \bigwedge_{i=1}^n I_i(l_i)$. *The set* E *consists of the transitions* $\mathbf{l} \xrightarrow{g,a,r} \mathbf{l'}$ *whenever: (1) there exists* $(\alpha_1, \ldots, \alpha_n) \in \prod_{i=1}^n (\Sigma_i \cup \{\bot\})$ *such that* $f(\alpha_1, \ldots, \alpha_n) = a$, f *is a mapping function; (2) if* $\alpha_i = \bot$ *then* $l_i' = l_i$; *(3) if* $\alpha_i \neq \bot$ *then there exist a transition* $l_i \xrightarrow{g_i, \alpha_i, r_i} l_i'$ *in* E_i; *(4)* $g = \bigwedge \{g_i | \alpha \neq \bot\}$ *and* $r = \bigcup \{r_i | \alpha_i \neq \bot\}$.

The transition system of timed automata is infinite because clocks are real numbers, therefore, timed automata are not adequate for model checking. A zone representation of clock constraints is one of the most used and efficient representation of the state space for timed automata. Zones are efficiently represented as difference bounded matrices (DBM). A zone region $\langle l, Z \rangle$ is a pair of a location l and a DBM of a clock zone Z. Transitions of a timed automata symbolically translated into zones as follows. We define an zone update $Z \uparrow = \{u + d | u \in Z, d \in \mathbb{R}_+\}$ and a zone reset $r(Z) = \{[r : 0]u | u \in Z\}$. Let $\rightarrowtail$ denote the symbolic transition relation over symbolic states defined by the following rules: (1) $\langle l, Z \rangle \rightarrowtail \langle l, Z \uparrow \wedge I(l) \rangle$; (2) $\langle l, Z \rangle \rightarrowtail \langle l', r(Z \wedge g) \wedge I(l') \rangle$ if

$l \xrightarrow{g,a,r} l'$. Rules (1) and (2) are interpretations of time and discrete transitions of timed automata, respectively.

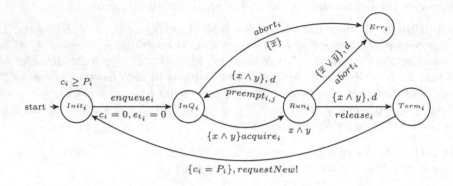

Fig. 1. A task model τ_i

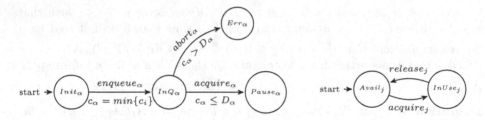

Fig. 2. An abstract task model τ_α **Fig. 3.** A processor model π_j

3.1 A Scheduler Model

A scheduler model is the arrival pattern of tasks for queuing in a scheduling system. The typical states of tasks in the model are *running, ready* and *blocked* [21]. Tasks in the ready state are contained in a queue data structure where they wait for their turn to be executed by a processor at the *running* state. In a real-time task model, a periodic and sporadic real-time task is an executable program characterized by a triple $\tau = (W, D, P)$ where W is the worst case execution time (WCET), D is a deadline and P is a period. RTOS task scheduler models are represented as timed automata.

A task model is a transition system that is formed as a parallel composition of timed automata which are derived from two types of components: tasks and processors. Figure 1 shows a task model for an arbitrary task $\tau_i = (W_i, D_i, P_i)$, $i \in \mathbb{N}$. The automaton for τ_i has a single clock variable c_i which keeps track of the 'lifetime' of the task from *instantiated* until *terminated*. It also has a variable $e_{t_i} \in \mathbb{R}_{\geq 0}$ which keeps record of task's clock execution elapse time. For a compact representation, the real-time predicates are defined over the following atomic predicates:

- $x = (c_i \leq D_i)$: (the clock valuation must not be greater than the deadline)
- $y = (e_{t_i} \leq W_i)$: (the execution time must not be greater than the WCET)
- $Front(q, \tau_i)$: (*true* iff task τ_i is in the front of queue q)
- $Available(\pi_j)$: (*true* iff a processor automaton π_j is in state $avail_j$)

The task queue, denoted by q, has a capacity $|q| \in \mathbb{N}$. Items in q are tracked by the variable $n_q \in \mathbb{N}, n_q \leq |q|$. The task queue has two synchronous actions *enqueue*$_i$ and *dequeue*$_i$ to add (resp. remove) some task τ_i to (resp. from) q. The operations correspond to the following guarded commands:

- $enqueue_i = assume(n_q < |q|) : q := q \cup \{\tau_i\}; n_q := n_q + 1;$
- $dequeue_i = assume(Front(q, \tau_i) \wedge n_q > 0); q := q \backslash \{\tau_i\}; n_q := n_q - 1;$

Fig. 3 shows a timed automaton for an arbitrary processor, denoted $\pi_j, j \in \mathbb{N}$. A processor π_j is in state $InUse_j$ if there exists a task τ_i which has acquired π_j. It is in state $Avail_j$ after τ_i has been released from π_j. The action $acquire_j$ corresponds to the guarded command: $assume(Front(q, \tau_i) \wedge Available(\pi_j))$.

The initial state of a task model is $Init_i$ where the task is to instantiate and release with all the required variables initialized e.g. clocks. We assume that each released task is schedulable. A detailed description of timed automata for schedulable task release step is available in [3]. A schedulable task release automaton models a representation that each task is released within its period. An initialized task is then added to the queue q. For a queued task all constraints x and y must always hold. An ejected task from q will either attempt to acquire a processor, provided all constraints hold and a processor is available for use, or it will be aborted, if any constraint is violated.

If the task model is preemptive then a task τ_i running on some processor π_j may be preempted to join the queue q. Moreover, the variable e_{t_i} is updated with the delay duration $d_i \in \mathbb{R}^+$. At the Run_i state, the real-time invariant: $\{x \wedge y\}$ must hold throughout the task execution. If the constraints x or y are violated at any state, a transition to an error state is taken. If the invariant stays true and the task execution was completed after some delay d, the task is released to a terminated state $Term_i$. For sporadic tasks, at the $Term_i$ state a successive task instance invocation at $Init_i$ is separated by at least the period P time units.

3.2   The Abstract Task Models

Before a model checking algorithm commences, it is required that the queue of tasks q is partitioned into a spotlight and a shade, $q = Spot \cup Shade$. The abstract task $\tau_\alpha = (W_\alpha, D_\alpha, P_\alpha)$ which is a summary of concrete tasks in the shade is be defined as follows. We define the abstract task based on properties that hold for all the tasks contained in the shade. τ_α is defined by properties that will maintain an invariant for all tasks in the shade. We define the clock of τ_α as the minimum clock value from the clocks in the shade i.e. $c_\alpha = min\{c_i|\tau_i \in Shade\}$. This clock c_α advances synchronously with other clocks. Moreover, $W_\alpha = min\{W_i|\tau_i \in Shade\}$ and $P_\alpha = min\{P_i|\tau_i \in Shade\}$. For each task τ_i in the shade, we calculate the difference $diff_{\tau_i} = \{D_{\tau_i} - c_{\tau_i}|\tau_i \in Shade\}$. Then the static deadline is defined as $D_\alpha = min\{diff_{\tau_i}|\tau_i \in Shade\}$. The deadline clock constraint for τ_α becomes $c_\alpha \leq D_\alpha$. This clock constraint becomes invariant in all locations of the timed automata of τ_α. Specifying the deadline over τ_α helps in an EDF scheduler whereby either preempted tasks or recently released tasks with higher priorities than τ_α are positioned ahead of τ_α in the abstract queue. In a FIFO policy, recently released tasks are added at the back of the abstract queue, therefore, the location of τ_α in the queue will not be affected. During model checking, if the deadline constraint of τ_α is violated then at least one task in the shade has missed a deadline.

Figure 2 shows an automaton corresponding to an abstract task τ_α. The abstract task is initialized with task a clock c_α and a deadline D_α as described in the previous paragraph. The abstract task can be added to (resp. removed from) a scheduler queue. An attempt to acquire a processor by task τ_α will not be successful because τ_α is an abstract task that is a summary of multiple concrete tasks. Therefore, the transition goes to a configuration called $Pause_\alpha$, provided the clock constraints to $c_\alpha < D_\alpha$ holds. The $Pause_\alpha$ pauses a *run* of a scheduler automaton. All clocks are also paused. If $c_\alpha < D_\alpha$ does not holds the transition goes into an Err_α state.

Another form of task abstraction is a task denoted τ_β. All tasks that have successfully terminated in the previous abstraction steps are collapsed into a single state abstract timed automaton and the state is $Term_\beta$.

4   An Example: Model Checking Schedulability for FIFO RTOS Scheduler

In this section, we demonstrate the functioning of our spotlight abstraction technique for queued tasks based on an example. Consider a FIFO scheduler consisting of a processor π and a queue q that contains a set of tasks $T = \{\tau_1(2,2,2), \tau_2(1,3,3), \tau_3(2,5,5), \tau_4(1,6,6)\}$ where the first value of each triple is the worst case execution time, the second value is the deadline and the third value is the period. The schedulability property φ is verified for the set T. Based on spotlight abstraction on queues, we construct an abstract queue q'. We assume an abstraction interval of $k = 2$. In the initial iteration q' contains τ_1, τ_2 and τ_α, with τ_1 and τ_2 in the spotlight. Task τ_α represents the shade which is an abstraction of the subset $\{\tau_3, \tau_4\}$ of T. The *network of timed automata* (NTA) corresponding to this abstraction is derived from the parallel composition of timed automata of $\tau_1, \tau_2, \tau_\alpha$, and π.

Figure 4 depicts the *partial* branching structure in the first iteration of abstraction with τ_1 and τ_2 in the spotlight. The branching structure is *partial*

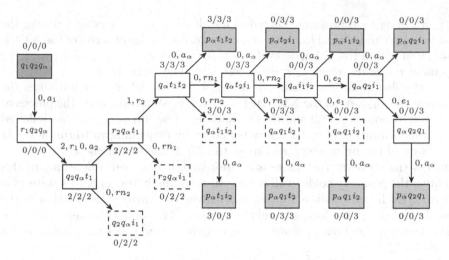

Fig. 4. A partial trace of model checking in the first iteration

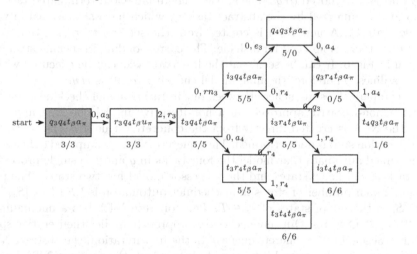

Fig. 5. A trace of model checking in the second iteration

because there are traces from states with *dotted* nodes that are not captured in the figure. This is due to page space limitations. The nodes that are filled with blue (red) color represent an initial (a $Pause_\alpha$) state. The state of the processor is $InUse_\pi$ whenever a node in the figure has a label r_i, otherwise it is in the $Avail_\pi$ state. Figure 5 depicts the branching structure, i.e. all possible runs of the NTA, in the second iteration with τ_3 and τ_4 in the spotlight. In each node of the figures, the labels $i_i, q_i, r_i, t_i, a_\pi, u_\pi$ are abbreviations for the state compositions of the NTA which are $Init_i, inQueue_i, Run_i, Term_i, Avail_\pi, InUse_\pi$ respectively, where the subscript i is the task identifier. The labels above or below the node, in the forms $X_1/X_2/X_\alpha$ or X_3/X_4, denote the clock valuations of tasks

$\tau_1, \tau_2, \tau_\alpha$ or τ_3, τ_4 (always in this order) for all tasks in the spotlight during the first iteration and second iteration respectively. Each edge of a run of the NTA is associated with a transition delay $d \in \mathbb{N}$ and an action. The actions e_i, a_i, r_i, rn_i represent $enqueue_i, acquire_i, release_i, requestNew_i$ respectively.

In the first iteration, illustrated in Fig. 4, the model checker initializes the run at state $q_1 q_2 q_\alpha a_\pi$ of the NTA. At $t = 0$, task τ_1 starts to run on the processor π for a duration of $d_1 = 2$ and then terminates. The run of τ_1 is either followed by a re-initialization of τ_1 for a new period or by dequeuing τ_2 to run next. At each state of the branching structure of the NTA, the model checker verifies φ, which is the property that there is no task that has missed a deadline. In this example the property holds in all states. All runs finally converge to a state with $Pause_\alpha$. Each state with a $Pause_\alpha$ label saves the current information of the model checker e.g. the location and clock values. The model checker returns the result $true$ on the $Pause_\alpha$ states because there are no tasks that has missed a deadline.

In the subsequent iteration of abstraction, the remaining two tasks of q, which are τ_3 and τ_4, are moved to q'. The already schedulable and terminated tasks τ_1 and τ_2 are summarized by the abstract task τ_β which have an automaton with a single state t_β. A new NTA is created from the set $\{\tau_3, \tau_4, \tau_\beta, \pi\}$. Since q is now empty, there is no need for a shade. The corresponding branching structure is shown in Fig. 5. It can be seen that the last two tasks can be executed within their deadlines. Therefore, the final model checking result is $true$.

We compare the state spaces between our iterative model checking approach against a non-iterative approach. In a non-iterative model checking approach where the NTA is created directly from the concrete queue $q = \{\tau_1, \tau_2, \tau_3, \tau_4\}$, the abstraction step is not performed. The concrete NTA is composed of five component timed automata that model the four tasks in q and the single processor. Each task model has 6 states and the processor model has two states. The possible maximum number of states in a scheduler automaton is $(|S_i|^{|T|} \times |S_j|^{|\Pi|})$, where S_i is the set of states of $\tau_i \in T$. The concrete NTA has a maximum of $(6^4 \times 2^1) = 2592$ states. Our model checking approach applies the iterative spotlight abstraction on the concrete queue q. In the first iteration, the abstract NTA has 108 states. In the second iteration of abstraction, the abstract NTA has 36 states. It can be seen that the state spaces to be explored in our abstraction-based approach are an order of magnitude smaller than the state space of the concrete NTA. Hence, our spotlight abstraction technique enables a significant reduction of the complexity of model checking schedulability properties.

5   Model Checking Real-Time Queues Using Spotlight Abstraction

In this section we present our developed algorithms for abstraction (Algorithm 1) and for model checking (Algorithm 2). The input of the abstraction algorithm is a $ready$ queue q that contains $n \in \mathbb{N}$ tasks and a set of processors Π. The schedulability property for a task τ_i is given by φ_i which states that τ_i must execute and terminate within its deadline. The schedulability property of all tasks in the queue is φ which is a conjunct formula of the schedulability properties of all tasks in the queue q. The formula φ expresses the property that all queued tasks will eventually terminate execution within their deadlines. The verification of the schedulability property is reduced into a reachability safety property. Given an automaton A, decide if there exists an accepting run. Based on the automata definition in Sect. 3, a run that reaches an Err_i state signals a violation of the schedulability property φ.

Algorithm 1 3vSpotAbstraction	**Algorithm 2** 3vChecker
Input: k, q, Π;	Input: $nta, \varphi', visited$
1: $\varphi = $ true;	1: $z = nta(\langle l_0, Z_0 \rangle)$;
2: $visited = A = \emptyset$;	2: $wait = paused = \emptyset$
3: **while** $(q \neq \emptyset)$ **do**	3: $wait.add(\langle l_0, Z_0 \rangle)$;
4: **for** $(\tau_i \in q[0, k])$ **do**	4: **while** $(wait \neq \emptyset)$or$(paused == \emptyset)$ **do**
5: $p = q.pop()$;	5: $z = wait.pop()$;
6: $q'.add(p)$;	6: **if** $(z \not\models \varphi')$ **then**
7: **end for**	7: **return** false;
8: **if** $(q \neq \emptyset)$ **then**	8: **end if**
9: $q'.add(\tau_\alpha)$;	9: **if** $(Z \not\subseteq Z', \forall \langle l, Z \rangle \in visited)$ **then**
10: **end if**	10: $visited.add(z)$;
11: $A.add(\tau_\beta)$;	11: **for** $\langle l', Z' \rangle : \langle l, D \rangle \rightarrowtail \langle l', D' \rangle$ **do**
12: $A.addAll(q')$;	12: **if** $(l' \notin Pause_\alpha)$ **then**
13: $nta = buildNTA(A, \Pi)$;	13: $wait.add(z')$;
14: $\varphi' = abstractProperty(A)$;	14: **else**
15: $\varphi = 3vChecker(nta, \varphi', visited)$;	15: $paused.add(z)$;
16: **if** $(\varphi == $ false$)$ **then**	16: **end if**
17: **return** not schedulable;	17: **end for**
18: **end if**	18: **end if**
19: **end while**	19: **end while**
20: **return** schedulable;	20: **return** true;

5.1 The Abstraction Algorithm Commences

The first line shows that the verified property φ is initialized by a *true* value. This means that the property is assumed to hold and the model checking algorithm will attempts to show that the property is not violated. The set of visited states is initialized in line 2 of Algorithm 1. In lines 4–10 the concrete queue q is translated into an abstract queue q': The first k tasks of q are moved to q'. This part is considered as the spotlight. The remaining tasks τ_{k+1} to τ_n are kept in q. Additionally, an abstract task τ_α, that approximates the behavior of tasks in the shade, is then added to the back of q'. Tasks τ_α is formed as per the description in Sect. 3.2. An example of the concrete queue q is depicted in Fig. 6 and a corresponding abstract queue q' is shown in Fig. 3. The tasks in the spotlight will be executed in the near future while the tasks in the shade will be still idle. The spotlight tasks are the ones whose schedulability properties will be model checked in the current iteration of abstraction.

Lines 11–12 of Algorithm 1 show the initialization of an array A that contains all the tasks in q' and the two abstract tasks τ_β and τ_α. Task τ_β is a summary of all the tasks that have terminated in previous iterations and it is created as described in Sect. 3.2. The method $buildNTA(A, \Pi)$ that is called in line 13 builds the network timed automaton that represents a scheduler system. The NTA is generated from the finite set of timed automata corresponding to the tasks in the spotlight, the abstract task τ_α and the processors in Π. In the initial state of the NTA each automaton corresponding to a task is in the state $InQueue$ and each automaton corresponding to a processor is in the state $Avail$. In line 14, an abstract property φ' which correspond with the the abstract NTA is defined by invoking the method $abstractProperty(A)$. Using all the tasks in array A, an abstract property φ' that summarizes φ is computed as $\varphi' = \varphi_\alpha \wedge \varphi_\beta \wedge (\wedge_{i=1}^{k} \varphi_i)$.

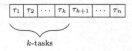

k-tasks

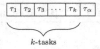

k-tasks

Fig. 6. A queue with n tasks

Fig. 7. Queue from Fig. 6 in abstract form

5.2 Calling the Reachability Analysis Algorithm

In line 15 of Algorithm 1, the model checker $3vChecker()$ shown in Algorithm 2 is invoked. Algorithm 2 is a modification of the typical forward symbolic reachability analysis algorithm [7]. It takes the following input arguments: the NTA, the abstract property to be verified φ', and the passed states $visited$ of the NTA. The variables $wait$ and $paused$ are initially empty containers that keep track of states waiting to be visited and states that invoke a command to pause the checker, respectively. Initially, the abstract property φ' is assumed to hold, and the algorithm automatically checks if there exists a task in the spotlight that violates the schedulability property. The model checker returns one of the two truth values: $true, false$ i.e. $\{t,f\}$.

In Algorithm 2 the abstract NTA is iteratively model checked as follows: The $wait$ set is initialized with the start state of the NTA. Iteratively, while in the $wait$ list there are states that have not been explored, a zone z is removed from the $wait$ list. The recently popped out zone z is added to the set of passed zones $visited$. In lines 6–8, the schedulability property φ' is checked for the current zone z, see Definition 4. Between lines 9–14, a transition is taken from z to z' on some action a_i over a duration d and z' is added to the $wait$ list. Then an attempt to reach to each successor state of z is made.

Definition 4. *Let z be a zone and φ be a property under verification, the semantics of $z \models \varphi$ is as follows: 1) $z \not\models \varphi$ does not hold if z contains an Err_i (error) location for some task $\tau_i \in Spot$, and, 2) $z \models \varphi$ holds if all $\tau_i \in Spot$ reaches $Term_i$ (terminate) location.*

The main modification of the reachability analysis algorithm is in lines 15–17 of Algorithm 2 where the current zone z is placed in a $paused$ list if task τ_α

attempts to acquire a processor. The checker goes to a successor zone z' which contains $Pause_\alpha$. There is no definite edge for it in the partial NTA because the task belongs to the shade. The corresponding transitions between the spotlight tasks and the shade are unknown. In order to continue, the model checker must *pause* the state space exploration for the path at z to allow the abstraction algorithm to move additional tasks to the spotlight. Thus, the NTA moves to the state with $Pause_\alpha$ and saves the partial result for later re-use. A partial result is a run of the NTA that maintains the assumed *true* model checking outcome. In the $Pause_\alpha$ state the following is done: Firstly, all reached zones in *visited* are also saved as part of the partial result. Secondly, all clocks $c_i \in C$ values that are in the abstract system are paused and saved for the next iteration.

Model checking a partial NTA that contains the abstract task τ_α can either return f or t. A t result indicates that all tasks in the abstract NTA satisfy the abstract schedulability property φ'. A f result is returned if at least one task in the spotlight violates the schedulability property.

5.3   The Abstraction Algorithm Resumes

After the partial result has been saved in the list *visited*, the execution of Algorithm 1 is continued. If model checking yields f, then in lines 16–18 the algorithm terminates and additionally outputs a counterexample run of the combined NTAs that shows the violation of the schedulability property. If the model checking result is t and the queue q is not empty then the algorithm continues with the subsequent iteration of the algorithm in line 3 and the schedulability property is assumed to hold. The next iteration step creates a new spotlight and shade from tasks that were previously in the shade q and tasks that were recently released into the abstract queue q. A corresponding synchronous product automaton NTA is built. The model checker is then resumed with the new NTA as an input. Note that the schedulability of tasks that were in the spotlight in the previous iteration has already been model checked. Therefore, these tasks will be part of the τ_β abstract task in the new iteration.

Refinement steps are iteratively repeated until a definite schedulability result is obtained. The concrete queue q is now empty, as such there are no more tasks to keep in the shade represented by τ_α. A definite final result, t or f exists at the last cycle of iteration when all tasks of the concrete queue in $q[0, n]$ have been explored by the model checker.

Lemma 1. *Algorithm 1 returns 'schedulable' iff all tasks in q can be executed within their deadlines by Π and it returns 'not schedulable' iff there exists a task in q that cannot be executed within its deadline by Π.*

Proof. We present a proof by induction for Lemma 1. Assume a FIFO queue that contains m tasks. The size of the concrete queue can be expressed as $m = xk + y$ where $k, x, y \in \mathbb{N}$, k is a constant and $1 \leq y \leq k$. Let φ_i be the schedulability property for task τ_i. Let $\varphi = \wedge_{i=0}^m (\varphi_i)$ be the schedulability property of all tasks in the scheduler system. Let φ_α denote the schedulability property for the abstract task. Let φ_t denote the schedulability property for all tasks that have previously executed and terminated successfully. Let $\varphi' = \varphi_t \wedge \varphi_\alpha \wedge (\wedge_{i=1}^{k}\varphi_i)$ be the abstract representation of the schedulability property of the scheduler system that approximates φ.

Base case: The base case is such that the total number is smaller than the size of the spotlight i.e. $1 \leq m \leq k$ then $x = 0$ and $m = y$. Algorithm 1 builds an abstract queue $q' \neq \emptyset$ and the concrete queue becomes $q = \emptyset$. The abstract property $\varphi' = \varphi = \wedge_{i=1}^{m}(\varphi_i)$. To continue with the base case we distinguish the following two cases.

In case 1, for all the tasks in queue the each task's property φ_i holds, we want to show that Algorithm 1 will return schedulable. An abstract network of timed automata NTA and the property φ' becomes input to Algorithm 2 whose return value is true. This is because Algorithm 2 will not reach a state such that $s \not\models \varphi'$ holds. and you should also explain in the proof why it holds. Since $q = \emptyset$ and φ holds, Algorithm 1 returns 'schedulable'.

In case 2, there exist at least one task in the queue with a schedulability property that does not hold, we want to show that The NTA and the property φ' becomes input to Algorithm 2 whose return value is false. Algorithm 2 returns false if a state is reached such that $s \not\models \varphi'$ holds. Because φ does not hold, Algorithm 1 returns 'not schedulable'. For the base case Lemma 1 holds.

Inductive hypothesis: Assume that the Algorithm 1 works correctly for the concrete queue with m tasks, then $m = (u)k + v$ and $u, v \in \mathbb{Z}_{\geq 0}$ and φ holds.

Inductive step: We now consider the inductive step where the size of the queue q is $m + 1$. Then $m = (u)k + v + 1 = (u)k + z$ where $z = v + 1$. There are two cases to distinguish, either $1 \leq z \leq k$ with $m = (u)k + z$ or $z = k + 1$ with $m = (u)k + (1)k + 1 = (w)k + 1, w = u + 1$. The first case means that the newly added task at location $m + 1$ of the queue joins the $u + 1$ iteration of the Algorithm 1. The second case means that the added task in q will be excluded from the $u + 1$ iteration that will have k tasks already, then the task will be executed in a new iteration.

In the first case, the last iteration of Algorithm 1, the verified property is $\varphi' = \varphi_\beta \wedge (\wedge_{i=1}^{z}\varphi_i) = \varphi_t \wedge (\wedge_{i=1}^{z-1}\varphi_i) \wedge \varphi_z$. From the inductive hypothesis, φ_t is known to holds for the first $(u)k$ tasks which means that the first $(u)k$ tasks are schedulable. In the last iteration of Algorithm 1, the base case applies whereby $\wedge_{i=0}^{z-1}\varphi_i$ is known true (from the inductive hypothesis). Lastly, if model checking φ_z is known to hold and Algorithm 1 returns 'schedulable' or φ_z holds and Algorithm 1 returns 'non schedulable'.

In the second case case where $z = k + 1$ then $m = (w)k + 1$. In the final iteration of Algorithm 1 the verified property is $\varphi' = \varphi_t \wedge \varphi_1$. From the inductive hypothesis, φ_t holds for the first $(w)k$ tasks, which means that the $(w)k$ tasks are schedulable. The last iteration of Algorithm 1 returns 'schedulable' if the property φ_1 is true otherwise Algorithm 1 returns 'non schedulable'. For the inductive step Lemma 1 holds, therefore, the Lemma holds everywhere.

For priority based queues such as EDF, a concrete task may be placed at an index that is behind that of the abstract task in the abstract queue q'. This is due to priority based actions such as preemption. It follows that during an iteration of $0 \leq y \leq k$ tasks in Algorithm 1, a model checking algorithm call may be terminated while some tasks in the abstract queue were not explored. The tasks that were not checked in an iteration are then included for verification of another k tasks of the subsequent iteration.

6   Experimental Results

We implemented the algorithms in the Java programming language. The timed automata transitions were transferred into symbolic zone exploration. We utilized zone manipulating algorithms from [7] that are integral to the Uppaal DBM library. We used a synthetic task set generating model from [8] to generate random task sets.

We evaluated our algorithms on two types of queues; FIFO and EDF queues. We show the version of the algorithms when the abstraction algorithm is applied on the concrete queue. We also show the counter part cases when the abstraction was not applied. Moreover, in each case we report on the number of states and the execution times. We also counted the number of iterations employed for our abstraction approach.

Table 1 displays the results of our experiments. The experiments were run on an Intel i7 at 2.30 Ghz processor running on Windows. Based on the runtimes, the algorithm that employs our abstraction approach performed better with FIFO queues than with EDF queues. Moreover, applying our approach causes the EDF queues have many iterations than FIFO queues. In case when the abstract task has a higher deadline priority than other tasks, the abstraction algorithm is tasked with generating more abstract queues when the EDF policy is applied on input queue. For task sets with sizes larger than 5, we do not present the case whereby abstraction is not applied because it is computationally expensive to manipulate large DBMs from multiple tasks with many clocks. This shows that the most efficient timed automata contain few clocks per iteration. Our approach attempts to breakdown the large system with multiple clocks into smaller manageable abstract models with fewer clocks. This avoids the state space complexity problem in model checking schedulability on the concrete models which did not complete execution due to program heap space exhaustion. Our abstraction-based model checking tool is available at https:// github.com/MadodaNxumalo/TVMC-On-RTOS.

Table 1. Results of schedulability analysis for FIFO and EDF task-sets at intervals of 4 tasks per iteration. "States/ite" stands for number of states per iteration.

		With Abstraction				No Abstraction		
Case	Tasks	States/ite	Iterations	Time(s)	Schedulable?	States	Time(s)	Schedulable?
FIFO	5	1536	2	1.585s	Yes	2304	4.125	Yes
	10	1536	3	1.769	Yes	*	*	
	50	1536	14	7.062	No	*	*	
	100	1536	25	13.785	No	*	*	
	200	1536	50	29.377	No	*	*	
	500	1536	125	76.189	No	*	*	
EDF	5	1536	2	1.127	Yes	2304	4.298	Yes
	10	1536	4	1.758	No	*	*	
	50	1536	19	9.217	No	*	*	
	100	1536	34	15.931	No	*	*	
	200	1536	71	33.740	No	*	*	
	500	1536	143	78.650	No	*	*	

7   Conclusion and Outlook

In this paper we presented a new model checking technique for verifying the schedulability of queued real-time tasks. Our approach is based on spotlight abstraction in which we partition a task queue into a 'spotlight' and a 'shade'. The spotlight contains the tasks that appear to a specified depth at the front-side of the queue. The shade contains all other tasks in the queue: they are represented as a single 'abstract task' that approximates their collective behavior. This abstraction, which is made to shrink the size of our formal models' state space, entails a particular loss of information.

Our formal model of such a scenario is a 'cross-product' of several timed automata: one for each task in the spotlight, one for the abstract task in the shade, and one for each each processor. Our model checking algorithm explores this model until a definite schedulability result (t or f) is obtained. After the result of an abstraction and model checking iteration, more tasks are moved out of the shade into the spotlight, a modified state space model is constructed accordingly, and the next iteration begins. Our approach divides a model checking problem with a very large state space into several smaller problems which can be tackled in a sequence of steps. Experimental results demonstrated that the state space of a large concrete model can be reduced to smaller state spaces that can executed by the available computer resources.

Combining clocks constraints of tasks in the shade into abstract zones where clock valuations on zones result into values in $\{t, f, u\}$ is another direction for future work. Unknown clock valuations are evident in cases whereby the difference clock constraints, of the form $x - y \sim d$ where $x, y \in C, d \in \mathbb{N}$, are used. For example, clock x belongs to the spotlight and y to the shade and the result becomes u. Furthermore, some form of optimization to the algorithms is another future study. For example the number of the components in the spotlight could possibly be determined dynamically by suitable automated parameter tuning techniques [17]. Future work should also look into the probabilistic nature of many real-time queuing systems: for comparison see [18] in which three-valued abstraction was applied to models of continuously timed Markov chains.

References

1. Abdeddaïm, Y., Maler, O.: Preemptive job-shop scheduling using stopwatch automata. In: Katoen, J.-P., Stevens, P. (eds.) TACAS 2002. LNCS, vol. 2280, pp. 113–126. Springer, Heidelberg (2002). https://doi.org/10.1007/3-540-46002-0_9

2. Alur, R., Dill, D.L.: A theory of timed automata. Theor. Comput. Sci. **126**(2), 183–235 (1994)

3. Amnell, T., Fersman, E., Mokrushin, L., Pettersson, P., Yi, W.: TIMES: a tool for schedulability analysis and code generation of real-time systems. In: Formal Modeling and Analysis of Timed Systems: First International Workshop, FORMATS 2003, Marseille, France, 6–7 September 2003. Revised Papers, pp. 60–72 (2003)

4. André, É., Fribourg, L., Kühne, U., Soulat, R.: IMITATOR 2.5: a tool for analyzing robustness in scheduling problems. In: Giannakopoulou, D., Méry, D. (eds.) FM 2012. LNCS, vol. 7436, pp. 33–36. Springer, Heidelberg (2012). https://doi.org/10.1007/978-3-642-32759-9_6

5. Ball, T., Majumdar, R., Millstein, T.D., Rajamani, S.K.: Automatic predicate abstraction of C programs. In: Proceedings of the 2001 ACM SIGPLAN Conference on Programming Language Design and Implementation (PLDI), Snowbird, Utah, USA, 20–22 June 2001, pp. 203–213 (2001)

6. Bauer, K., Gentilini, R., Schneider, K.: A uniform approach to three-valued semantics for μ-calculus on abstractions of hybrid automata. Int. J. Softw. Tools Technol. Transf. **13**(3), 273–287 (2011)

7. Bengtsson, J., Yi, W.: Timed automata: semantics, algorithms and tools. In: Desel, J., Reisig, W., Rozenberg, G. (eds.) ACPN 2003. LNCS, vol. 3098, pp. 87–124. Springer, Heidelberg (2004). https://doi.org/10.1007/978-3-540-27755-2_3

8. Bertout, A., Forget, J., Olejnik, R.: Minimizing a real-time task set through task clustering. In: Jan, M., Hedia, B.B., Goossens, J., Maiza, C. (eds.) 22nd International Conference on Real-Time Networks and Systems, RTNS 2014, Versaille, France, 8–10 October 2014, p. 23. ACM (2014)

9. Bini, E., Natale, M.D., Buttazzo, G.C.: Sensitivity analysis for fixed-priority real-time systems. Real-Time Syst. **39**(1–3), 5–30 (2008)

10. Bouyer, P., Fahrenberg, U., Larsen, K.G., Markey, N., Ouaknine, J., Worrell, J.: Model checking real-time systems. In: Handbook of Model Checking, pp. 1001–1046 (2018)

11. Fersman, E., Pettersson, P., Yi, W.: Timed automata with asynchronous processes: schedulability and decidability. In: Katoen, J., Stevens, P. (eds.) Tools and Algorithms for the Construction and Analysis of Systems, 8th International Conference, TACAS 2002, Held as Part of the Joint European Conference on Theory and Practice of Software, ETAPS 2002, Grenoble, France, 8–12 April 2002, Proceedings. Lecture Notes in Computer Science, vol. 2280, pp. 67–82. Springer (2002)

12. Fitting, M.: Kleene's three valued logics and their children. Fundam. Inform. **20**(1/2/3), 113–131 (1994)

13. Govind, R., Herbreteau, F., Srivathsan, B., Walukiewicz, I.: Revisiting local time semantics for networks of timed automata. In: Fokkink, W.J., van Glabbeek, R. (eds.) 30th International Conference on Concurrency Theory, CONCUR 2019, 27–30 August 2019, Amsterdam, the Netherlands. LIPIcs, vol. 140, pp. 16:1–16:15. Schloss Dagstuhl - Leibniz-Zentrum für Informatik (2019)
14. Grumberg, O.: 2-valued and 3-valued abstraction-refinement in model checking. In: Logics and Languages for Reliability and Security, pp. 105–128 (2010)
15. Henzinger, T.A., Kopke, P.W., Puri, A., Varaiya, P.: What's decidable about hybrid automata? J. Comput. Syst. Sci. **57**(1), 94–124 (1998)
16. Herbreteau, F., Srivathsan, B., Walukiewicz, I.: Better abstractions for timed automata. Inf. Comput. **251**, 67–90 (2016)
17. Huang, C., Li, Y., Yao, X.: A survey of automatic parameter tuning methods for metaheuristics. IEEE Trans. Evolut. Comput. **24**(2), 201–216 (2019)
18. Katoen, J.-P., Klink, D., Leucker, M., Wolf, V.: Three-valued abstraction for continuous-time Markov Chains. In: Damm, W., Hermanns, H. (eds.) CAV 2007. LNCS, vol. 4590, pp. 311–324. Springer, Heidelberg (2007). https://doi.org/10.1007/978-3-540-73368-3_37
19. Roussanaly, V., Sankur, O., Markey, N.: Abstraction refinement algorithms for timed automata. In: Dillig, I., Tasiran, S. (eds.) CAV 2019. LNCS, vol. 11561, pp. 22–40. Springer, Cham (2019). https://doi.org/10.1007/978-3-030-25540-4_2
20. Schrieb, J., Wehrheim, H., Wonisch, D.: Three-valued spotlight abstractions. In: Cavalcanti, A., Dams, D.R. (eds.) FM 2009. LNCS, vol. 5850, pp. 106–122. Springer, Heidelberg (2009). https://doi.org/10.1007/978-3-642-05089-3_8
21. Stallings, W.: Operating Systems - Internals and Design Principles, 7th edn, Pitman (2011)
22. Timm, N., Gruner, S.: Three-valued bounded model checking with cause-guided abstraction refinement. Sci. Comput. Program. **175**, 37–62 (2019)

Verifying Pipeline Implementations in OpenMP

Maik Wiesner$^{(\boxtimes)}$ (ID) and Marie-Christine Jakobs$^{(\boxtimes)}$ (ID)

Department of Computer Science, Technical University of Darmstadt,
Darmstadt, Germany
wiesner@svps.tu-darmstadt.de, jakobs@cs.tu-darmstadt.de

Abstract. OpenMP is a popular API for the development of parallel, shared memory programs and allows programmers to easily ready their programs to utilize modern multi-core processors. However, OpenMP-compliant programs do not guarantee that the OpenMP parallelization is functionally equivalent to a sequential execution of the program. Therefore, several approaches analyze OpenMP programs. While some approaches check functional equivalence, they are either general purpose approaches, which ignore the structure of the program and the design pattern applied for parallelization, or they focus on parallelized for-loops. In this paper, we propose a verification approach that aims at pipeline parallelism. To show functional equivalence, our approach mainly computes the dependencies that a sequential execution imposes on the pipeline stages and checks whether these dependencies are incorporated in the OpenMP parallelzation. We implemented our verification approach in a prototype tool and evaluated it on some examples. Our evaluation shows that our approach soundly detects incorrect pipeline implementations.

Keywords: OpenMP verification · Functional equivalence · Pipeline parallelism · Parallel design pattern

1 Introduction

For several years, the CPU frequency has stayed the same, while the number of cores per CPU is increasing. To take full advantage of today's hardware, we need multi-threaded programs. However, many programs are still not multi-threaded.

OpenMP [17] is an API that allows one to easily transform sequential programs into multi-threaded ones, which are even platform independent. To parallelize a sequential program, one often only needs to insert OpenMP directives.

One problem of OpenMP parallelization is that not all OpenMP-compliant programs are correct [17]. For example, an OpenMP-compliant program may contain data races or deadlocks. Even worse, correctly applying OpenMP is

---

This work was funded by the Hessian LOEWE initiative within the Software-Factory 4.0 project.

© Springer Nature Switzerland AG 2021
A. Laarman and A. Sokolova (Eds.): SPIN 2021, LNCS 12864, pp. 81–98, 2021.
https://doi.org/10.1007/978-3-030-84629-9_5

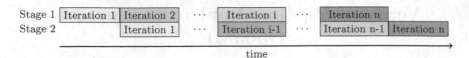

Fig. 1. Pipeline parallelism with a two-stage pipeline

```
1  void foo(int *a, int *b, int N)
2  {
3    #pragma omp parallel
4    {
5      #pragma omp single
6      for(int i=1; i<N; i++)
7      {
8        #pragma omp task depend(in: a[i-1]) depend(out: b[0:i+1])
9        b[i] = a[i-1];
10       #pragma omp task depend(in: b[i]) depend(out: a[0:i+1])
11       a[i] = b[i]-a[i];
12     }
13   }
14 }
```

Listing 1.1. An example for a parallelization that uses the pipeline pattern

difficult [5]. Therefore, we need verification methods to check whether a program parallelized with OpenMP is correct, i.e., we want to show that every execution of the parallelized program is *functionally equivalent* to a sequential execution that ignores the OpenMP directives.

Several approaches [2–4,13,14,19,20,23,28] look into correctness threats of OpenMP parallelizations, e.g., data races [2–4,14,23], deadlocks [14,20], etc. However, these approaches do not guarantee functional equivalence. In contrast, equivalence checkers like Pathg [27], CIVL [22], PEQCHECK [7], or the approach proposed by Abadi et al. [1] aim at proving functional equivalence. These equivalence checkers are general purpose checkers that ignore how a program is parallelized and, thus, regularly fail to show equivalence.

To overcome this problem, PatEC [6], AutoPar's correctness checker [12] and CIVL's OpenMP simplifier [22] take the kind of parallelization into account. However, they only support parallelizations utilizing data parallelism, e.g., parallelizations of loops whose iterations are independent of each other. In this paper, we propose a verification approach that aims at *pipeline parallelism*.

The pipeline pattern is a parallel design pattern [15,16] that may be used for loops whose iterations depend on each other. The idea of the pipeline pattern is similar to a processor pipeline. The sequential loop iteration is split into a sequence of stages such that each stage consumes data from the previous stage and provides data to the next stage. To exploit parallelism, the execution of consecutive loop iterations are overlapped as shown in Fig. 1.

Our verification approach assumes that the pipeline is implemented as follows. Stages are encapsulated in OpenMP tasks and depend clauses or synchronization directives describe the dependencies between stages. The loop itself is enclosed in a combination of a parallel and single OpenMP directive. Listing 1.1

shows an example for a pipeline with two stages. For demonstration purposes, we assume that a and b do not overlap. Hence, we do not require an in-dependency for a[i] in line 10. Read entry a[i] can only be modified in the same task.

Given a pipeline implementation of that form, our approach first determines the dependencies between tasks. In our example, the first task of iteration i depends on the second task of iteration $i - 1$, which declares a dependency on the first $i-1$ elements of array a. Moreover, the second task of iteration i depends on the first task of iteration i. In addition, the first (second) task in iteration i depend on all first tasks (second) tasks generated in iterations $j < i$. Next, our approach looks at all read-after-write (RAW), write-after-read (WAR), and write-after-write (WAW) dependencies in the sequential execution that cross stage boundaries. In our example, we have two RAW dependencies.[1] For each of these dependencies, our approach checks whether this dependency is captured by the task dependencies. For write-after-read dependencies, our approach also inspects whether the parallelized program uses data-sharing attributes that allow the read to access the value of the write. In our example, the RAW and WAR dependency is captured by the task dependencies and variable a and b are shared, i.e., writes to a and b are visible to all threads. Finally, our approach examines whether all variables modified by and live at the end of the pipeline use data-sharing attribute shared, which makes the modification visible.

As a proof-of-concept, we implemented our verification procedure in a prototype and evaluated it on several example programs. Our evaluation shows that our implementation soundly detects all incorrect pipeline implementations.

2   Using OpenMP to Implement Pipelines

OpenMP [17] is a standard that programmers can use to implement parallel programs for shared-memory systems. Programmers typically only insert OpenMP directives into the code, which the compiler considers to generate the parallel program. In the following, we describe the important features needed to implement a parallel pipeline in OpenMP. We start with the OpenMP directives.

OpenMP Directives in Parallel Pipelines. We assume that the parallel pipelines are realized with the following five directives:

parallel. Defines a parallel region that multiple threads execute in parallel.
single. Defines a region, typically nested inside a parallel region, that is executed by exactly one thread.
task. Defines a code region that is executed by an arbitrary thread in parallel with e.g., other tasks.
barrier. Introduces an explicit barrier that must be reached by all threads of the enclosing parallel region before any thread can continue.

---

[1] In iteration i, the second task reads memory location b[i] after it is written by the first task. Similarly, the first task reads memory location a[i-1] in iteration i after the second task writes to it in iteration $i - 1$.

taskwait. Forces the task, `single` region, etc. to wait on the completion of its generated child tasks.[2]

Data-Sharing Attributes. The data-sharing attribute defines the visibility of a variable, e.g., whether it is shared among the threads or each thread uses its own local copy, and how information is exchanged between the original variable and its copies. Our analysis supports the following attributes, which primarily occur in parallel pipelines.

private. Each thread has a local copy of the variable, which is uninitialized.
firstprivate. Similar to private, each thread gets its own local copy. In addition, the variable is initialized to the value of the original variable at the point the directive (`parallel`, `single`, `task`) is encountered.
shared. The variable is shared among all threads.

Data-sharing attributes can be specified explicitly by adding data-sharing clauses to the above directives. If not specified explicitly, the data-sharing attribute is determined implicitly via rules. For example, variables declared inside a region are typically private. Variables declared outside the parallel pipeline are shared and for tasks all other variables are normally firstprivate.

Depend Clauses. By default, tasks are executed independently, e.g., concurrently or in arbitrary order. However, pipeline parallelism requires a certain partial order on tasks. Depend clauses, which can be added to the task directive, allow one to enforce such order constraints[3]. The general structure of these clauses is

$$\mathbf{depend}(type : varList),$$

where $type \in \{\mathtt{in}, \mathtt{out}, \mathtt{inout}\}$ and *varList* denotes a list of variables and array sections as shown in Listing 1.1[4] The dependence type specifies how the mentioned variables are accessed, i.e., read (`in`), written (`out`), or both (`inout`).

Semantically, depend clauses specify a dependency between tasks. A task cannot execute before all tasks that it depends on and that are generated before it finished. The following definition formalizes the dependency between tasks.

Definition 1. *Tasks T_1 and T_2 are dependent if there exists a depend clause $\mathbf{depend}(t_1{:}l_1)$ for T_1 and a depend clause $\mathbf{depend}(t_2{:}l_2)$ for T_2 such that*

- *$(t_1, t_2) \neq (in, in)$ and*
- *there exist $a_1 \in l_1$ and $a_2 \in l_2$ such that a_1 and a_2 designate the same memory location.*

---

[2] Note that we currently do not support `taskwait` directives with depend clauses.
[3] In general, the constraints apply to sibling tasks only. Due to the construction of tasks in parallel pipeline implementations that we support, all tasks are siblings.
[4] The OpenMP standard also allows other variants of the depend clause but we stick to these because they are the main ones used when realizing the pipeline pattern. Ignoring other types is sound but can lead to false positives.

In our verification approach, we only look at task constructs (task directive plus associated code region), not tasks generated for task constructs. Thus, we may only introduce dependencies between task constructs if a dependency always exists for all respective tasks generated by the pipeline. This property is fulfilled for all dependencies built on scalar variables or array subscripts that are loop invariant, i.e., whose value does not change during pipeline execution. Also, task construct T_1 depends on task construct T_2 if every task of T_2 depends on every previously constructed task of T_2 and each task generated for T_1 depends on the last task generated for T_2. The following definition captures the first two cases and demonstrates the latter for pipelines with incrementing loops, i.e., loops that only change the loop counter at the end of each loop iteration and that change increments the loop counter by one. Supporting further loops, e.g., decrementing loop or loops with another step size, or supporting multi-dimensional arrays is rather straightforward.

Definition 2. *Task construct T_1 depends on task construct T_2 if there exists a depend clause* **depend**$(t_1{:}l_1)$ *for T_1 and a depend clause* **depend**$(t_2{:}l_2)$ *for T_2 such that*

- $(t_1, t_2) \neq (in, in)$ *and*
- *there exist $a_1 \in l_1$ and $a_2 \in l_2$ such that either*
  1. *$a_1 = a_2$ and a_1, a_2 are scalar variables,*
  2. *$a_1 = a_2$, and a_1, a_2 are array subscripts, and the subscript expressions are loop invariant, or*
  3. *the pipeline uses an incrementing loop with loop counter i and there exists an array a such that either*
     (a) $a_2 = a[0 : i + 1], a_1 = a[i]$ and T_2 occurs after T_1 in the loop body,
     (b) $a_2 = a[0 : i + 2], a_1 = a[i]$ and T_2 occurs after T_1 in the loop body,
     (c) $a_2 = a[0 : i + 1], a_1 = a[i - 1]$ and T_2 occurs before T_1 in the loop body.

Pipeline Structure. Pipelines can be realized in different ways in OpenMP. We assume that the pipeline is structured as shown in Listing 1.2. This is a common structure for a pipeline implementation and it is e.g., used by the auto-parallelization tool DiscoPoP [10]. As shown in Listing 1.2, the pipeline is implemented in a **parallel** region. Inside the **parallel** region, a **single** region

```
 1    #pragma omp parallel
 2    {
 3        : //Declarations
 4    #pragma omp single
 5        {
 6            : //Declarations
 7            for /*or while*/ (...) {
 8
 9                //Tasks, statements, barriers
10            }
11        }
12    }
```

Listing 1.2. General structure of a pipeline implementation

Algorithm 1: Verification algorithm

Input: program - source code of program with pipeline to verify

1 dependGraph := BUILDDEPENDENCYGRAPH(program)
2 potentialViolations := CHECKRWDEPENDENCIES(dependGraph)
3 violation := CHECKPOTENTIALVIOLATIONS(potentialViolations)
4 **if** violation = ⊥ **then**
5 | violation := CHECKREMAININGDEPENDENCIES(dependGraph)
6 **return** witness

---

constructs the pipeline stages in a loop[5]. Thereby, each instance of a pipeline stage becomes a task, which must not include tasks itself, i.e. task constructs must not be nested. Furthermore, we allow declarations of temporary variables at the beginning of the **parallel** or **single** region. In addition to task constructs, the loop body may contain statements, which prepare the different stages, and barriers (**barrier** or **taskwait**) to further order tasks. Task constructs, statements, and barriers are sequentially composed, especially, task constructs and statements must not contain task constructs or barriers.

3   Verifying Correctness of Pipeline Implementations

The goal of our verification is to determine whether a code segment parallelized with the pipeline pattern behaves functionally equivalent to its sequential execution. Our verification algorithm shown in Algorithm 1 consists of four steps. First, it constructs a task dependency graph (Sec. 3.1) that represents the specified constraints on the execution order of the tasks. Then, it inspects which of the RAW and WAR dependencies in the sequential execution that cross task boundaries are reflected in the task dependency graph (Sec. 3.2). Read-write conflicts (i.e., RAW or WAR dependencies) that are not represented in the task dependency graph may be eliminated with barriers or proper data-sharing attributes, e.g., the variable can be private in both tasks. The third step checks this. Finally, the last step (Sec. 3.3) analyzes write-after-write dependencies and ensures that the tasks get the correct input values and make their output available. Algorithm 1 will return ⊥ if it can prove that the pipeline pattern is correctly implemented.[6] Otherwise, it outputs a read-write or write-write conflict on variable v, which may threaten functional equivalence.

3.1   Constructing Task Dependency Graphs

A task dependency graph provides information about execution constraints, especially order constraints, on tasks. A vertex of the graph represents a task construct (task directive plus associated code region) or a statement that is not part

---

[5] Currently, we support *for* and *while* loops.

[6] Note that Algorithm 1 assumes, but does not check that the checked code segment follows the pipeline structure described in the previous section. Therefore, its result is only reliable for those segments.

of a task construct but occurs in the pipeline's single region. In the following, we use $V_T := \{t_1, \ldots, t_n\}$ to denote the set of task constructs and $V_S := \{s_1, \ldots, s_m\}$ to denote the statements. An edge $(v_1, v_2) \in (V_T \cup V_S) \times (V_T \cup V_S)$ describes a dependency between v_1 and v_2, e.g., if $v_1 \in V_T$, then a task generated for task construct v_2 (statement v_2) must be executed after all previously generated tasks for task construct v_1 finished. Note that our task dependency graph does not include dependencies from $V_S \times V_S$ because the statements in V_S are executed by a single thread, which executes them in the same order as in the sequential execution. Next, let us discuss how to compute the edges.

Dependency Edges from Depend Clauses. First, let us consider dependencies between task constructs that origin from depend clauses. Remember that our depend definition (Def. 2) captures these dependencies. In the task dependency graph, these order constraints are represented by the depend edges.

$$E_{\text{depend}} := \{(t_i, t_j) \in V_T \times V_T \mid t_j \text{ depends on } t_i\} \tag{1}$$

Dependency Edges from Barriers. Next to depend clauses, also barriers (`barrier` or `taskwait` directives) introduce dependencies. For example, a barrier ensures that no two tasks of the same task construct can execute in parallel. There exists a self-dependency for all task constructs if the set of barriers B is non-empty.

$$E_{\text{self}} := \begin{cases} \varnothing & \text{if } B = \varnothing \\ \{(v, v) \in V_T \times V_T\} & \text{otherwise} \end{cases} \tag{2}$$

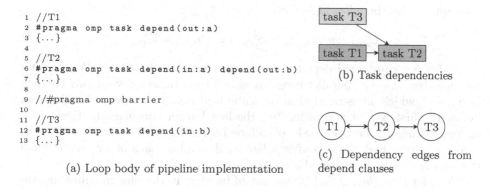

```
1  //T1
2  #pragma omp task depend(out:a)
3  {...}
4
5  //T2
6  #pragma omp task depend(in:a) depend(out:b)
7  {...}
8
9  //#pragma omp barrier
10
11 //T3
12 #pragma omp task depend(in:b)
13 {...}
```

(a) Loop body of pipeline implementation

(b) Task dependencies

(c) Dependency edges from depend clauses

Fig. 2. Demonstrating unsoundness of transitive dependency edges

Similarly, we use barriers to add some of the transitive edges from E_{depend}. Since our graph only considers task constructs and cannot distinguish tasks generated in different iterations of the enclosing loop, not all transitive edges from E_{depend} can be considered without becoming unsound.[7] For example, consider

---

[7] In contrast, leaving out some of those edges only makes our approach imprecise.

the pipeline implementation sketched in Fig. 2a. Figure 2b shows task T3 constructed for task construct T3 in iteration i, tasks T1 and T2 constructed for task constructs T1 and T2 in iteration i+1, and their dependencies. In addition, Fig. 2c shows the task dependencies E_{depend}.[8] We observe that the transitive edge $(T3, T1)$ is not present in Fig. 2b, although T3 is generated before T1. Thus, edge $(T3, T1)$ must not be added to the task dependency graph. When adding transitive edges, we use that the barrier ensures that at most one task per task construct exists at any point in time and a task belongs to either iteration i (task constructs after the barrier) or iteration i+1 (task constructs before the barrier). Thus, we can safely add transitive dependency edges between task constructs that occur both either before or after the barrier. The transitive edges introduced by a barrier are:

$$E_{\text{trans}}^b := \left((V_{\text{before}}^b \times V_{\text{before}}^b) \cap E_{\text{depend}} \right)^+ \cup \left((V_{\text{after}}^b \times V_{\text{after}}^b) \cap E_{\text{depend}} \right)^+,$$

$$(3)$$

where $V_{\text{before}}^b \subseteq V$ and $V_{\text{after}}^b \subseteq V$ denote the sets of task constructs before and after barrier b respectively.

In addition, a barrier introduces dependencies between tasks from V_T and statements from V_S. A barrier b enforces the single thread to wait until all tasks preceding the barrier finished. Therefore, statements after the barrier (S_{after}^b) depend on the task constructs before the barrier (V_{before}^b). Furthermore, when the barrier was passed new tasks for task constructs before the barrier are only constructed in the next loop iteration, i.e., all statements after the barrier have been executed. Thus, there also exists a dependency between the statements after the barrier and the task constructs before the barrier. These dependencies are captured by the following set of edges.

$$E_{\text{stmts}}^b := \left(V_{\text{before}}^b \times S_{\text{after}}^b \right) \cup \left(S_{\text{after}}^b \times V_{\text{after}}^b \right)$$

$$(4)$$

So far, we considered dependencies caused by a single barrier. When using multiple barriers, the parallel program either runs tasks between two barriers in parallel, which are generated in the same iteration, or we execute tasks from before the first barrier and tasks after the last barrier concurrently. Even if we cannot distinguish between tasks of different iterations, we know that all tasks before a barrier and all tasks after a barrier depend on each other except when they occur before the first and after the last barrier.[9]

Now, let $B = \{b_1, \ldots, b_n\}$ be the list of barriers in the pipeline implementation such that the barriers in the list are ordered in source code order. Furthermore, let $V_{\text{before}}^{b_i}$ be the statements and task constructs that occur in the pipeline before barrier b_i and $V_{\text{after}}^{b_i}$ those occurring after barrier b_i. We use these sets to

---

[8] Note that Fig. 2b does not contain dependencies between tasks T2 and T1 and tasks T2 and T3 because $T3$ and $T1$ are generated before $T1$.

[9] The same holds for pairs of tasks and statements.

Algorithm 2: checkRWEdges($G = (V, E)$)

Input: G - depend graph, where $V = V_T \cup V_S$
1   *potentialViolations* := $\varnothing$
2   **foreach** $v \in Vars$ **do**
3   T_R := READIN(V, v)   ▷ returns tasks in which v is read
4   T_W := WRITTENIN(V, v)   ▷ returns tasks in which v is written
5   **foreach** $(t_r, t_w) \in$ GETDEPS(T_R, T_W) $\setminus (V_S \times V_S)$ **do**
6   **if** $(t_r, t_w) \notin E$ **then**
7            $potentialViolations := potentialViolations \cup (t_r, t_w, v)$
8   **return** *potentialViolations*

---

define the dependencies discussed above.

$$E_{\text{barrier}}^B := \bigcup_{i=1}^{|B|} \left\{ (v_b, v_a), (v_a, v_b) \mid v_b \in V_{\text{before}}^{b_i} \setminus V_{\text{before}}^{b_1} \wedge v_a \in \times V_{\text{after}}^{b_i} \setminus V_{\text{after}}^{b_n} \right\}$$

(5)

Summing up, the dependency edges from a set of barriers B are:

$$E_{\text{barrier}} := E_{\text{self}} \cup E_{\text{barrier}}^B \cup \bigcup_{b \in B} \left(E_{\text{trans}}^b \cup E_{\text{stmts}}^b \right)$$

(6)

Now, we have everything at hand to define the task dependency graph.

Definition 3. *A task dependency graph is a directed graph*

$$G = (V_T \cup V_S, E_{depend} \cup E_{barrier}).$$

3.2 Inspecting RAW and WAR Dependencies

In this check, we inspect if the read-after-write and write-after-read dependencies of the sequential execution are respected by the parallel pipeline, i.e., the dependencies occur in the task dependency graph, or they are safely removed from the parallel pipeline. First, we use Algorithm 2 to check which of the dependencies are present in the task dependency graph. Thereafter, we call Algorithm 3 to check whether all dependencies not present in the task dependency graph are safely removed by the pipeline implementation.

To compare the program dependencies with the task dependency graph, Algorithm 2 iterates over the variables. For each variable, it first computes which component, i.e., task construct or statement in the pipeline, reads and which writes the variable. Then, it calls the method getDeps to compute all pairs (t_r, t_w) of reading and writing components that have a RAW or WAR conflict on variable v. Note that this is sufficient and we do not need to distinguish between RAW and WAR dependencies because OpenMP and our task dependency graph do not distinguish them.[10] Next, Algorithm 2 checks whether all

---

[10] While one can reflect RAW and WAR dependencies with OpenMP depend clauses, a RAW depend specification can prevent a WAR dependency and vice versa.

Algorithm 3: checkPotentialViolations(*potentialViolations*)

```
1  foreach (t_r, t_w, v) ∈ potentialViolations do
2  │   d_r := GETDATASHARINGATTRIBUTE(t_r, v)
3  │   d_w := GETDATASHARINGATRRIBUTE(t_w, v)
4  │   if d_r = firstprivate ∧(d_w ≠ shared ∨
5  │       d_w = shared ∧ G.EXISTSBARRIERBETWEEN(t_r, t_w)) then
6  │   │   continue;
7  │   if FIRSTWRITE(t_r, v) < FIRSTREAD(t_r, v)
8  │       ∧ (d_r ≠ shared ∨ d_w ≠ shared) then
9  │   │   continue;
10 │   return (t_r, t_w, v)
```

---

those pairs are reflected in the task dependency graph. However, it excludes all pairs (t_r, t_w) from $V_S \times V_S$ because they are executed in sequential order. If the task dependency graph does not contain a corresponding edge (t_r, t_w) and the dependency is not an intra-task dependency, a potential dependency violation is found and stored in the set of `potentialViolations`.

In a second step, Algorithm 3 checks the potential violations. Under certain conditions a parallel pipeline is still correctly implemented although it misses a dependency. In general, the variable must not be shared, i.e., at least one of the components uses a thread-local copy to prevent data races, and the read access must still return the same value as a sequential execution. Currently, we support two cases. First, the read variable is allowed to be `firstprivate` if the written variable is either not `shared` or is `shared` and there exists a barrier between the read and write accesses that ensures that the read variable is initialized with the correct value. Second, if a component always writes to variable v before it reads variable v, the read does not depend on other components and could be performed on a different copy without altering the behavior. Therefore, a dependency can be missing if the component always writes to variable v before it reads variable v and variable v is (first)private. Note that Algorithm 3 only checks that the read-write conflicts are eliminated, but does not check whether the elimination affects the functional behavior. The latter is considered by the next algorithm.

3.3   Checking WAW Dependencies and I/O Availability

In this check, we examine whether all WAW dependencies in the sequential execution are handled appropriately, whether all read accesses in the pipeline see the same value as a sequential execution, and whether the computation result is available after the pipeline execution. To inspect the WAW dependencies, we inspect all variables v and check that all pairs of pipeline components (task constructs or statements from V_S) that write to v are either ordered or at least one component uses a thread-local copy of the variable. Thus, we ensure that writes to the same variable cannot interfere.

Algorithm 4: checkRemainingDependencies($G = (V, E)$)

Input: G - depend graph

```
1  // check write-write dependencies
```
2 **foreach** $(t_{w_1}, t_{w_2}) \in ((T_W \times T_W) \setminus (V_S \times V_S))$ **do**

3   **if** GETDATASHARINGATTRIBUTE$(t_{w_1}, v) = $ ***shared*** $\wedge$
      GETDATASHARINGATTRIBUTE$(t_{w_2}, v) = $ ***shared*** $\wedge$ $(t_{w_1}, t_{w_2}) \notin E$ **then**

4   **return** (t_{w_1}, t_{w_2}, v)

5

```
6  //check reads
```
7 **foreach** $t_r \in T_R$ **do**

8     $d_r := $ GETDATASHARINGATTRIBUTE(t_r, v)

9   **if** $d_r = $ ***private*** $\wedge$ FIRSTWRITE$(t_r, v) > $ FIRSTREAD(t_r, v) **then**

10   **return** $(t_r, -, v)$

11

```
12 //check output availability
```
13 **foreach** $v \in $ GETLIVEVARS **do**

14   **foreach** $t_w \in T_W$ **do**

15       $d_w := $ GETDATASHARINGATTRIBUTE(t_w, v)

16   **if** $d_w \neq $ ***shared*** **then**

17   **return** $(-, t_w, v)$

18

19 **foreach** $v \in Vars$ **do**

20     $T_R := $ READIN(V, v) $\triangleright$ returns tasks in which v is read

21     $T_W := $ WRITTENIN(V, v) $\triangleright$ returns tasks in which v is written

22   **foreach** $(t_r, t_w) \in T_R \times T_W$ **do**

23       $d_r := $ GETDATASHARINGATTRIBUTE(t_r, v)

24       $d_w := $ GETDATASHARINGATTRIBUTE(t_w, v)

25   **if** FIRSTWRITE$(t_r, v) < $ FIRSTREAD(t_r, v) **then**

26   **continue**;

27   **if** $d_r = $ ***firstprivate*** $\wedge$ $d_w = $ ***shared***
28         $\wedge$!G.EXISTSBARRIERBEFOREORAFTER(t_r, t_w) **then**

29   **return** (t_r, t_w, v)

30

31 **return** $\perp$

After we checked the RAW, WAR, and WAW dependencies, we know that reads and writes are ordered as in the sequential execution or they are performed on local copies. To show functional equivalence between the parallel pipeline and the sequential execution, it remains to be shown that a variable read returns the same value in both cases and we get the same values when reading variables after the pipeline. To ensure that the correct value can be read in the pipeline, the algorithm checks that read variables are only `private` if they are defined in a node (task construct or statement) before they are read. To allow that a write can be propagated to a read in or after the pipeline, we check that all variables written in the pipeline that are live have data-sharing attribute `shared`, i.e., we can access the modified value. Finally, we need to check whether we read the correct value in the pipeline. We already know that for each read-write pair, there either exists a dependency edge, i.e., the read and write cannot occur concurrently, or Algorithm 3 already checked that the correct values are read. In addition, a read variable can only be `private` if it is defined in the node before it is read. The only reason why an incorrect value might be read are `firstprivate` variables, which are initialized at task creation. `Firstprivate` variables are unproblematic if the initialization value is irrelevant (i.e., they are defined before read) or a barrier between reading and writing node ensures that during task generation the same value as in a sequential execution is used for initialization.

3.4   Handling of Loop Header

To include the statements of the loop header into our analysis we consider them to be part of the loop body. The condition test is the first statement of the body while increment statements are placed right at the end. All these statements are executed by the single thread and can be treated the same way as regular statements placed outside of tasks.

3.5   Implementation

We implemented the algorithms in a prototype tool to check pipeline parallelizations of C programs. Our prototype builds on the ROSE compiler framework [18]. Next, we describe how we implemented the predicates used in the algorithms.

`readIn/writtenIn`. We use ROSE's def-use analysis to determine the variable usages and definitions (AST nodes) in the loop. Based on the position of the AST node in the code, we identify the corresponding node (task construct or statement from V_S) in the pipeline. Arrays are treated like scalar variables, i.e. array indices are ignored.

`getDeps`(T_R, T_W). Based on the nodes reading or writing a variable v, our prototype compute a coarse, but fast overapproximation of the read-write dependencies on variable v in the sequential program, namely the Cartesian product $T_R \times T_W$ of nodes reading and writing variable v.

`getDataSharingAttribute`(t, v). We try to determine the data-sharing attribute based on the corresponding OpenMP declarative and fallback to the rules if it is not explicitly specified.

`firstRead`(t, v)/`firstWrite`(t, v). To compute these predicates, we take all reads into account, but only consider write accesses that occur on every execution path, i.e., that are not part of a branch or loop body. Since our algorithms only check whether there always exists a write to v before any read of v, this approximation is sound, but imprecise. However, the approximation allows us to use source code lines in the implementation of the predicates. More concretely, the predicates return the source line number of the first read access of v in t and the first write access of v in t that is considered. In case there is no read and write access respectively, the source line number of the end of t is returned.

`existsBarrierBetween`(t_r, t_w). We use code lines to decide this predicate. Note that this is only valid because we assume that tasks, barriers, and statements (from V_S) are sequentially composed and must not be nested.

Let $t.\textbf{loc}$ and $b.\textbf{loc}$ be the source code line of the beginning of a node $t \in V_T \cup V_S$ and a barrier b. To determine the truth value of the predicate, our implementation checks the following formula by iterating over all barriers b.

$$\exists b \in B : \min(t_r.\textbf{loc}, t_w.\textbf{loc}) < b.\textbf{loc} < \max(t_r.\textbf{loc}, t_w.\textbf{loc})$$

`existsBarrierBeforeOrAfter`(t_r, t_w). Similar to `existsBarrierBetween`, we use code lines and iterate over the barriers b to decide the following formula.

$$\exists b \in B : b.\textbf{loc} < t_r.\textbf{loc} \lor b.\textbf{loc} > t_w.\textbf{loc}$$

`getLiveVars`. Our implementation returns all modified variables.[11]

So far, our prototype realizes a restricted implementation of the verification technique, which was sufficient for our initial evaluation. For example, the implementation is limited to scalar variables and arrays and, as already mentioned, arrays are handled like scalar variables, i.e. so we do not distinguish different indices. However, the algorithm is not limited to these data types. Adding basic struct support is simple. One could handle struct accesses similar to arrays. To soundly support pointers one however requires a points-to analysis. Using a more fine grained notion of variables, e.g., on the basis of memory locations, allows one to differentiate between different array elements.

Also, recursive function calls are currently not supported. They might violate the assumptions that tasks are not nested. Since nested task are not siblings of all other tasks, a depend clause of a non-sibling tasks has no effect. To support recursion, we, therefore, need to analyze which tasks are siblings and consider this when determining the dependency edges from depend clauses.

Furthermore, the implementations of `readIn`, `writtenIn`, `firstRead`, and `firstWrite` are intra-procedural. In our context, the current implementation of `firstWrite` is sound. To soundly support function calls in `readIn` and `writtenIn`, we could e.g., assume that called functions read and write all global variables and passed parameters. For `firstRead`, we could also assume that called functions read all global variables and associate those reads with the called functions.

In addition, the precision of the prototype can be further improved by using more precise implementations of the above predicates. For example, the `getDeps` predicate could take the control-flow into account. The `getLiveVars` can be refined by applying ROSE's live variable analysis. Furthermore, one can use definition-use chains to improve the predicates `firstRead` and `firstWrite`.

---

[11] Although read-only variables are excluded, this is sufficient because Algorithm 4 only checks live and modified variables.

Table 1. Evaluation results showing for each example, the expected and reported result, the size of the task dependency graph, and the number of barriers B

Task	Expected result	Reported result	$\|V_S\| + \|V_T\|$	$\|E\|$	$\|B\|$
DRB072-taskdep1-orig-no.c	✓	✓	0+2	3	0
DRB072-taskdep2-orig-no.c	✓	✓	0+2	4	0
DRB072-taskdep3-orig-no.c	✓	✓	0+3	5	0
DRB120-barrier-orig-no.c	✓	✓	2+0	4	1
DRB131-taskdep4-orig-yes-omp45.c	✓	✗	4+3	16	1
DRB132-taskdep4-orig-no-omp45.c	✗	✗	4+3	25	1
DRB133-taskdep5-orig-no-omp45.c	✗	✗	4+3	29	1
DRB134-taskdep5-orig-yes-omp45.c	✓	✗	4+3	20	1
DRB135-taskdep-mutexinoutset-orig-no.c	✗	✗	0+6	17	0
DRB136-taskdep-mutexinoutset-orig-yes.c	✓	✗	0+6	9	0
DRB165-taskdep4-orig-yes-omp50.c	✓	✗	2+3	8	1
DRB166-taskdep4-orig-no-omp50.c	✗	✗	2+3	15	1
DRB167-taskdep4-orig-no-omp50.c	✗	✗	2+3	19	1
DRB168-taskdep5-orig-yes-omp50.c	✓	✗	2+3	12	1
eos-mbpt-hf-interpolate/pipeline_1:27.c	✓	✗	0+2	3	0
Kastors/strassen-task-dep.c	✓	✓	0+19	305	8
Kastors/strassen-task.c	✓	✓	0+19	361	1

4   Evaluation

Our goal is to demonstrate the applicability of our verification approach. Note that we could not compare our approach to the closely related approach of Royuela et al. [19] because we failed to find out how to run their analysis.

Benchmark Tasks. We looked at the DataRaceBench [11] and KASTORS benchmark [25] and selected all examples that contain task parallelism and use **depend** clauses. Our selection results in 14 examples from the DataRaceBench and two from the KASTORS benchmark. To get a syntactical pipeline implementation, we added a loop to the tasks. In addition, we consider one potential pipeline implementation suggested by the auto-parallelizer DiscoPoP [10] (`eos-mbpt-hf-interpolate/pipeline_1:27.c`). In total, we use 17 examples.

Environmental Setup. We run our experiments 5-times on an Ubuntu 18.04 machine with an Intel Core i7 CPU and 32 GB of RAM.

4.1   Experimental Results

RQ 1: Is our algorithm sound and does it detect correct pipelines? Table 1 shows for each of the 17 tasks the expected result, the reported result, the number of nodes and edges in the task dependency graph as well as the number of barrier statements in the pipeline implementation. Looking at Table 1, we observe that our algorithm rejects all incorrect results. Thus, it is sound on out examples. Also, it detects 50% of the correct pipeline implementations, but rejects the

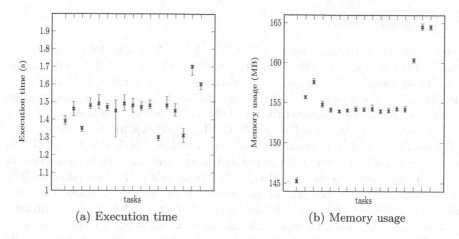

(a) Execution time   (b) Memory usage

Fig. 3. Per task, average, maximum and minimum execution time (left) and average, maximum and minimum memory usage (right) of five executions

other half. The main reason for rejection is that the algorithm fails to detect that inter-iteration depenendencies can be ignored for loops with one iteration.

RQ 2: How does our algorithm scale? To analyze the scalability, we consider the size of the task dependency graph, which includes the number of tasks ($|V_T|$) and statements ($|V_S|$), as well as the number of barriers in the program. The last three columns of Table 1 provide these numbers. While our set of tasks is too small to come to a definite conclusion, we can observe that the number of edges increases superlinear with the number of tasks and statements (the nodes of the task dependency graph). Furthermore, the last two rows show two parallelizations of the same sequential program. One uses barriers and the other depend clauses. We observe that for the two examples, barriers are more efficient.

RQ 3: How efficient is our algorithm? To evaluate the efficiency of our algorithm, we consider the execution time and memory usage shown in Fig. 3a and 3b. For each example, the two plots show the average of five executions together with the maximum and minimum value. The examples are ordered as in Table 1.

We observe that the execution times and memory usage are rather low and often similar. The reason is that for our examples the parsing dominates the execution time and memory usage. Furthermore, we observe that for the analysis of the larger KASTORS tasks (last two examples) we require significantly more time and memory. We also see that the first example requires significantly less memory than the others because it does not call library functions. Another outlier is the DiscoPoP example (third last). The task itself contains more code than most of the other tasks, which leads to larger memory usage. However, the pipeline section itself is rather small. Thus, the analysis time is short.

5   Related Work

Several static and dynamic analyses [2–4, 9, 13, 14, 19–21, 23, 28] for OpenMP programs exist. We focus on the static analyses [3, 4, 13, 19, 20, 23, 28]. Some of the static analyses specialize on specific properties like concurrent access [13, 19, 28], the absence of data races [4, 23, 26] or deadlocks [20]. In contrast, we examine behavioral equivalence between the parallel and sequential execution.

Equivalence checkers like Pathg [27], CIVL [22], PEQCHECK [7], or the approach of Abadi et al. [1] examine equivalence, but these checkers are general purpose checkers, which ignore applied parallel design patterns and the structure of the parallelization. In contrast, PatEC [6], AutoPar's correctness checker [12], CIVL's OpenMP simplifier [22], or ompVerify [3] analyze equivalence of sequential and parallelized for loops, but they do not support pipeline implementations.

The approach closest to ours is the one by Royuela et al. [19]. Like our approach, they focus on tasks and analyze depend and data-sharing clauses. While we construct a task dependency graph, they represent the task dependencies in an extended control-flow graph. Furthermore, we explicitly check equivalence while Royuela et al. [19] only look for common parallelization mistakes.

Finally, we would like to mention that there exist approaches [8, 24] that verify whether a sequential loop optimization that aims at a better utilization of the processor pipeline is correct.

6   Conclusion

While the CPU frequency remains static, the number of cores per CPU increases. To speed up a program, one must execute it on multiple CPU cores.

OpenMP is a widely used API that programmers utilize to transform their programs into multi-threaded programs. To this end, the programmers typically only insert OpenMP directives. Unfortunately, not all OpenMP-compliant programs are correct. Thus, programmers should analyze whether an OpenMP parallelization is behavior preserving.

In this paper, we propose an automatic technique to support a programmer with this analysis task. Our technique utilizes that programmers often consider parallel design patterns when parallelizing programs. More concretely, we develop a specific technique to verify that a parallelization that applies the pipeline pattern is behavior preserving. To ensure that the behavior is preserved, our technique aims to check that a read access to a variable returns the same value in the sequential and parallelized program. Therefore, it analyzes whether the dependencies on variables accesses that exist in the sequential program are properly considered in the parallelization and that data-sharing attributes do not prevent reading the proper values.

To test our technique, we implemented it in a prototype tool and evaluated it on 17 examples. Our technique overapproximates, and, thus, our implementation failed to detect all correct parallelizations, i.e., it is not complete. While completeness is desirable, soundness is important. In our evaluation, our implementation behaved soundly and successfully detected all incorrect parallelizations.

References

1. Abadi, M., Keidar-Barner, S., Pidan, D., Veksler, T.: Verifying parallel code after refactoring using equivalence checking. Int. J. Parallel Program. **47**(1), 59–73 (2018). https://doi.org/10.1007/s10766-017-0548-4
2. Atzeni, S., et al.: ARCHER: effectively spotting data races in large OpenMP applications. In: Proceedings IPDPS, pp. 53–62. IEEE (2016). https://doi.org/10.1109/IPDPS.2016.68
3. Basupalli, V., et al.: ompVerify: polyhedral analysis for the OpenMP programmer. In: Proceedings IWOMP, pp. 37–53. LNCS 6665, Springer (2011). https://doi.org/10.1007/978-3-642-21487-5_4
4. Bora, U., Das, S., Kukreja, P., Joshi, S., Upadrasta, R., Rajopadhye, S.: LLOV: a fast static data-race checker for openMP programs. TACO **17**(4) (2020). https://doi.org/10.1145/3418597
5. Goncalves, R., Amaris, M., Okada, T.K., Bruel, P., Goldman, A.: OpenMP is not as easy as it appears. In: Proceedings HICSS, pp. 5742–5751. IEEE (2016). https://doi.org/10.1109/HICSS.2016.710
6. Jakobs, M.: PatEC: pattern-based equivalence checking. In: Laarman, A., Sokolova, A. (eds.) SPIN 2021, LNCS, vol. 12864, pp. 120–139 (2021). https://doi.org/10.1007/978-3-030-84629-9_7
7. Jakobs, M.C.: PEQcheck: localized and context-aware checking of functional equivalence. In: Proceedings FormaliSE, pp. 130–140. IEEE (2021), https://doi.org/10.1109/FormaliSE52586.2021.00019
8. Leviathan, R., Pnueli, A.: Validating software pipelining optimizations. In: Proceedings CASES, pp. 280–287. ACM (2002). https://doi.org/10.1145/581630.581676
9. Li, J., Hei, D., Yan, L.: Correctness analysis based on testing and checking for OpenMP Programs. In: Proceedings ChinaGrid, pp. 210–215. IEEE (2009). https://doi.org/10.1109/ChinaGrid.2009.12
10. Li, Z., Atre, R., Huda, Z.U., Jannesari, A., Wolf, F.: Unveiling parallelization opportunities in sequential programs. J. Syst. Softw. 282–295 (2016). https://doi.org/10.1016/j.jss.2016.03.045
11. Liao, C., Lin, P.H., Asplund, J., Schordan, M., Karlin, I.: DataRaceBench: a benchmark suite for systematic evaluation of data race detection tools. Proc. SC. ACM (2017). https://doi.org/10.1145/3126908.3126958
12. Liao, C., Quinlan, D.J., Willcock, J., Panas, T.: Extending automatic parallelization to optimize high-level abstractions for multicore. In: Proceedings IWOMP, pp. 28–41. LNCS 5568, Springer (2009). https://doi.org/10.1007/978-3-642-02303-3_3
13. Lin, Y.: Static Nonconcurrency analysis of OpenMP programs. In: Proceedings IWOMP, pp. 36–50. LNCS 4315, Springer (2005). https://doi.org/10.1007/978-3-540-68555-5_4
14. Ma, H., Diersen, S., Wang, L., Liao, C., Quinlan, D., Yang, Z.: Symbolic analysis of concurrency errors in OpenMP programs. In: Proceedings ICPP. pp. 510–516. IEEE (2013). https://doi.org/10.1109/ICPP.2013.63
15. Mattson, T.G., Sanders, B.A., Massingill, B.L.: Patterns for parallel programming. Addison-Wesley Professional (2013)
16. McCool, M., Reinders, J., Robison, A.: Structured Parallel Programming: Patterns for Efficient Computation. Morgan Kaufmann Publishers Inc., Burlington (2012)
17. OpenMP: OpenMP application programming interface (version 5.1). Technical report OpenMP Architecture Review Board (2020). https://www.openmp.org/specifications/

18. Quinlan, D., Liao, C.: The ROSE source-to-source compiler infrastructure. In: Cetus users and compiler infrastructure workshop, in conjunction with PACT, vol. 2011, p. 1. Citeseer (2011)
19. Royuela, S., Ferrer, R., Caballero, D., Martorell, X.: Compiler analysis for OpenMP tasks correctness. In: Proceedings CF, pp. 11–19. ACM (2015). https://doi.org/10.1145/2742854.2742882
20. Saillard, E., Carribault, P., Barthou, D.: Static Validation of barriers and work-sharing constructs in openmp applications. In: Proceedings IWOMP, pp. 73–86. LNCS 8766, Springer (2014). https://doi.org/10.1007/978-3-319-11454-5_6
21. Salamanca, J., Mattos, L., Araujo, G.: Loop-carried dependence verification in OpenMP. In: Proceedin IWOMP, pp. 87–102. LNCS 8766, Springer (2014). https://doi.org/10.1007/978-3-319-11454-5_7
22. Siegel, S.F., et al.: CIVL: the concurrency intermediate verification language. In: Proceedings SC, pp. 61:1–61:12. ACM (2015). https://doi.org/10.1145/2807591.2807635
23. Swain, B., Li, Y., Liu, P., Laguna, I., Georgakoudis, G., Huang, J.: OMPRacer: a scalable and precise static race detector for OpenMP programs. In: Proceedings SC. IEEE (2020). https://doi.org/10.1109/SC41405.2020.00058
24. Tristan, J., Leroy, X.: A simple, verified validator for software pipelining. In: Proceedings POPL, pp. 83–92. ACM (2010). https://doi.org/10.1145/1706299.1706311
25. Virouleau, P., Brunet, P., Broquedis, F., Furmento, N., Thibault, S., Aumage, O., Gautier, T.: Evaluation of OpenMP dependent tasks with the KASTORS benchmark suite. In: Proceedings IWOMP, pp. 16–29. LNCS 8766, Springer (2014). https://doi.org/10.1007/978-3-319-11454-5_2
26. Ye, F., Schordan, M., Liao, C., Lin, P., Karlin, I., Sarkar, V.: Using polyhedral analysis to verify openmp applications are data race free. In: Proceedings CORRECTNESS@SC, pp. 42–50. IEEE (2018). https://doi.org/10.1109/Correctness.2018.00010
27. Yu, F., Yang, S., Wang, F., Chen, G., Chan, C.: Symbolic consistency checking of openmp parallel programs. In: Proceedings LCTES, pp. 139–148. ACM (2012). https://doi.org/10.1145/2248418.2248438
28. Zhang, Y., Duesterwald, E., Gao, G.R.: Concurrency analysis for shared memory programs with textually unaligned barriers. In: Proceedings LCPC, pp. 95–109. LNCS 5234, Springer (2007). https://doi.org/10.1007/978-3-540-85261-2_7

Tool Papers

C-SMC: A Hybrid Statistical Model Checking and Concrete Runtime Engine for Analyzing C Programs

Antoine Chenoy, Fabien Duchene[✉], Thomas Given-Wilson, and Axel Legay

UCLouvain, Louvain-La-Neuve, Belgium
antoinechenoy@outlook.be,
{fabien.duchene,thomas.given-wilson,axel.legay}@uclouvain.be

Abstract. Finding programming errors is one of the major challenges in software development. Formal methods such as model checking have become a popular approach to address this problem because of their guarantees about error status. However, one of the greatest challenges is to have correct information about complex internal details such as memory, registers, and system state. In this paper we describe the C-SMC tool and methodology developed to find programming errors in C programs by leveraging statistical model checking and runtime information. Our prototype shows that our approach can complement many existing software verification tools.

1 Introduction and Motivation

The advantages of formal methods over traditional approaches, such as testing, are formal methods' capability to provide guarantees about results. Another advantage is in using expressive temporal logic to elegantly express and verify complex temporal properties. Approaches such as *model checking* (MC) [13] are able to produce examples of errors (falsification of properties) or guarantee the absence of errors, albeit at the cost of building a model and checking every possible state.

Over past years, formal methods were restricted to the verification of system's abstractions such as transition systems that would directly be provided by the user. The situation has changed with the arrival of a series of new tools that allows us to verify C code (among others) directly. There are many tools for C code analysis that use a variety of approaches including: heuristics [1,2,8]; model checking [17,18,21,25,34] and variations [29,32]; other formal methods [38,39]; symbolic verification [19], and runtime analysis [11,36]. All those tools either suffer from the state-space explosion problem or from difficulties in handling the memory model of the system under verification.

Advances on MC such as *statistical model checking* (SMC) [12,30,31] provide an efficient balance by resolving many complexity and state-space problems from MC, albeit at the cost of certainty [15,24].

This work has been partially supported by a Cisco grant.

A. Laarman and A. Sokolova (Eds.): SPIN 2021, LNCS 12864, pp. 101–119, 2021.
https://doi.org/10.1007/978-3-030-84629-9_6

SMC simulates multiple executions of a system and monitors them in regards to properties. Then, SMC uses statistical algorithms to extrapolate to the global system. While SMC can efficiently find errors and avoid complexity problems, the trade-off is that SMC provides only a statistical likelihood of the absence of errors and a confidence in this result, not a formal guarantee. So far, SMC has been applied to verify safety/liveness requirements of (stochastic) models of systems, but not security.

The application of SMC to verify specifications of high-level code is limited to very specific reachability properties and restricted fragments of languages [36]. Consequently the verification of security properties that depends on space and time memory failures have not yet been explored. Such failures are prominent in popular languages such as C.

This is because one great challenge for many formal methods is how to accurately model true possible values within the program and also the complex internal information related to the program being analyzed. The true possible values of a program execution can be difficult to determine due to abstract approaches having extremely large domains to consider (e.g. all 64-bit Integers) or complex runtime relationships between values that are very hard to track. Similarly, memory organization may extremely complex to accurately model in an abstract manner. The choices of the compiler or of the operating system may be opaque to a verification engine. This can lead to inaccuracies and hence to security vulnerabilities that are difficult to define or analyze.

In this paper we develop the *C Statistical Model Checker* (C-SMC) approach and tool that is able to address these challenges by combining the strengths of SMC with a runtime engine to connect the model with the real execution of the program. The SMC aspects allow for many executions of the program to be handled independently and their checking results to be effectively combined using statistics on the overall likelihood to satisfy properties. The runtime engine allows for the model and states to gain real information that is apparent from the execution without having to simulate and model the entire hardware and operating system's behaviour in the model. The advantage of the approach used by C-SMC is that formal results are obtained for understanding the coverage and limitations of the analysis, i.e. the advantages of SMC. Also by using a real runtime debugging engine (here GDB [5]) to inform the analysis, the true instantiations of memory and internal system hardware can be exploited to determine concrete values and verify complex temporal properties.

The implementation of C-SMC is achieved by combining aspects of both static and dynamic analysis. A static model of the program is constructed and given to an SMC engine (Plasma Lab [16,33]), with information about the source code added as tags in the model. Then when Plasma Lab is analyzing the model, a link is made from the checker in Plasma Lab to an instance of the program being executed (by GDB) so that Plasma Lab can have access to a dynamic execution with real information based on areas that are difficult to model (e.g. memory layout, registers, true variable values, etc.). To validate the effectiveness of C-SMC we compare to other well regarded tools that are dedicated to the same challenge such as CBMC [29], Coverity [1], CPPCheck [2] and PVS Studio [8] Our results indicate that C-SMC performs extremely well at detecting errors, particularly those that rely upon runtime information and that it is able to detect bugs that no other evaluated tool can. These results also show that although the SMC and runtime approach comes at a cost in terms of execution time and resource consumption, the trade-off is the reduction of significant abstraction both in finding good executions and avoiding complexity problems. A Virtual-Box [7] Virtual Machine (VM) containing C-SMC, its source code and all the examples used in this paper is available at https://c-smc.csvl.eu/C-SMC.ova.

2   Systems: From Specification to Verification

This paper offers a *Statistical Model Checking* (SMC) approach to verifying safety and security properties of complex C programs. The technique works by inferring statistic properties from the monitoring of successive executions of a program written in C source code.

SMC applies to stochastic systems, while execution of C programs are inherently sequential except for two sources. The choice of initial arguments that may depends on users; and the governance of process interleaving. These two sources are inherently non-deterministic to the program. This paper is restricted to non-concurrent systems. Consequently the only source of non-determinism is the choice of initial software parameters. In order to account for this source of non-determinism, this work assumes the existence of a stochastic oracle that generates initial parameters in a uniform manner. Here the *uniform distribution* is the distribution with the maximal entropy.

Here a *state* specifies all the current information related to a C program. In particular a state not only includes current values of program's variables, but also the value of others elements used by the program. This includes, e.g., the current program counter, memory (stack and heap), registers, etc. A given program has one (or more) entry points which are here defined to be the *initial state[s]*. Such states are generated by uniformly selecting an initial value for the input parameters. As usual, a C program moves from one state to another via *transitions* that represents program's instructions. An *execution trace* is a sequence of states generated from one initial state by following a sequence of transitions of the software. Observe that such transitions not only modify program's values, but also other information like the CPU flags or the instruction pointer.

From the above, a C program can entirely be defined by the set of all of its executions. Moreover, by definition of the stochastic oracle and the restriction to non concurrent systems, one can define a unique probability distribution on such set. Consequently, SMC applies to our setting.

2.1   Trace Execution Properties

Expressing properties formally is key in software verification. Based on definitions from above, the properties about a program can be defined in terms of properties over states, over individual traces, and over sets of traces. We first focus on the first two types of properties. The last one, which corresponds to the verification of the whole program, will be handled in the next (sub-)section.

A propositional logic can define properties about each state individually. To be able to consider all the states of an execution trace, this propositional logic needs to be extended. One popular extension is *Linear Temporal Logic* LTL [37]. LTL allows us to make hypothesis of unbounded traces via temporal operators. As SMC restricts to finite trace executions, we consider a bounded version of LTL, where each temporal operator is bounded the number of states to which it applies.

Bounded Linear Temporal Logic (BLTL) is an enhancement of LTL that adds bounds expressed in step or time units. The syntax of BLTL is as follows and adapted from LTL:

$$\phi, \psi ::= \ p \mid \phi \vee \psi \mid \neg\phi \mid \phi U_{\leq t} \psi \mid X_{\leq t} \phi \,. \tag{1}$$

The p is propositional variables, disjunction $\phi \vee \psi$ and negation $\neg\phi$ are all as in LTL. The formula $X\phi$ is true if ϕ is true in the next state from the current state. The formula $\phi U_{\leq t} \psi$ is true if both: ψ becomes true before t in the sequence from the current state; and ϕ remains true in every state before the state where ψ becomes true. For a formal definition of BLTL semantics, see [41]. A BLTL formula is expressed with respect to a trace. It is also helpful to have conjunction ($\phi \wedge \psi$) and implication ($\phi \Rightarrow \psi$) that are defined in the usual manner. Similarly the *always* (G) and *eventually* (F) operators can be defined using the BLTL syntax above as follows. Eventually is defined as $F_{\leq t}\phi = \mathbf{true}\, U_{\leq t}\, \phi$ and means that the formula ϕ should become true before t. Always is defined as $G_{\leq t}\phi = \neg F_{\leq t}\neg\phi$ and means that ϕ must always hold for the next t.

Let $w = s_0, s_1, ..., s_L, ...$ be an execution trace, and denote by $w^j = s_j, ..., s_L, ...$ the portion of the trace starting from j (included). The truthfulness of the formulas can be decided using the rules described in Table 1.

Table 1. BLTL rules

$w \models F_{\leq t}\phi$	iff $w \models \mathbf{true}\, U_{\leq t}\phi$
$w \models G_{\leq t}\phi$	iff $w \models \neg(F_{\leq t}\neg\phi)$
$w \models \phi U_{\leq t}\psi$	iff $\exists i, t_0 \leq t_i \leq t_0 + t$ and $w^i \models \psi$ and $\forall j, 0 \leq j < i, w^j \models \phi$
$w \models X_{\leq t}\phi$	iff $\exists i, i = max(j \mid t_0 \leq t_j \leq t_0 + t)$ and $w^i \models \phi$
$w \models X_{\leq}\phi$	iff $w^1 \models \phi$
$w \models \phi \vee \psi$	iff $w \models \phi$ or $w \models \psi$
$w \models \phi \wedge \psi$	iff $w \models \neg\phi \vee w \models \neg\psi$
$w \models \phi \Rightarrow \psi$	iff $w \models \neg\phi \vee \psi$
$w \models \neg\phi$	iff $w \not\models \varphi$
$w \models \mathbf{true}$	always
$w \models \mathbf{false}$	never

BLTL allows us to express reachability properties such as "the software should eventually reach a state where variable x is equal to 1". The logic can also be used to express more elaborated causalities such as "always, if the software reaches a state where x is equal to 1, it will eventually reach a state where y is equal to 1". This expressive power allows us to express a wide range of safety and security properties. BLTL properties can be verified with monitoring procedures [26]. Such procedures, inspect successive states of an execution trace until it can decide whether the property is satisfied. Note that the BLTL is well suited to reason on system's model where states are abstracted by Boolean variables. As we are working with C code, we will assume that such variables can be replaced by Boolean predicates on states. Such predicates can express, e.g., Boolean properties on program's variables or register in a given state. These concepts are illustrated in Sect. 3.2 where the architecture of C-SMC is presented.

2.2 Probabilistic Verification

We now turn to properties defined over sets of trace executions, that is properties defined on the whole system. We are interested in solving the probabilistic BLTL problem, that is to compute the probability for the system to satisfy a BLTL property ϕ. Such probability being defined as the probability that a random trace of the system satisfies ϕ.

Statistical model checking [30] has been proposed as an efficient approach to solve such problem. SMC statistically measures the truthfulness of properties over a smaller number of traces. This is done by performing a fixed number of simulations of the system and using an algorithm to estimate the probability that the system satisfies the property. As the number of observed executions is finite, this answer comes together with a confidence interval [30].

There is a wide range of statistics algorithms that can be used to estimate the probability to satisfy a given property [30]. As the study of those algorithms is not the topic of this paper, we propose to work with the most simple one that is based on the Monte Carlo estimator. The estimator relies on the following proportion:

$$\bar{\gamma} = \frac{\sum_{i=1}^{N} \mathbf{1}(w_i \models \phi)}{N} \text{ where } \mathbf{1}(x) = \begin{cases} 1 & \text{if } x \text{ is true} \\ 0 & \text{otherwise.} \end{cases} \tag{2}$$

where N is the number of simulation being performed. Let γ be the true probability to satisfy ϕ and P be a probability evaluation. Let ϵ (precision) and δ (confidence) be small values. The Chernoff-Hoeffding bound [27] guarantees that $P(|\bar{\gamma} - \gamma| \geq \epsilon) \leq \delta$ is given by $N = \lceil \frac{\ln 2 - \ln \delta}{2\epsilon^2} \rceil$. Consequently, by controlling the number of trace executions to be verified, the user entirely controls the preciseness of the $\bar{\gamma}$ estimator.

2.3 Implementation: Plasma Lab

In this section, we focus on tools that implement Statistical Model Checking algorithms. As seen in the previous section, SMC mainly depends on sub-parts

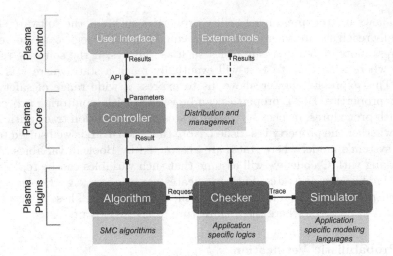

Fig. 1. Overview of the Plasma Lab architecture.

that include the type of execution trace property that has to be monitored and on the statistical algorithm used to compute the stochastic guarantee. Implicitly, SMC also depends on the type of system under verification and on the capacity to generate an arbitrary number of execution traces from this system.

In [40], the authors proposed YMER, a tool that can be used to verify BLTL properties of Markov Chains with an hypothesis testing procedure. That is, the tool decides between two hypothesis rather than computing an exact probability. In [23] Monte Carlo is applied to verify properties of Metric Temporal Logic over stochastic timed automata. Those tools have been shown to be very efficient on various problems. However, they are rather static in the sense that they do not exploit the intrinsic modularity of SMC. As an example, YMER does not permit replacing the hypothesis testing algorithm by a Monte Carlo one. None of those tools allows replacing classical BLTL with an algorithm that would consider debugger expression. On the top of this, none of those tools consider C code.

In [16,33], we introduced Plasma Lab a Statistical Model Checking (SMC) [30] tool that can provide the ability to create custom statistical model checkers. As shown in Fig. 1, Plasma Lab consists of three different layers. The first one is the *control layer*. It allows us to express various type of stochastic systems written in command-guarded language via a user interface. It also permits one to plug other system descriptions such as C code via an API for external control. The second one is the *core* that manages the model checking experiments, that is the interaction between all SMC components. The third one is the *plugins* that permits modularity and tool customization by introducing new SMC subparts.

Plasma Lab supports three types of plugins: Algorithm, Checker and Simulator. An *Algorithm* plugin manages the entire process and will begin by requesting new traces from the Checker. This is here that one choice between algorithms

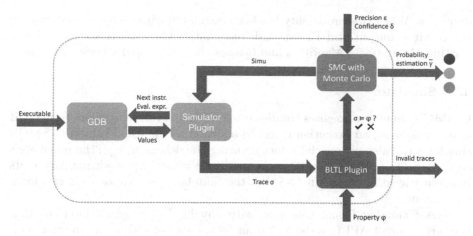

Fig. 2. C-SMC architecture with GDB as the runtime engine.

such as Monte Carlo or hypothesis testing. The user can also propose her own statistic algorithm. The *Checker* will then proceed to the monitoring of the property. To do so, the *checker* will ask the *Simulator* to initialize a new execution trace and control the simulation by requesting new states to check properties against. When the Checker obtains a verdict from the traces, the Algorithm is notified, aggregates the results statistically and sends the results through the controller API.

Several plugins provided with Plasma Lab already allow control guarded-command languages or tools such as Matlab/Simulink. In this paper, we will use the external tool to plug C programs. We will then use GDB as a simulator for trace execution of such programs. Finally, we will provide a Checker that extends Plasma's BLT checker with debugger predicates (and hence a link with GDB). By doing so, we will instantiate a new SMC tools to verify C code. Such tool shall be described in the next section.

3   Architecture of C-SMC

This section describes the architecture of C-SMC that allows us to estimate BLTL properties over C programs. Our tool builds on combining the facilities of Plasma Lab and GDB by using the plugins system described in Sect. 2.3.

An overview of C-SMC's architecture is shown in Fig. 2. The Algorithm (in orange, here SMC with Monte Carlo) will request a simulation from the Simulator (in yellow). The Simulator executes the executable instruction-by-instruction using GDB and generates a trace. The trace is then analyzed by the Checker (in green) that will send results back to the Algorithm. If the simulation resulted in the property not being satisfied, the Checker will output the complete execution trace to a file to be analyzed by the user. This cycle is executed several times to allow the Monte Carlo algorithm to estimate the probability of the outcomes. When this probability has been estimated with acceptable confidence the result is output and Plasma Lab terminates. C-SMC uses Plasma Lab's existing Monte Carlo Algorithm and has new Simulator and Checker plugins.

3.1 Simulator

C-SMC's Simulator executes binaries using GDB and retrieves values from GDB in order to build an execution trace. In addition to the usual values, C-SMC's simulator can also use special values by using the debugger, e.g., the processor's carry flag CF, overflow flag OF, or a predicate indicating stack memory edits between execution steps. In C-SMC, the Simulator is composed of two main components.

The *Simulator Plugin* can work with any kind of program interface that supports a small API (see the VM from Sect. 1 for details) for interaction with the execution. This plugin is able to produce an execution trace that Plasma Lab can use, and can then provide the information required for the Checker.

C-SMC's *GDB Communication Interface* is the component that links the Simulator Plugin with GDB. Using GDB's structured language GDB/MI [4] the GDB Communication Interface allows the Simulator Plugin to generate traces from GDB's execution of an executable. The GDB Communication Interface contains an MI message parser and generator to communicate with GDB via I/O streams.

The leftmost part of Fig. 2 shows the workflow of the Simulator Plugin in which GDB is controlled via the GDB Communication Interface to execute the executable instruction-by-instruction and retrieve the values to generate a trace. The trace is then sent to the Checker for validation.

3.2 Checker

The role of C-SMC's Checker is to verify BLTL properties on a trace coming from the Simulator. For doing so, we need an extension to Plasma Lab's existing BLTL plugin to add new expressions that relate to elements accessed by GDB. We will thus consider BLTL properties whose atoms are extended by debugger predicates, i.e., Boolean predicates on the values of variables and elements associated to each state (see Sect. 2.1).

As an example, the existing BLTL plugin already uses variables defined in the simulator plugin (like the line number and the program counter) with the syntax G <= 100 line != 10. The syntax of the BLTL plugin is extended to support debugger expression between two $ characters, allowing expression like G <= 100 $table[5] == 15$. These expressions are evaluated directly by the debugger and a Boolean result is returned.

C-SMC is also able to produce execution traces in XML format to provide a insight into the simulations. An XML execution trace contains a chronological list of all the states encountered during the execution. As illustrated in Fig. 3, each state contains information tracked in the analysis; here the program counter pc, line number `line`, variables `r` and `x`, and a property `_891715540_id_0`. This provides a deep understanding of the execution flow that may lead to an error. By default, the Checker only outputs the traces of executions that lead to a property violation (`BAD/INVALID` traces), but can be configured to also output traces for executions that lead to no properties violations (`GOOD` traces) and executions that lead to a crash like a segmentation fault (`CRASHED` traces).

```
1   <state>
2     <expr name="pc" expr="$pc">9.3824992236082E13</expr>
3     <expr name="line" expr="line">37.0</expr>
4     <expr name="r" expr="r">1.6843009E9</expr>
5     <expr name="x" expr="x">100.0</expr>
6     <expr name="__891715540_id_0" expr="x!=100">0.0</expr>
7   </state>
```

Fig. 3. Example of a State.

3.3   C-SMC Configuration

C-SMC comes with 2 types of configuration files both in TOML syntax: the model file and the requirement files.

The model file contains the configuration of the simulator inside Plasma Lab. It allows one to specify all the needed configurations for the execution to proceed. An example of such a file is shown in Listing 1.1. The first two lines `executable` and `function` respectively allow the configure the executable to be executed and the function to be monitored inside that executable. The `[simulator]` section allow specifying which of Plasma Lab's simulators is to be used. In C-SMC, we use the `gdb` simulator that we created. The `[simulator.options]` section contains the parameters of the simulator selected in the previous section. Our GDB simulator supports several options such as those from the example detailed below.

- CF: this enables the monitoring of the `Carry Flag`. This flag is used to indicate when an arithmetic carry or borrow out of the most significant arithmetic logic unit bit position.
- OF: this enables the monitoring of the `Overflow Flag`. This flag is used to indicate that an arithmetic overflow happened during the last instruction.
- STACK_M: the `Stack Modification` evaluates to true if the stack above the one of this function has been edited since the last operation (useful to detect buffer overflows).
- gdb_path: is the path of the `gdb` executable on the local system.

The last section, `variables` allows defining the variables we want the debugger to track for us (and use to verify properties). These variables are named expressions that will be evaluated during the simulation and accessible by their name in the properties. These expressions need to fit in a Java double value to be usable from the Plasma Lab interface. In Listing 1.1, the first line creates a variable x that will contain the value of the variable x of the main function and a variable y that contains the value of the index 5 of the array buffer.

```
1   executable = "../path/to/
       binary"
2   function = "main"
3   [simulator]
4   name = "gdb"
5   [simulator.options]
6   CF = true
7   OF = true
8   STACK_M = true
9   gdb_path = "/usr/bin/gdb"
10  [variables]
11  x = "x"
12  y = "(int)␣buffer[5]"
```

Listing 1.1. Example of a model file configuration.

```
1   [traces]
2   type = "one␣per␣file"
3   printall = "true"
4   folder = "../path/to/results/"
5   prefix = "example_prefix"
6   [BLTL]
7   G <= #1000 x > 10 =>
8       $choosenString != NULL$
```

Listing 1.2. Example of a requirement file configuration.

To specify the conditions that should be checked while running the program, C-SMC uses requirement files as the one shown in Listing 1.2. Several requirement files might be specified for the same program. A requirement file starts with the **traces** section. This section allows configuring the output of the generated execution traces. The **type** option specifies if the trace must be output on the standard output, in several files or in a single file. The BLTL section contains the BLTL formula to be checked on the program. In the example from Listing 1.2, the BLTL formula contains 3 parts. The first part G <= #1000 specifies the bound (1000 steps in this case). The second part x > 10 uses the variable x defined in Listing 1.1 to compare it against the value 10. The last part, $choosenString != NULL$ is a predicate that uses a debugger expression (see Sect. 3.2) to check if the variable **choosenString**, defined inside the program, is not null.

3.4   Running C-SMC

To illustrate how to run C-SMC let us start with the simple example in Listing 1.3. In this example, the function **contains** is searching for **elem** in the array **arr**. To do so, **contains** iterates over the array. When the desired value is found **contains** memorizes it by storing the value 1 inside the variable **found** and then stops the loop by using a **break**. When **contains** exits the loop, the value of **found** is checked to verify is the value was present in the array. If so, the index of the value is returned, otherwise the function return -1.

```
1   /* return the index of elem in arr, returns -1 if absent */
2   int contains(int arr[], int size, int elem) {
3           int i = 0, current = 0, found = 0;
4           for (i=0; i < size; i++) {
5                   current = arr[i];
```

```
6            found = (current == elem);
7            if (found)
8                    break; // BUG if replaced by continue;
9            }
10           if (found) {
11                   return i;
12           } else {
13                   return -1;
14           }
15   }
```

Listing 1.3. A simple Example.

To demonstrate the ability of C-SMC to perform an in-depth inspection of the behavior of a program, we will configure the tool in order to monitor the evolution of internal state of the **contains** function from Listing 1.3. In order for this code to work properly, once the **found** value has been set to 1 it should never go back to another value. If for some reason **found** goes back to another value, the result of the function will be incorrect. This could for instance be caused by a programming mistake where the **break** from line 8 is replaced by a **continue**. In this case, when the value is found, the loop will continue and the value of **found** will be overwritten.

To check this example with C-SMC the first step is to define the configuration model described in Sect. 3.3. In this file, shown in Listing 1.4, the **executable** and **function** will be set to the name of the binary (**check_array**) and the name of the function (**contains**) respectively. For this example, we do not need to track the values of the flags or to look for modifications of the stack. Thus, the next section to be configured is the **variables** section. In this section we will configure C-SMC to track the values of the variables **found**, **elem** and **i** during the execution of the program. To do so we create variables that tracks the value of the variables inside the program. For the sake of clarity we keep the same name, but we could have chosen another variable name.

```
1    executable = "./check_array"
2    function = "contains"
3    [simulator]
4    name = "gdb"
5    [simulator.options]
6    CF = false
7    OF = false
8    STACK_M = false
9    gdb_path = "/usr/bin/gdb"
10   [variables]
11   found = "found"
12   elem = "elem"
13   i = "i"
```

Listing 1.4. Model file configuration for the contains function.

```
1    [traces]
2    type = "one␣per␣file"
3    printall = "true"
4    folder = "../path/results/"
5    prefix = "check_array"
6    [BLTL]
7    G <= #1000 (found = 1 =>
8        (G <= #1000 found = 1))
```

Listing 1.5. Requirement file for the contains function.

Now that the variables that need to be tracked by C-SMC have been configured the next step is to express the behavior that needs to be verified. This part is done by adding requirement files as presented in Sect. 3.3. The requirement file for this example is shown in Listing 1.5. In the traces section we configure the format of the execution traces. The section BLTL contains the requirement we want to express. In this case we need to express the fact that once found has reached the value 1 it shouldn't change afterwards. This requirement is not trivial to express, but as explained in Sect. 2.1 BLTL allows the expression of elaborate causalities. With this ability, it is possible to translate "Once the value of bound switches to 1, this value should stay to 1 in the subsequent steps of the execution" into G <= #1000 (found = 1 => (G <= #1000 found = 1)). Now that the configuration is done, we can run C-SMC by launching Plasma Lab using our plugins described in Sect. 3 to check the properties and execute the code. For a small illustration, our oracle will search for the value 2 in the array {1,2,3,4,5,6,7,8}, i.e. with the value 2 at the index 1.

```
./plasmacli.sh launch -m model.toml:software-simulator -r req_01.
    toml:software-bltl-checker -a montecarlo -A"Total samples"=10
+----------------+---------------+-------------------------+--------+
| Name           | # Simulations | # Positive Simulation   | Result |
+----------------+---------------+-------------------------+--------+
| req_01.toml    | 10            | 10                      | 1.0    |
+----------------+---------------+-------------------------+--------+
```

In this case, C-SMC informs us that over the 10 executions of the code, the property held 10 times. The Result column gives us the probability of the property holding (this value might be set to -1 when the execution crashed). For the remainder of this example we replace the break by a continue. If we run C-SMC again; the output will change to inform us that none of the execution succeeded (0 positive simulation). Understanding why the property didn't hold can be done by inspecting the executions traces to follow the flow of the execution. For this example, the end of the trace will look like this:

```
<trace>
....
<state>
<expr name="pc" expr="$pc">9.3824992235894E13</expr>
<expr name="elem" expr="elem">2.0</expr>
<expr name="line" expr="line">6.0</expr>
<expr name="i" expr="i">2.0</expr>
<expr name="found" expr="found">1.0</expr>
</state>
<state>
<expr name="pc" expr="$pc">9.3824992235897E13</expr>
<expr name="elem" expr="elem">2.0</expr>
<expr name="line" expr="line">7.0</expr>
<expr name="i" expr="i">2.0</expr>
<expr name="found" expr="found">0.0</expr>
</state>
</trace>
```

This shows that between the last two states the value of found indeed changed from 1 to 0. The trace shows that this happened while the loop was inspecting the index 2. Because the value 2 was at the index 1, we can deduce that the loop went too far and look at the `continue` statement.

4   Use Cases

This section presents three clear examples of errors that are difficult for tools to discover. These errors rely on accurate understanding of the state of the program that is difficult to model or approximate without expensive analysis.

```
1   int main(int argc,char **argv){
2       int x = 42;
3       char buf[8];
4       memset(buf,'\0',sizeof(buf));
5       srand(time(NULL));
6       int r = rand() % 14;
7       printf("%d\n", r);
8       // overflow on x when r=13
9       strncpy(buf,"ddddddddddddddddd",
            r);
10      if (x == 100){
11          printf("secret");
12      } else {
13          printf("%s\n", buf);
14      }
15      return 0;
16  }
```

Listing 1.6. Buffer Overflow Example.

```
1   int search(int arr[],int size,
            int elem) {
2       int l = 0;
3       int r = size; //not size-1
4       int m = 0;
5       while (r >= 1) {
6           m = (l+r) / 2;
7           if (arr[m] == elem) {
8               return m;
9           } else if (arr[m] > elem) {
10              r = m - 1;
11          } else {
12              l = m + 1;
13          }
14      }
15      return -1;
16  }
```

Listing 1.7. Binary Search Example.

```
1   int main(int argc, char **argv) {
2       char **myArray = malloc(ARRAY_SIZE*sizeof(char*));
3       fillArrayWithValues(myArray); // put values in the array
4       if ((rand() % 10) == 1) { // randomly insert null sometimes
5           myArray[rand() % ARRAY_SIZE] = NULL; // NULL at a random index
6       }
7       printf("%s\n", myArray[rand() % ARRAY_SIZE]);
8   }
```

Listing 1.8. Pointer-to-pointer Example.

Consider the buffer overflow in Listing 1.6. A buffer of size 8 is overflowed with the character d (that has value 100 when converted to an integer). Because the variable x is located next to buf on the stack, the x variable can be overwritten by an incorrect write to buf. In this case, the x variable protects the access to a sensitive part of the code that is not supposed to be accessed in this context. The challenge for detecting this error relies upon determining that an overrun of buf leads to a specific modification of x leading to the `secret`.

Another difficult challenge for tools is to maintain context information that may not be local and accurately detect errors. Listing 1.7 shows an example where the relation between function arguments is vital to correct behavior and detecting the error. Observe that the `size` should give the size of `arr` and is incorrectly used to initialize `r`. This dependency can lead to an out of bounds access that is very difficult to detect accurately, particularly if the `search` function is called with different arguments at different times. Because C is not a reflective language, when the function receives an array (or a pointer to an array), C has no way to determine the size of that array, hence the need for a `size` parameter. Because of this limitation, most tools will consider the size of the array to be unknown and will not be able to perform a bounds check analysis. C-SMC is able to compare the value of m against the value of `size` at runtime, without needing to approximate, making this bound check possible. To detect this error C-SMC monitors the value of the variable m using the formula $m = 0|(0 <= m \& m < size)$.

Listing 1.8 presents a simplified version (full version in the VM from Sect. 1) of an error where a pointer-to-pointer is randomly set to `NULL`. A random value of the array is then printed, potentially leading to a segmentation fault if the `NULL` is selected. Because of the complexity incurred by replicating a memory model supporting pointers-to-pointers and the low probability of the error happening, this error is challenging to accurately detect. Since the probability of `NULL` being inserted in the array and then being selected to be printed is very low, this example outlines some challenges for C-SMC in term of confidence. The use of SMC as the core execution engine makes C-SMC unable to guarantee program correctness. SMC is able to provide a measure of confidence in the results based on the coverage of the possible executions. To make the verdict as accurate as possible, solutions are discussed in Sect. 6.

5   Examples and Evaluation

To evaluate C-SMC one clear source of evaluation examples and effectiveness is to ensure that C-SMC can detect errors that other tools on the market can detect. The following tools were used as sources for evaluation. *CBMC* [29] is chosen as another C analysis engine that uses a variation of MC to find errors, also CBMC is freely available and has examples of errors that may benefit from runtime information. *Coverity* [1], a static-analysis tool that integrates with Github [6] and Travis-CI [10] is chosen as an easy and free way for open source projects to scan their code for errors. *CPPCheck* [2] is chosen as being an open source freely available C/C++ analysis tool. *PVS Studio* [8] is chosen as another static analyser tool that can be trialed on C [8].

5.1   Methodology

The methodology used for analysis here is to gather a collection of different examples of errors that at least one of the other tools is able to detect and verify that C-SMC is able to detect this kind of error. Examples are collected from the documentation for each tool and also some examples from this paper (see Sect. 4 and the VM from Sect. 1). All the tools in their default configuration are run on all the examples to see if the errors were detected. Note that the focus is to evaluate whether C-SMC detects all the different kinds of errors, and thus all possible configurations for other tools were not explored (this makes direct comparison difficult, however this is not the goal here).

To avoid having too many variations of similar errors, when multiple tools announce support for a similar kind of error (e.g. division by 0) a "merged" single example is created. These merged examples are identified as "Multiple" for origin. The evaluation examples and brief descriptions are in Fig. 4 with the source code available in the Virtual Machine from Sect. 1.

Example	Origin	Description
static out-of-bounds	CPPCheck	Hard-coded array out-of-bounds.
dynamic out-of-bounds	CPPCheck	`rand()` valued array access that may go out-of-bounds.
divide by zero	Multiple.	A hard-coded a division by 0.
buffer overflow	This paper.	A potential buffer overflow, see Listing 1.6.
local binary search	CBMC	Binary search going out-of-bounds of local array.
parameter binary search	This paper.	Binary search going out-of-bounds, see Listing 1.7.
pointer to pointer	This paper.	Use of potential NULL pointer, see Listing 1.8.
read-only memory	Multiple.	Write into read-only memory.
integer overflow	This paper.	Addition resulting in an integer overflow.

Fig. 4. Evaluation Examples

	CBMC	Coverity	CPPCheck	PVS Studio	C-SMC
static out-of-bounds	X	X	X	X	X
random out-of-bounds	X	X	-	X	X
divide by zero	X	X	X	-	X
buffer overflow	-	X	-	X	X
local binary search	X	-	-	-	X
parameter binary search	-	-	-	-	X
pointer to pointer	-	-	-	-	X
read-only memory	-	-	X	X	X
integer overflow	X	-	-	-	X

Fig. 5. Evaluation results for tools on all source code samples with errors. Detected represented as X and Missed by -.

The results of running a tool on an evaluation example are classified into two possible outcomes. *Detected* where the tool accurately detected the error and *Missed* where the tool did not detect any error (of the right kind).

5.2   Results

The results of the evaluation are summarized in Fig. 5. If one of the other tools was able to detect an error, then the goal was for C-SMC to also detect the error. With that objective being met, observe that there are two examples that only C-SMC is able to detect. The first is the `parameter binary search` described in Sect. 4. It is expected that this kind of error would be hard for tools to detect because of C not being a reflective language. When the function under inspection receives an array (or a pointer to an array), C has no way to determine the size of that array, hence the need for a `size` parameter. Because of this limitation, most tools will consider the size of the array to be unknown and will not be able to perform a bounds check analysis. However, C-SMC is able to compare the value of m against the value of "size" making this bound check possible. The second is the `pointer-to-pointer error`. C-SMC detects it but, as discussed in Sect. 4, this is an example of where C-SMC may not find the error. Depending on the probability of the pointer-to-pointer being NULL, C-SMC might have to run many executions to find the error. If insufficient executions are run, the error will not occur and thus C-SMC would report that the program is clean (with some confidence) when it is not (this is discussed further in Sect. 6). For this specific example, by running 4883 simulations, C-SMC detects the presence of the bug and evaluate its probability to 0.75773090313% with a precision of 10^{-1} and a confidence of 10^{-5}.

Performance: By design C-SMC is executing and instrumenting the binary code of a program, this comes at a cost in term of interaction with the debugger which is itself expensive in resources. Thus other approaches can have significantly better performance in terms of execution time and resource consumption. However, the SMC approach and GDB values allow for the reduction of significant abstraction both in finding good executions and avoiding explosion problems. Some of the tools performing static analysis will outperform C-SMC in terms of execution time and resources consumption. While we can't easily reduce this overhead, future work will optimize C-SMC for performance.

6   Conclusion and Future Work

Finding programming errors is a hard challenge, particularly when they rely on detailed runtime information. C-SMC's approach to combine SMC with runtime information proves effective in finding a variety of (causality) errors that are difficult or beyond the capabilities of many tools. This indicates that C-SMC's approach is useful to finding some of these specific kinds of errors, and helps in broadening the effective tools available.

Future work can proceed in various directions. One directions is to handle concurrent C programs. This would require either definition of a stochastic semantics for such programs, or using non-deterministic SMC algorithms such as those in [22]. In addition, this would require modifying C-SMC to support multi-threading instructions from GDB. We would also be interested in using debuggers with other capabilities, e.g. HP Wildebeest Debugger [3] or Radare2 [9].

Another direction is in using more efficient SMC algorithms such as those based on guided search [14,20,28,31]. This would allows us to handle rare bugs in a more efficient manner.

Finally, in C-SMC properties have to be expressed with BLTL properties extended with debugger predicates. It would be worth defining a pattern-based language to express BLTL properties in a language that can be understood by engineers. This could be achieved by extending the work presented in [35] to debugger predicates. It would also be worth testing further kinds of checks such as memory allocation and freeing would be interesting to add since runtime information could resolve many complexities related to pointer aliasing.

References

1. Coverity Scan. https://scan.coverity.com/. Accessed 18 Jan 2021
2. CPPCheck: A tool for static C/C++ code analysis. http://cppcheck.sourceforge. net/. Accessed 18 Jan 2021
3. Debugging Dynamic Memory Usage Errors Using HP WDB. http://www.3kranger. com/HP3000/mpeix/en-hpux/PDF/5014-0301.pdf. Accessed 21 Jan 2021
4. Debugging with GDB: GDB/MI. https://sourceware.org/gdb/onlinedocs/gdb/ GDB_002fMI.html. Accessed 21 Jan 2021
5. GDB: The GNU Project Debugger. https://www.gnu.org/software/gdb/. Accessed 14 Oct 2020
6. GitHub. https://github.com/. Accessed 18 Jan 2021
7. Oracle VM VirtualBox. https://virtualbox.org/. Accessed 20 Apr 2021
8. PVS-Studio. https://www.viva64.com/en/pvs-studio/. Accessed 18 Jan 2021
9. Radare2 - A free/libre toolchain for easing several low level tasks like forensics, software reverse engineering, exploiting, debugging. https://rada.re/n/radare2.html. Accessed 21 Jan 2021
10. Travis-CI. https://travis-ci.com/. Accessed 18 Jan 2021
11. Valgrind: an instrumentation framework for building dynamic analysis tools. https://valgrind.org/. Accessed 21 Jan 2021
12. Agha, G., Palmskog, K.: A survey of statistical model checking. ACM Trans. Model. Comput. Simul. **28**(1), 6:1–6:39 (2018). https://doi.org/10.1145/3158668
13. Baier, C., Katoen, J.P.: Principles of Model Checking. MIT Press, Cambridge (2008). google-Books-ID: 5dvxCwAAQBAJ
14. Barbot, B., Haddad, S., Picaronny, C.: Coupling and importance sampling for statistical model checking. In: Flanagan, C., König, B. (eds.) Tools and Algorithms for the Construction and Analysis of Systems, pp. 331–346. Springer, Heidelberg (2012). https://doi.org/10.1007/978-3-642-28756-5_23
15. Basu, A., Bensalem, S., Bozga, M., Delahaye, B., Legay, A.: Statistical abstraction and model-checking of large heterogeneous systems. Int. J. Softw. Tools Technol. Transf. **14**(1), 53–72 (2012)
16. Boyer, B., Corre, K., Legay, A., Sedwards, S.: Plasma-lab: a flexible, distributable statistical model checking library. In: Joshi, K., Siegle, M., Stoelinga, M., D'Argenio, P.R. (eds.) Quantitative Evaluation System, pp. 160–164. Springer, Heidelberg (2013). https://doi.org/10.1007/978-3-642-40196-1_12

17. Bradley, M., Cassez, F., Fehnker, A., Given-Wilson, T., Huuck, R.: High performance static analysis for industry. Electron. Notes Theor. Comput. Sci. **289**, 3–14 (2012)

18. Bradley, M., Cassez, F., Fehnker, A., Given-Wilson, T., Huuck, R., Junker, M.: Goannasmt-a static analyzer with smt-based refinement (2012)

19. Cadar, C., et al.: Symbolic execution for software testing in practice: preliminary assessment. In: Taylor, R.N., Gall, H.C., Medvidovic, N. (eds.) Proceedings of the 33rd International Conference on Software Engineering, ICSE 2011, Waikiki, Honolulu, HI, USA, 21–28 May 2011, pp. 1066–1071. ACM (2011). https://doi.org/10.1145/1985793.1985995

20. Chockler, H., Ivrii, A., Matsliah, A., Rollini, S.F., Sharygina, N.: Using cross-entropy for satisfiability. In: Shin, S.Y., Maldonado, J.C. (eds.) Proceedings of the 28th Annual ACM Symposium on Applied Computing, SAC 2013, Coimbra, Portugal, 18–22 March 2013, pp. 1196–1203. ACM (2013). https://doi.org/10.1145/2480362.2480588

21. Clarke, E., Kroening, D., Lerda, F.: A tool for checking ANSI-C programs. In: Jensen, K., Podelski, A. (eds.) Tools and Algorithms for the Construction and Analysis of Systems, pp. 168–176. Springer, Heidelberg (2004). https://doi.org/10.1007/978-3-540-24730-2_15

22. D'Argenio, P.R., Legay, A., Sedwards, S., Traonouez, L.: Smart sampling for lightweight verification of Markov decision processes. Int. J. Softw. Tools Technol. Transf. **17**(4), 469–484 (2015). https://doi.org/10.1007/s10009-015-0383-0

23. David, A., Larsen, K.G., Legay, A., Mikucionis, M., Poulsen, D.B.: Uppaal SMC tutorial. Int. J. Softw. Tools Technol. Transf. **17**(4), 397–415 (2015). https://doi.org/10.1007/s10009-014-0361-y

24. David, A., Larsen, K.G., Legay, A., Mikučionis, M.: Schedulability of Herschel revisited using statistical model checking. Int. J. Softw. Tools Technol. Transfer **17**(2), 187–199 (2014). https://doi.org/10.1007/s10009-014-0331-4

25. Havelund, K., Pressburger, T.: Model checking JAVA programs using JAVA PathFinder. Int. J. Softw. Tools Technol. Transfer (STTT) **2**(4), 366–381 (2000)

26. Havelund, K., Roşu, G.: Synthesizing monitors for safety properties. In: Katoen, J.-P., Stevens, P. (eds.) TACAS 2002. LNCS, vol. 2280, pp. 342–356. Springer, Heidelberg (2002). https://doi.org/10.1007/3-540-46002-0_24

27. Hoeffding, W.: Probability Inequalities for Sums of Bounded Random Variables, pp. 409–426. Springer, New York (1994). https://doi.org/10.1007/978-1-4612-0865-5_26

28. Jegourel, C., Legay, A., Sedwards, S.: Importance splitting for statistical model checking rare properties. In: Sharygina, N., Veith, H. (eds.) Computer Aided Verification, pp. 576–591. Springer, Heidelberg (2013). https://doi.org/10.1007/978-3-642-39799-8_38

29. Kroening, D., Tautschnig, M.: CBMC - C bounded model checker. In: Ábrahám, E., Havelund, K. (eds.) Tools and Algorithms for the Construction and Analysis of Systems, pp. 389–391. Springer, Heidelberg (2014). https://doi.org/10.1007/978-3-642-54862-8_26

30. Legay, A., Delahaye, B., Bensalem, S.: Statistical model checking: an overview. In: Barringer, H., et al. (eds.) Runtime Verification, pp. 122–135. Springer, Heidelberg (2010). https://doi.org/10.1007/978-3-642-16612-9_11

31. Legay, A., Lukina, A., Traonouez, L.M., Yang, J., Smolka, S.A., Grosu, R.: Statistical model checking. In: Steffen, B., Woeginger, G. (eds.) Computing and Software Science. LNCS, vol. 10000, pp. 478–504. Springer, Cham (2019). https://doi.org/10.1007/978-3-319-91908-9_23

32. Legay, A., Nowotka, D., Poulsen, D.B., Tranouez, L.-M.: Statistical model checking of LLVM code. In: Havelund, K., Peleska, J., Roscoe, B., de Vink, E. (eds.) FM 2018. LNCS, vol. 10951, pp. 542–549. Springer, Cham (2018). https://doi.org/10.1007/978-3-319-95582-7_32

33. Legay, A., Sedwards, S., Traonouez, L.M.: Plasma lab: a modular statistical model checking platform. In: Margaria, T., Steffen, B. (eds.) Leveraging Applications of Formal Methods, Verification and Validation: Foundational Techniques, pp. 77–93. Springer International Publishing, Cham (2016). https://doi.org/10.1007/978-3-319-47166-2_6

34. Li, J., Dureja, R., Pu, G., Rozier, K.Y., Vardi, M.Y.: SimpleCAR: an efficient bug-finding tool based on approximate reachability. In: Chockler, H., Weissenbacher, G. (eds.) CAV 2018. LNCS, vol. 10982, pp. 37–44. Springer, Cham (2018). https://doi.org/10.1007/978-3-319-96142-2_5

35. Mignogna, A., Mangeruca, L., Boyer, B., Legay, A., Arnold, A.: Sos contract verification using statistical model checking. In: Larsen, K.G., Legay, A., Nyman, U. (eds.) Proceedings 1st Workshop on Advances in Systems of Systems, AiSoS 2013, Rome, Italy, 16th March 2013. EPTCS, vol. 133, pp. 67–83 (2013). https://doi.org/10.4204/EPTCS.133.7

36. Ngo, V.C., Legay, A., Joloboff, V.: PSCV: a runtime verification tool for probabilistic SystemC models. In: Chaudhuri, S., Farzan, A. (eds.) CAV 2016. LNCS, vol. 9779, pp. 84–91. Springer, Cham (2016). https://doi.org/10.1007/978-3-319-41528-4_5

37. Pnueli, A.: The temporal logic of programs. In: 18th Annual Symposium on Foundations of Computer Science (SFCS 1977), pp. 46–57. IEEE, Providence, RI, USA, September 1977. http://ieeexplore.ieee.org/document/4567924/

38. Raad, A., Berdine, J., Dang, H.H., Dreyer, D., O'Hearn, P., Villard, J.: Local reasoning about the presence of bugs: Incorrectness separation logic. In: Lahiri, S.K., Wang, C. (eds.) Computer Aided Verification, pp. 225–252. Springer International Publishing, Cham (2020). https://doi.org/10.1007/978-3-030-53291-8_14

39. Švejda, J., Berger, P., Katoen, J.-P.: Interpretation-based violation witness validation for C: NITWIT. TACAS 2020. LNCS, vol. 12078, pp. 40–57. Springer, Cham (2020). https://doi.org/10.1007/978-3-030-45190-5_3

40. Younes, H.L.S.: Ymer: A statistical model checker. In: Etessami, K., Rajamani, S.K. (eds.) Computer Aided Verification, 17th International Conference, CAV 2005, Edinburgh, Scotland, UK, July 6–10, 2005, Proceedings. Lecture Notes in Computer Science, vol. 3576, pp. 429–433. Springer, Cham (2005). https://doi.org/10.1007/11513988_43

41. Zuliani, P., Platzer, A., Clarke, E.M.: Bayesian statistical model checking with application to stateflow/simulink verification. Formal Methods Syst. Design 43(2), 338–367 (2013). https://doi.org/10.1007/s10703-013-0195-3

PatEC: Pattern-Based
Equivalence Checking

Marie-Christine Jakobs$^{(\boxtimes)}$ (iD)

Department of Computer Science, Technical University of Darmstadt,
Darmstadt, Germany
`jakobs@cs.tu-darmstadt.de`

Abstract. Program parallelization is a common software engineering
task, in which parallel design patterns are applied. While the focus of
parallelization is on performance, the functional behavior should be kept
invariant, i.e., sequential and parallelized program should be functionally
equivalent. Several verification techniques exist that analyze properties
of parallel programs, but only a few approaches inspect functional equivalence between a sequential program and its parallelization. Even fewer
approaches consider parallel design patterns when checking equivalence.

In this paper, we present PATEC, which checks equivalence between
sequential programs and their OpenMP parallelizations. PATEC utilizes
the knowledge about the applied parallel design pattern to split equivalence checking into smaller subtasks. Our experiments show that PATEC
is effective, efficient, and often outperforms existing approaches.

1 Introduction

To efficiently use today's computer systems, we require parallel programs. Existing, sequential programs should be parallelized. Furthermore, programmers still
often start with a sequential program and, later, parallelize it. Hence, program
parallelization is important in software engineering and can be supported by
parallel design patterns [24,25] (i.e., well-established parallelization solutions).

OpenMP [29] is an API that is widely-used in high performance computing
to realize shared-memory parallel programs. It allows programmers to easily
implement platform-independent parallelizations by adding OpenMP directives.

However, the OpenMP specification [29] states that an OpenMP-compliant
program may be incorrect. In addition, correct parallelization with OpenMP is
difficult [15] and optimistic, automatic parallelization tools like DiscoPoP [19]
may suggest incorrect parallelizations. While parallelization focuses on performance, one must also ensure that the parallelization keeps the functional behavior, i.e., that sequential and parallelized program are functionally equivalent.

Several approaches [7,11,23,35,36,39] exist that detect correctness issues of
OpenMP programs, but they do not necessarily guarantee functional equivalence.

This work was funded by the Hessian LOEWE initiative within the Software-Factory
4.0 project.

© Springer Nature Switzerland AG 2021
A. Laarman and A. Sokolova (Eds.): SPIN 2021, LNCS 12864, pp. 120–139, 2021.
https://doi.org/10.1007/978-3-030-84629-9_7

Listing 1.1. Sequential program

```
int foo_s(unsigned int *a, int N)
{
  int x = 0;
  for(int i=0; i<N; i++)
    if(a[i]%2==1) x++;
  return x;
}
```

Listing 1.2. Parallelized program

```
int foo_p(unsigned int *a, int N)
{
  int x = 0;
  #pragma omp parallel for reduction(+: x)
  for(int i=0; i<N; i++)
    x+=a[i]%2;
  return x;
}
```

Fig. 1. An example for a parallelization that uses the Reduction pattern and also optimizes the program's code

In contrast, Blom et al. [9,10], Pathg [42], AutoPar [21], and CIVL's OpenMP simplifier component [37] check whether all executions of an OpenMP program are equivalent to a sequential execution of the same program.

This is not sufficient to show that our example shown in Fig. 1 is correctly parallelized. The problem is that the parallelized program uses an optimized computation in the loop body. Thus, the sequential program and the sequential execution of the parallelized program are not identical.

Equivalence checkers like CIVL [37], PEQcheck [17], and the one proposed by Abadi et al. [1] support parallelizations like the one shown in Fig. 1. However, they are general checkers that encode equivalence problems into program verification tasks and ignore design patterns applied for parallelization. Thus, they neglect valuable knowledge about the performed parallelization and in contrast to our approach, PEQcheck fails to verify equivalence of our example.

To overcome this problem, we propose PatEC, which checks functional equivalence of a sequential program and its OpenMP parallelization. PatEC relies on the applied parallel design pattern to decompose equivalence checking into several subtasks. In case of our example in Fig. 1, in which the Reduction pattern is applied, PatEC inspects whether the loop bodies of the sequential and parallelized program are equivalent. Furthermore, PatEC checks that the loop iterations of the parallelized program do not interfere with each other. Note that this is the case because variable a is read-only and due to the reduction clause there exist thread-local copies for variable x. Finally, PatEC checks that the loop iterations get the correct inputs and produce the correct outputs. Since variable a is shared, no copy of variable a is used and all parallel loop iterations access the same value as a sequential execution. PatEC detects that variable x is only used to perform data reduction, which can be performed out of order. Therefore, we can perform data reduction per thread using local copies of x, starting with the neutral element 0. At the end, the original value of x and the final values of the thread local copies can be combined via addition (the reduction operator). This is exactly what the reduction clause induces.

In this paper, we describe how to decompose equivalence checking for two popular parallel design patterns. Both patterns are taught in every parallel programming course that covers OpenMP. One of them is the Reduction pattern used in our example. Our experiments on 91 benchmark programs demonstrate that PATEC is effective and efficient. Furthermore, we compare PATEC with two competitive approaches and show that PATEC outperforms those competitors.

2 Background

We aim to prove functional equivalence of a sequential program and its parallelization. We ignore termination and focus on partial functional equivalence.

Definition 1. *Two programs (code segments) are* partially functional equivalent *if they start in the same state and terminate, they will end in the same state.*[1]

To determine partial functional equivalence, we must know how variables are used in the code, in particular in code segments. We consider the three usages:

Liveness. A variable is live at a program location if there exists an execution starting at the location that reads the variable before it is redefined (written).

Modification. A variable is modified in a code segment if there exists an execution of the code segment that writes to the variable.

Use Before Definition. Similar to uninitialized variable usage, we say that in a code segment a variable will be used before definition if there exists an execution of the code segment in which the variable is read before it is written.

To find out which of the three usages apply to a variable and when, we use two static analyses: a definition-use analysis and a liveness analysis. Similar to a reaching definition analysis [28], the *definition-use analysis* computes for each variable and program statement which definitions of the variable may reach the program statement. Additionally, it computes which variables are used in a statement. The *liveness analysis* [28] (also known as live variable analysis) determines for each program location which variables may be live.

OpenMP. In this paper, we assume that programs use OpenMP [29] to implement parallelism. OpenMP is an interface to write platform-independent parallelization code. Therefore, the programmer adds OpenMP directives that instruct the compiler and the runtime system how to realize the parallelization. To understand our approach, it is important to know the semantics of OpenMP's data-sharing attributes, which define whether thread-local copies are used and how information is passed between the original variable and its copies. In the following, we describe OpenMP's data-sharing attributes.

Shared. The original variable is shared among the threads.
Private. Each thread has its own local copy of the variable and uses the copy instead of the original variable. The local copy is not initialized.

---

[1] We assume that sequential programs are deterministic. To deal with non-determinism caused by random methods or I/O functions, one can consider those inputs as part of the starting state.

Firstprivate. An extension of private that initializes the thread-local copies to the value of the original variable.

Lastprivate. An extension of private that causes the original variable to be overwritten. At the end of the parallel execution, the original variable is set to the value of the copied variable used in the sequentially last iteration of the loop. In case of modifier conditional, the sequentially last iteration that modified the variable is considered instead.

Reduction. Each thread has its own local copy of the variable and uses the copy instead of the original variable. The thread-local copies are initialized with the initializer value (the neutral element) of the respective reduction operator. At the end of the parallel execution, the specified reduction operator combines the value of the original variable with the values of the local copies and updates the original variable with the combined value.

Typically, each variable is assigned one of the above data-sharing attributes. However, variables can also be firstprivate and lastprivate. From now on, we use the artificial data-sharing attribute **firstlastprivate** to describe this case.

The data-sharing attribute of a variable is either declared explicitly with a data-sharing attribute clause or defined implicitly. The rules for implicit declarations state that the loop counter of a parallelized for loop and variables declared in the parallelized code are typically private. Except for corner cases, the variables declared outside of the parallelized code are shared.

Parallel Design Patterns. Parallel design patterns [24, 25] are well-known parallelization solutions. In this paper, we consider two parallel design patterns for embarrassingly parallel problems. More concretely, the two patterns describe how to parallelize (for) loops that exchange little or no information between loop iterations. Both patterns suggest to execute the loop iterations in parallel.

The *DoAll pattern* is applicable to (for) loops that do not exchange information between loop iterations, but loop iterations may write to the same memory. During parallelization of the loop iterations, these write-write conflicts must be resolved, e.g., by defining an appropriate data-sharing attribute in OpenMP.

The *Reduction pattern* can be used for loops with a particular shape of exchange between loop iterations. Computations that perform data reduction, e.g., compute the sum, the minimum, etc. of a set of values, are allowed to exchange the value of the reduction variable that stores the temporary and final result of the reduction. Additionally, two loop iterations may write to the same memory. During parallelization of the loop iterations, the reduction computation must be split among the threads, e.g., using an appropriate reduction clause, and similar to the DoAll pattern the write-write conflicts must be resolved.

3   Determining Equivalence for DoAll and Reduction

Our goal is to determine whether a sequential program is equivalent to a parallelized program, which is derived from the former. Thereby, we assume that

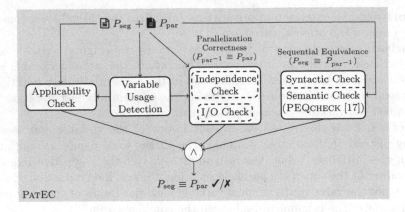

Fig. 2. Overview of PATEC approach

the parallelization applies DoAll or Reduction patterns. To simplify equivalence checking, we divide it into several subtasks. First, we inspect all parallelized code segments individually. Our equivalence checking will succeed, if it can show that all parallelized code segments P_{par} are equivalent to their counterparts P_{seg} in the sequential program. We further decompose each equivalence check of a pair of sequential and parallelized code segment to separately reason about parallelization and loop optimization. The *sequential equivalence check* examines whether the sequential code segment P_{seg} is equivalent to P_{par-1}, the unparallelized version of P_{par}, which is derived from P_{par} by removing the OpenMP directives. A second check analyzes whether the unparallelized code segment P_{par-1} and the parallelized code segment P_{par} are equivalent, i.e., P_{par} is *correctly parallelized*. Equivalence of the sequential and parallelized code segment is then determined based on the following formula: $P_{seg} \equiv P_{par-1} \wedge P_{par-1} \equiv P_{par} \implies P_{seg} \equiv P_{par}$.

Figure 2 gives an overview of our PATEC approach. It contains the mentioned sequential equivalence check and the check on correct parallelization, which use subchecks tailored to DoAll and Reduction patterns. Additionally, PATEC uses an applicability check that determines whether the preconditions for the other two checks are met. PATEC will succeed if all three checks succeed. Furthermore, PATEC contains a variable usage detection component that computes the required information for the checks. Next, all PATEC components are described.

1) Variable Usage Detection. The goal is to compute required information on how variables are used in the code segments P_{seg} and P_{par}, namely variable modification, variable liveness, and use-before-definition.

Detecting Variable Modifications. We use intraprocedural definition-use analyses to overapproximate the variables modified by a code segment. For all read accesses of a variable v in the code segment, we look up v's definitions that may reach the access and declare variable v modified if one of the definitions belongs to the code segment. Similarly, we detect variables modified in functions reachable from the code segment, but we only consider global variables and variables that alias with variables of the code segment (due to parameter passing).

Detecting Variable Liveness. To detect which variables are live after the code segment (information we require for the I/O check), we run an intraprocedural liveness analysis [28]. Then, we declare a variable live if (1) the liveness analysis detects that a variable is live after the loop, (2) it is a global variable, or (3) it is a pointer passed to the function enclosing the code segment. Conditions (2) and (3) overapproximate the interprocedural behavior. For the decomposition into sequential equivalence and parallelized correctness to be sound, we add the variables live after P_{seg} to the set of variables live after P_{par}.

Detecting Use Before Definition Variable Accesses. Next, we determine which variables may be accessed in a code segment (i.e., for loop) before the loop iteration defines them. To detect such intra-segment accesses, we run an intraprocedural definition-use analysis. Then, we add all variables for which a use (read) access in the code segment exists for which (1) no definition is known, which can e.g. happen for global variables, (2) a definition from before the code segment reaches the use, or (3) a definition from the loop body reaches the use and the variable is live at the beginning of the loop body. To incorporate the behavior of functions reachable from the code segment, we add non-scalar variables passed to a called function and all global variables accessed in those functions.[2]

2) Checking Applicability. PATEC aims at checking equivalence of parallelizations of for loops that use the DoAll or Reduction pattern and will output inequivalent (✗) if its applicability check detects that PATEC is not applicable to a given pair of sequential and parallelized code segment.

The patterns require that the sequential and parallelized code segments are for loops. In addition, the parallelized code segment must be preceded by OpenMP directives appropriate for a DoAll or Reduction pattern. PATEC supports the most commonly used directive `parallel for`, the `simd` directive, and a combination of the `parallel` directive with the `for` directive or the `simd` directive. To allow PATEC to identify reduction variables, the Reduction pattern must be realized with data-sharing attributes (e.g., `reduction`), which is the simplest and most common solution for reduction. Furthermore, PATEC currently does not support nested pattern applications[3] and, thus, disallows OpenMP directives in the loop body or in functions reachable from the loop body.

PATEC's equivalence check focuses on the loop bodies. Therefore, we assume that the for loops only differ in the loop bodies.[4] PATEC syntactically checks that the sequential and the parallelized for loop only differ in their loop bodies.[5]

---

[2] This is sufficient because we do not support aliasing.

[3] Nested pattern applications can be checked recursively when being careful with the data-sharing attributes, but it is inefficient and misses equivalences.

[4] Note that we make the assumption because (i) it simplifies the sequential equivalence check and (ii) most parallelizations we have seen fulfill the assumption. One can easily get rid of this assumption by letting the sequential check inspect P_{seg} and $P_{\text{par}-1}$.

[5] In our implementation, we rely on the unparse function of the AST to avoid that formatting differences influence the check.

Moreover, PATEC inspects several requirements on OpenMP parallelizations of for loops with the DoAll or Reduction pattern. Since PATEC cannot inspect external functions, it only allows external calls to a subset of the system's library, which contains functions that are thread-safe and pure.

Finally, we forbid to declare variables in the loop body whose name is identical to the name of the loop counter or to the name of a variable that is used, but not declared in the loop body. Note that this is a technical limitation caused by our decision to only use variable names and to ignore their scope when assigning data-sharing attributes declared by OpenMP directives.

3) Checking Correctness of Parallelization. This step checks whether the unparallelized version $P_{\mathrm{par}-1}$, which is derived from P_{par} by deleting all OpenMP directives, is equivalent to the parallelized code segment P_{par}. We split the check into an independence and an I/O check. Both are explained below.

3a) Checking Independence of Loop Iterations. This task inspects whether all loop iterations can be executed without interfering with each other, i.e., the loop iterations are independent. To this end, the task relies on the information about variable modifications to determine whether there exist read-write, write-read, or write-write conflicts between variable accesses in different loop iterations. Also, it considers the variables' data-sharing attribute because a data-sharing attribute may rule out conflicts when making a variable thread local. Given this information, we inspect the variables occurring in the loop body.

Scalar Variables. If a scalar variable, e.g., an integer variable, is modified in the loop body and its data-sharing attribute is shared, there might be a write-write conflict. Thus, the independence check fails. In all other cases, the variable does not threaten the independence of loop iterations.

Non-scalar Variables. We assume that no aliasing occurs and pointers do not overlap. Hence, variables not modified in the loop body do not threaten the independence between loop iterations. The same is valid for variables declared in the loop body, which are thread-local.[6] For all other variables, their independent access must be analyzed. So far, we only support array and pointer variables.

Let us look at *arrays* first. We analyze array accesses when they may threaten the independence of loop iterations, namely if the array is shared. In addition, we analyze accesses to arrays with variable length, i.e., a length that cannot be determined at compile time because not all compilers support non-shared data-sharing attributes for those arrays. For each such array, our access analysis extracts all *accesses* to the array occurring in the loop body [7] and then checks whether each set of access pairs $(a_1, a_2) \in accesses$ is independent.

---

[6] There exists some corner cases in which those variables are not thread-local like static variables. However, we do not support these rare cases.

[7] Since it is sufficient that an array access is independent in one dimension, we only extract the complete accesses, e.g., from x[i][j] > 0 we collect x[i][j] but not x[i].

To check independence of an arbitrary access pair (a_1, a_2), we first check that the accesses have the same dimension. Then, we traverse the dimensions and report independence if and only if we find an independent dimension.

To check the independence of index expressions i_{a_1} and i_{a_2} in dimension i, we translate them into SMT bitvector formulae $f_{i_{a_1}}$ and $f_{i_{a_2}}$. Constant values are translated to bitvector values and variables are translated to bitvector constants with the same name. To consider that modified variables may have different values in different iterations, we extend modified variables with the suffix @r in $f_{i_{a_2}}$. N-ary expressions are translated recursively by translating the operands and then combining the resulting SMT formulae with the SMT operator corresponding to the expression operator. After translation, we query SMT solver Z3 [27] whether $f_{i_{a_1}} == f_{i_{a_2}}$ is satisfiable. To improve the result, we inform Z3 that the values of the loop counter are different. If the SMT solver returns unsatisfiable, the independence check of access pair $\{a_1, a_2\}$ will succeed. With our current translation, this is only reliable if an evaluation of an index expression does not cause any side-effects. Our check considers this.

To simplify the independence check of access pairs (a, a), we precede the general check described above with a syntactical check. The difference to the general check is that the syntactic check of index expression i_a inspects whether index expression i_a is semantically equivalent to loop counter plus constant value. Therefore, the check determines whether the loop counter occurs exactly once in i_a, all other variables accessed are not modified (i.e., they have a constant value throughout the loop execution), and only addition or subtraction operations are used. From experience, many index expressions meet these criteria.

Next, let us consider *pointer variables*. We analyze pointer access independently of the data-sharing attribute because non-shared data-sharing attributes might introduce aliasing. To avoid dealing with pointer arithmetic, we check that all accesses to pointer variables look like array references (e.g., x[0]). Then, we apply the independence check for array accesses.

3b) I/O Check: Are Same Inputs and Outputs Ensured? If all variables are shared, iteration dependence is sufficient for a correct parallelization. However, non-shared data-sharing attributes introduce thread-local copies, which may prohibit that required information is exchanged between loop iterations or between the code segment and its surrounding code. The I/O check investigates whether the used data-sharing attributes cause such input/output availability problems and fails when it detects a problem.

I/O Check for DoAll Parallelizations. First, let us discuss the I/O check performed when considering a DoAll pattern. For input availability, we only check variables that are used in the loop body, but not declared in the loop body because only those variables can cause problems. The first four rows of the left table in Table 1 show when inputs become available for the DoAll pattern. The shared attribute is unproblematic. If the variable is always defined in an

Table 1. Overview on when data-sharing attributes guarantee that the required inputs are available during a loop iteration and that the required outputs are available after a loop iteration. Symbol ✓ (✗) means that the respective usage property must (not) be fulfilled. Symbol ● means ✓ or ✗.

Input availability

	modified	used before definition
shared	●	●
private	✓	✗
lastprivate	✓	✗
firstprivate/ firstlastprivate	✗	●
	●	✗
reduction	✓	●

Output availability

	modified	live after loop
shared	●	●
private/ firstprivate	✗	●
	●	✗
lastprivate	✓ (scalar)	●
	●	✗
firstlastprivate	✓ (scalar)	●
	✗	●
	●	✗
reduction	●	●

iteration before it is used, even any data-sharing attribute can be used.[8] Finally, a read-only variable must use the value of the original variable. Next to shared, also attributes firstprivate and firstlastprivate guarantee this.

For output availability, we only check variables that can be accessed after the loop execution. The four rows of the right table in Table 1 show when outputs are available for the DoAll pattern. The shared attribute is unproblematic. If a variable is not live after the loop, the variable may have any value. Furthermore, if a variable is not modified, one does not need to propagate its value, but one may propagate the value of the copied variables if it is initialized with the original value. For those cases, output availability is also guaranteed using attributes private, firstprivate, or firstlastprivate. Finally, if we write the modified value back into the original variable, the output is guaranteed. Data-sharing attributes lastprivate and firstlastprivate trigger writing back. Since OpenMP uses the value of the copied variable from the last iteration (modifying the variable), non-scalar copied variables might not incorporate all modifications[9]. Hence, we only support scalar variables when writing values back.

I/O Check for Reduction Parallelizations. The I/O check for a parallelization using the Reduction pattern is an extension of the I/O check for DoAll-based parallelizations, which also considers the data-sharing attribute reduction.

To forbid that reduction variables are misused as read-only, which is incorrect because reduction variables are initialized with the neutral element of the reduction operator, we require that the reduction variable is modified by some loop iterations (see last row in Table 1). However, this is not enough. Due to their initialization, reduction variables can only be safely used in reduction statements.

---

[8] Note that our check additionally requires that a variable with attribute private or lastprivate must be modified. Since we only check variables that occur in the loop body, variables that are not used before must be modified.

[9] Also, one must use the modifier conditional to ensure that the last write is considered.

Since we only support scalar reduction variables, a reduction statement can either be an assignment or a compound assignment, e.g., v+=x;, which assign a reduction variable. The right-hand side of the compound statement must not use the reduction variable. Similarly, the right-hand side of the assignment must be a binary expression that uses the reduction operator and the reduction variable as left (right) operand. Moreover, the right (left) operand must not use any reduction variable. In case of a reduction operation + (-), the reduction statement can also be an increment (decrement) of the reduction variable. We inspect safe usage of all reduction variables, but fail when the loop body calls a function and the reduction variable is global.

4) Checking Sequential Equivalence. The goal of this check is to show that the sequential code segment P_{seg} is equivalent to the unparallelized code segment P_{par-1}. Since two code segments may only differ in their loop body, we examine the equivalence of their loop bodies. First, a *syntactic* equivalence check examines whether the loop bodies and the functions transitively called from the loop bodies are syntactically identical.[10] If the first check fails, we use a *semantic* equivalence check using the existing PEQCHECK approach [17], which encodes the equivalence problem into verification tasks and verifies them.

Discussion of Soundness. Formally proving soundness, i.e., PATEC only reports equivalence (✓) if the sequential program and its parallelization are equivalent, is beyond the scope of this paper[11]. Nevertheless, let us briefly sketch our soundness arguments under the assumption no aliasing and no pointer overlap occur. The independence check inspects whether the memory locations modified in a loop iteration are disjoint from the memory locations considered in other loop iterations. Hence, this check ensures that all executions of the parallel program starting with the same input either all terminate and compute the same result or all do not terminate. Second, the I/O check examines whether P_{par-1} and the parallelized program P_{par} behave identically when P_{par} executes the iterations sequentially. To this end, it is sufficient to check whether the data-sharing attributes allow the required flows between write and read accesses. Together, independence and I/O check then ensure that $P_{par-1} \equiv P_{par}$ and their termination behavior does not differ. Third, soundness of PEQCHECK guarantees soundness of the semantic check. Fourth, deterministic sequential programs are equivalent to themselves and the syntactic check inspects whether the two sequential loop bodies are identical. Since we assume that sequential programs are deterministic, the sequential equivalence check is therefore sound and guarantees $P_{seg} \equiv P_{par-1}$. Since $P_{par-1} \equiv P_{par}$ and their termination behavior does not differ, we get the desired property $P_{seg} \equiv P_{par}$. While we may become unsound in case of aliasing and pointer overlap, all other assumption are checked and lead to rejection (✗).

---

[10] Again, our implementation relies on the unparse function of the AST.
[11] Especially note that all semantics we are aware of do not support all data-sharing attributes [12] or do not cover the data aspect [3].

Implementation. We implemented a prototype for the presented PATEC approach, which supports C programs. Our prototype is integrated in the framework FECheck[12] and builds on Z3's C++ API and the ROSE compiler framework [33] (v0.11.33.0.1). Our implementation assumes that the start and end of the parallelized code segment i and the sequential counterparts are marked via pragma directives `#pragma scope_i` and `#pragma epocs_i`. For our experiments, we added the annotations manually. Given annotated programs `seq.c` and `par.c`, one can run our prototype with the following command[13].

```
./FECheck -type=REDUCTION seq.c par.c
```

During execution, our prototype outputs for each pair of sequential and parallelized code segment whether it is checked successfully or a failure reason, e.g., incorrect data-sharing attributes or failure to show independence for variable x.

4   Evaluation

The goals of our evaluations are twofold. First, we aim to study the effectiveness of our PATEC approach. Second, we want to compare PATEC with existing approaches. We choose AutoPar [21] and PEQCHECK [17].

4.1   Experimental Setup

Benchmarks. In our evaluation, we utilize three benchmark sets. We use the DataRaceBench suite [20,40] (version 1.3.2), which contains programs with and without data races. Parallelized programs with data races cannot be equivalent to their sequential version. Therefore, this suite provides us with parallelized programs for which we know that they are inequivalent to their sequential version. In addition, we select the examples from the functional equivalence suite (FEVS) [38] already considered by PEQCHECK [17]. To evaluate our approach on more realistic examples, we choose the MILCmk benchmark set[14], which consists of representative microkernels that are taken from the MIMD Lattice Computation (MILC) collaboration code. From all benchmark sets, we select the tasks that only apply DoAll or Reduction patterns for parallelization. In total, we get 80 programs with DoAll patterns and 11 programs using Reduction patterns. Note that in all cases the parallelized versions enhance the sequential versions with OpenMP directives, but do not change code statements.

Environment. We execute our experiments on an Ubuntu 20.04 machine with an Intel i7-8565U CPU (frequency of 1.8 GHz) and 32 GB RAM. As competitors, we use AUTOPAR [21] in version 0.11.33.0.1 and PEQCHECK [17] in a configuration is similar to [17], which combines the PEQCHECK encoding[15] (revision PatEC-SPIN2021) with the verifier CIVL [37] (version 1.20_5259), which

---

[12] https://git.rwth-aachen.de/svpsys-sw/FECheck, revision PatEC-SPIN2021.

[13] To limit PATEC's checking to DoAll patterns, use -type=DOALL.

[14] https://asc.llnl.gov/coral-benchmarks.

[15] https://git.rwth-aachen.de/svpsys-sw/FECheck.

uses the theorem prover Z3 [27] (version 4.8.8). We restrict CIVL to two threads and 5 min and disable division by zero and memory leakage checks.

Availability. PATEC and our experimental data are available on Zenodo [16].

4.2   Experiments

RQ 1: Does PatEC reliably detect inequivalences? To answer this question, we look at all tasks of the DataRaceBench suite that contain data races. As explained above, these tasks represent inequivalent parallelizations. Table 2 describes the results for checking the DataRaceBench tasks with PATEC, AUTOPAR, and PEQ-CHECK. For each checker, the table reports the number of correctly detected (in)equivalences, the number of incorrectly detected equivalences[16] and inequivalences, and the number of inconclusive results (due to timeout, errors, etc.). The last row presents the total time each

Table 2. Per equivalence checker number of tasks in the DataRaceBench suite that are correctly solved plus the total checking time

	PATEC	AUTOPAR	PEQCHECK
Correct equivalence	21	13	2
Correct inequivalence	38	37	4
Incorrect equivalence	0	0	0
Incorrect inequivalence	1	9	0
Unknown	2	3	56
Total time (s)	744	453	10558

approach takes to check all tasks. We observe that PATEC does not report any incorrect equivalences, i.e., it never reports that a pair of sequential and parallelized program are equivalent although they are inequivalent. Hence, PATEC's behavior is sound. Furthermore, PATEC detects many of the incorrectly parallelized programs. PATEC reliably detects inequivalences.

RQ 2: How effective is PatEC? First, let us look at the tasks of the DataRaceBench suite. PATEC's results are presented in Table 2. The table shows that PATEC detects (in)equivalence correctly for most of the tasks. It only reports one incorrect result and two unknowns. In case of the incorrect inequivalence, PATEC is conservative and assumes that the used indirect array indexing is not iteration independent. Except for the two unknowns, which represent time outs of about 300 s each, PATEC's check takes only a few seconds,

Next, let us inspect the FEVS tasks. Table 3 represents the results. Incorrectly parallelized tasks are highlighted in red. For each task, Table 3 reports the pattern used for parallelization and for each of the three tools PATEC, AUTOPAR, and PEQCHECK, the checking time t and result s. Correct results are highlighted in blue. Looking at PATEC's columns, we observe that checking with PATEC takes a few seconds. Moreover, PATEC correctly reports the inequivalence of the two incorrect parallelizations. Also, it often correctly detects equivalence of the correctly parallelized tasks. Only in two cases, PATEC conservatively reports correctly parallelized programs as inequivalent. In case of `gausselim`, PATEC does not detect that the accesses to an array are independent. In case of `matmat`,

---

[16] An incorrectly detected equivalence is an inequivalent task reported as equivalent.

Table 3. Results of PATEC, AUTOPAR, and PEQCHECK on FEVS and MILCmk benchmark. For each tool, reports the time spent on checking equivalence and the result, i.e., equivalence (✓), inequivalence (✗), or failure due to an error (ERR), a timeout (TO), or another property violation (✗$_{mem}$). Correct results are shown in blue.

FEVS benchmark

Task	Pattern	PATEC		AUTOPAR		PEQCHECK	
		t (s)	s	t (s)	s	t (s)	s
adder-init	DoAll	2	✓	2	✓	307	TO
adder	Reduction	2	✓	2	✓	308	TO
adder-e	DoAll	2	✗	2	✗	612	TO
adder-nd	Reduction	2	✓	3	✗	76	✓
adder-s	Reduction	2	✓	2	✗	9	✓
diffusion1d	DoAll	2	✓	2	✗	16	✗$_{mem}$
diffusion1d-nd	DoAll	2	✓	2	✗	56	✗
factorial	Reduction	2	✓	3	✗	11	✓
gausselim	DoAll	3	✗	2	✗	36	✗$_{mem}$
gausselim-e	DoAll	3	✗	2	✗	11	✗$_{mem}$
integrate	Reduction	3	✓	3	✗	6	ERR
laplace-init	DoAll	2	✓	2	✓	7	ERR
laplace-jacobi	Reduction	2	✓	3	✓	7	ERR
matmat	DoAll	2	✗	2	✗	3	ERR
mean	Reduction	2	✓	3	✓	77	✓
wave1d	DoAll	3	✓	3	✗	23	✗$_{mem}$
wave1d-nd	DoAll	3	✓	3	✗	19	ERR

MILCmk benchmark

Task	Pattern	PATEC		AUTOPAR		PEQCHECK	
		t (s)	s	t (s)	s	t (s)	s
D3_D	DoAll	16	✓	11	✗	65	ERR
D3_M	DoAll	6	✓	9	✗	10	ERR
D3_r1	Reduction	6	✓	9	✗	10	ERR
D3_V_veq	DoAll	6	✓	9	✗	10	ERR
D3_V_vmeq	DoAll	6	✓	9	✗	10	ERR
D3_V_vpeq	DoAll	6	✓	9	✗	10	ERR
F3_D	DoAll	16	✓	11	✗	65	ERR
F3_M	DoAll	6	✓	9	✗	10	ERR
F3_r1	Reduction	6	✓	13	✗	10	ERR
F3_V_veq	DoAll	6	✓	9	✗	10	ERR
F3_V_vmeq	DoAll	6	✓	9	✗	10	ERR
F3_V_vpeq	DoAll	6	✓	9	✗	10	ERR

PATEC fails to find out that an array passed as function argument is accessed independently in the function.

Finally, let us consider the MILCmk tasks. PATEC's results are also shown in Table 3. We notice that PATEC always requires a few seconds to execute. More importantly, it reports equivalence (✓), the correct result, in all cases.

Summing up, PATEC is fast and often correctly detects (in)equivalences.

RQ 3: How does PatEC compare against state-of-the-art? We compare PATEC with two other approaches: AUTOPAR and PEQCHECK. AUTOPAR is a parallelization tool, which has a correctness checking mode. PEQCHECK is an approach that encodes the equivalence problem into program verification tasks and solves them with a program verifier.

1) Comparing PATEC *and* AUTOPAR. We run AUTOPAR in correctness checking mode[17], which reports the difference between the generated and the provided OpenMP directives. Since a reorder of data-sharing-attribute clauses or a reorder of variables in such clauses may cause differences, we inspect the differences and report an inequivalence if AUTOPAR does not suggest an OpenMP directive or the suggested and the existing directive differ semantically.

---

[17] We use the following command line: `autoPar -rose:unparse_tokens -rose:auto par:no_aliasing -rose:autopar:enable_diff -fopenmp program.c`.

Looking at the results for the DataRaceBench suite (Table 2), we observe that PATEC and AUTOPAR are nearly equally fast when ignoring timeouts[18], detect a similar number of correct inequivalences, and never report incorrect equivalences. However, AUTOPAR detects fewer equivalences because it often suggests more strict data-sharing attributes. Furthermore, a detailed result analysis reveals that PATEC solves all tasks correctly that AUTOPAR solves correctly.

For the FEVS and the MILCmk benchmarks (Table 3), the checking times are similar, too. While PATEC detects equivalence for most of the equivalent tasks, AUTOPAR only succeeds for five of the equivalent tasks. AUTOPAR's main problem is the difference in the data-sharing attributes.

Overall, PATEC and AUTOPAR are equally fast, but PATEC is more effective.

2) Comparing PATEC and PEQCHECK. We start to compare PATEC's and PEQCHECK's results on the DataRaceBench suite. Looking at Table 2, we observe that PEQCHECK has no incorrect results, while PATEC has one incorrect inequivalence. Nevertheless, PATEC detects (in)equivalence correctly more often and PEQCHECK often comes to no conclusion. About 50% of PEQCHECK's unknowns result from time outs. Another third is caused by errors occurring during encoding or verification. The remaining unknowns reflect other property violations like invalid dereference, out of bounds accesses detected in PEQ-CHECK's verification tasks. A detailed analysis of the results reveals that all tasks correctly solved by PEQCHECK (see Table 4) are also solved by PATEC. Considering the total times (last row of Table 2), PEQCHECK requires an order of magnitude longer. One reason is the many time outs. However, comparing the times for those tasks that are solved by both PATEC and PEQCHECK (see Table 4), we observe that PATEC is still faster.

Table 4. Excerpt of the results of PATEC and PEQCHECK on DataRaceBench benchmark showing the tasks correctly solved by PEQCHECK.

		PATEC		PEQCHECK	
Task	Pattern	t (s)	s	t (s)	s
DRB009	DoAll	2	✗	8	✗
DRB010	DoAll	2	✗	9	✗
DRB016	DoAll	2	✗	17	✗
DRB035	DoAll	2	✗	21	✗
DRB050	DoAll	2	✓	9	✓
DRB059	DoAll	2	✓	9	✓

When looking at the FEVS tasks (Table 3), we again notice that PEQCHECK only correctly solves tasks that PATEC correctly solves. Additionally, PATEC always reports a results while PEQCHECK often fails with a time out (TO)[19], an error (ERR), or the detection of a different property violation (✗_{mem}). Moreover, PEQCHECK's checking is less efficient, i.e., it requires more time.

For the MILCmk benchmark (Table 3), PATEC always succeeds, while PEQ-CHECK always fails due to the verifier CIVL, which cannot parse the verification tasks encoding the equivalence problem.[20]

---

[18] PATEC times out twice (2*300 s) and AUTOPAR only once (300 s).

[19] Note that the reported time for status TO in PEQCHECK can differ significantly because PEQCHECK may generate multiple verification tasks and we use a time out per task instead of one global time out for all tasks.

[20] The parsing problems occur in one of the MILCmk header files.

In summary, PATEC's pattern-based approach outperforms PEQCHECK's general approach.

Threats to Validity. Our evaluation uses benchmark programs. Since the DataRaceBench set contains parallelizations with common mistakes and the DataRaceBench as well as the MILCmk contain kernels from real applications, we think that they represent realistic scenarios.

The benchmark set is dominated by examples for the DoAll pattern. Our findings might not generally apply to the Reduction pattern. We do not think this is the case. Except for the I/O check, which is extended for the Reduction pattern, the checks are identical. Also, our experiments demonstrate that PATEC correctly detects missing reduction clauses[21] and correctly detects the equivalent tasks which contain a program parallelized with the Reduction pattern.

All programs in our benchmark set only add OpenMP directives. Thus, we never need the semantic check. We admit that PATEC might fail more often to detect equivalence if the semantic check is required. Nevertheless, we expect PATEC to still reliably detect inequivalences because theoretically the semantic check is sound and PEQCHECK uses a verifier that rarely reports false results. Also, we still expect that PATEC performs better than AUTOPAR and PEQ-CHECK. AUTOPAR cannot deal with modifications of instructions and our semantic check also uses PEQCHECK, but on a reduced problem.

The ground truth of the benchmark programs is not always known, which may invalidate our results. Our largest benchmark, the DataRaceBench, comes with programs for which it is known that they contain data races or are data-race free. Racy programs are typically not equivalent. In addition, we manually inspected the programs and cross-checked our classification with the assessment of the AutoParBench [26], a benchmark to evaluate the correctness of auto-parallelization tools. We confirmed that all tasks with data races are inequivalent and only one of the data race free tasks is inequivalent.[22] Furthermore, the MILCmk set consists of representative microkernels from a real-world problem, for which we are confident that their parallelizations are correct.

We only compared PATEC to two other approaches. The approaches work differently and PEQCHECK works similar as other equivalence checkers [1,37]. We are confident that PATEC also compares well to other approaches.

5   Related Work

Several approaches [5,6,13,14,18,30,34,43] check functional equivalence between two sequential programs. Often, these approaches perform equivalence checking on the level of functions. PATEC's sequential equivalence check combines a syntactic difference check and a semantic check with PEQCHECK [17].

CIVL [37], PEQCHECK [17], and Abadi et al. [1] support equivalence checking between sequential programs and programs parallelized with OpenMP. All three

---

[21] Parallelizations without the reduction clause are classified as DoAll.
[22] For our experiments, we therefore classified it inequivalent, too.

encode the equivalence problem into a program verification task and are not pattern-specific. While CIVL's equivalence check considers whole programs, the other two approaches check equivalence on the level of code segments.

Often, parallelization only adds OpenMP directives, but does not change program statements. In this case, it is sufficient to check whether the executions of the parallel program are equivalent to the sequential execution. PATEC's check on parallelization correctness pursues this property. Similarly, CIVL [37] incorporates an OMP simplifier that performs such a check for array-based parallel loops. The simplifier uses an array-dependence analysis and the data-sharing attributes to determine whether dependencies between loop iterations exist. The automatic parallelizer AUTOPAR [21] provides a checking mode which compares the provided parallelization (OpenMP annotation) with AUTOPAR's suggested parallelization annotations. Like PATEC, AUTOPAR requires a parallelized loop to be of a particular form, but it analyzes iteration independence based on dependence relations between variable references. Pathg [42] searches for data races and analyzes whether those races can cause an equivalence violation. omp-Verify [7] aims to verify that affine loops are correctly parallelized. Its checks are based on the polyhedra model and detect data races and variables that need to be declared private. Blom et al. [9,10] use separation logic to prove whether manually provided iteration contracts on for loops are valid. The validity of an iteration contract ensures functionally equivalence for the respective for loop.

Furthermore, there exist approaches that do not check full equivalence, but properties which may make parallelization incorrect. For example approaches like [4,7,11,23,39] aim at detecting data races. Next to data races, the OpenMP Analysis Toolkit (OAT) [23] also checks for deadlocks. Similarly, Saillard et al. [36] describe an analysis checking whether an implicit or explicit barrier may only be reached by a subset of the threads, which may cause a deadlock. Lin [22] and Zhang et al. [44] present a static analysis that determines whether two statements may be executed concurrently. The Mercurium compiler incorporates checks for task constructs [35] that detect data races and correctness issues caused by wrong data-sharing attributes or dependence clauses.

To determine whether array accesses in different iterations overlap, PATEC uses a constraint-based check encoded in SMT. PATEC's SMT-based check of array accesses is similar to the check for unbounded loops in OAT [23]. Both use SMT solvers to check satisfiability of the constraints, but PATEC considers the array dimensions individually, while OAT translates multi-dimensional arrays into one-dimensional ones. Moreover, PATEC uses a constraint to state that the loop counters are different, but in contrast to OAT it does not yet bound the loop counters to their (symbolic) start and end values. In contrast, CIVL relies on Omega testing [31,32] to find out whether the dependence constraints can be fulfilled. AUTOPAR [21] uses a Gaussian elimination algorithm to solve the array dependence constraints, which are a set of linear integer equations.

PATEC considers variable usage to classify which data-sharing attributes are appropriate to guarantee correctness. Parallelization tools perform a similar task, but also select one of the appropriate attributes. For example, AUTOPAR [21] considers the information from the live variable analysis and the dependence analysis to assign data-sharing attributes. Furthermore, DiscoPoP [2] assigns data-sharing attributes based on the variable type, whether a variable is written in the parallelized code segment and which read-after-write dependencies exist between the code segment and the code before and after the code segment.

Finally, note that PATEC is not the first pattern-specific approach that checks equivalence between sequential and parallelized programs. For example, Beckert et al. [8] suggest an interactive approach to prove the equivalence between a sequential program an a parallelization with an MapReduce algorithm. However, all pattern-specific approaches we are aware of do not target OpenMP.

6   Conclusion

To tap the full potential of today's computer systems, we require parallel programs. Nevertheless, many existing software programs are sequential and writing a sequential program is easier than writing a parallel program. Thus, programmers often start with the sequential version of a parallel program. Therefore, program parallelization is a common software engineering task.

OpenMP allows programmers to easily perform platform-independent parallelizations. Often, programmer only need to extend their code with parallelization directives. Parallel design patterns further guide the programmer during parallelization. While parallelization aims at improving performance, it must not alter the program's functional behavior. Several existing approaches verify certain properties, e.g., data-race freedom, of OpenMP programs. Also, a few approaches examine functional equivalence of a sequential program and its OpenMP parallelization, but they are either too strict or ignore the applied parallel design patterns, missing out to leverage knowledge about the parallelization.

To overcome these problems, we suggest PATEC. PATEC is an approach to check functional equivalence between a sequential program and its OpenMP parallelization. In particular, PATEC decomposes equivalence checking into several subtasks, which are tailored to specific parallel design patterns. Currently, PATEC supports two commonly used patterns, the DoAll and the Reduction pattern. Our experiments with PATEC on 91 benchmark programs show that PATEC is reliable. It detects all inequivalent parallel programs and most of the equivalent ones. Furthermore, a comparison with two competitive approaches reveals that PATEC outperforms those competitors.

Extending PATEC to support more patterns is possible, but likely requires new specific subchecks. Recently, we added support for the pipeline pattern [41].

References

1. Abadi, M., Keidar-Barner, S., Pidan, D., Veksler, T.: Verifying parallel code after refactoring using equivalence checking. International Journal Parallel Programming **47**(1), 59–73 (2019). https://doi.org/10.1007/s10766-017-0548-4
2. Arab, M.N., Wolf, F., Jannesari, A.: Automatic construct selection and variable classification in OpenMP. In: Proceedings of ICS, pp. 330–341. ACM, New York (2019). https://doi.org/10.1145/3330345.3330375
3. Atzeni, S., Gopalakrishnan, G.: An operational semantic basis for building an OpenMP data race checker. In: Proceedings of IPDPSW, pp. 395–404. IEEE (2018). https://doi.org/10.1109/IPDPSW.2018.00074
4. Atzeni, S., et al.: ARCHER: effectively spotting data races in large OpenMP applications. In: Proceedings of IPDPS, pp. 53–62. IEEE (2016). https://doi.org/10.1109/IPDPS.2016.68
5. Badihi, S., Akinotcho, F., Li, Y., Rubin, J.: ARDiff: scaling program equivalence checking via iterative abstraction and refinement of common code. In: Proceedings of FSE, pp. 13–24. ACM, New York (2020). https://doi.org/10.1145/3368089.3409757
6. Barthe, G., Crespo, J.M., Kunz, C.: Relational verification using product programs. In: Proc. FM. pp. 200–214. LNCS 6664, Springer, Berlin (2011), https://doi.org/10.1007/978-3-642-21437-0_17
7. Basupalli, V., Yuki, T., Rajopadhye, S.V., Morvan, A., Derrien, S., Quinton, P., Wonnacott, D.: ompVerify: Polyhedral analysis for the OpenMP programmer. In: Proc. IWOMP. pp. 37–53. LNCS 6665, Springer, Berlin (2011), https://doi.org/10.1007/978-3-642-21487-5_4
8. Beckert, B., Bingmann, T., Kiefer, M., Sanders, P., Ulbrich, M., Weigl, A.: Relational equivalence proofs between imperative and MapReduce algorithms. In: Proc. VSTTE. pp. 248–266. LNCS 11294, Springer, Cham (2018), https://doi.org/10.1007/978-3-030-03592-1_14
9. Blom, S., Darabi, S., Huisman, M.: Verification of loop parallelisations. In: Proc. FASE. pp. 202–217. LNCS 9033, Springer, Berlin (2015), https://doi.org/10.1007/978-3-662-46675-9_14
10. Blom, S., Darabi, S., Huisman, M., Safari, M.: Correct program parallelisations. STTT (2021). https://doi.org/10.1007/s10009-020-00601-z
11. Bora, U., Das, S., Kukreja, P., Joshi, S., Upadrasta, R., Rajopadhye, S.: LLOV: a fast static data-race checker for OpenMP programs. TACO **17**(4), 1–26 (2020) https://doi.org/10.1145/3418597
12. Bronevetsky, G., de Supinski, B.R.: Complete formal specification of the OpenMP memory model. International Journal of Parallel Programming **35**(4), 335–392 (2007). https://doi.org/10.1007/s10766-007-0051-4
13. Felsing, D., Grebing, S., Klebanov, V., Rümmer, P., Ulbrich, M.: Automating regression verification. In: Proceedings of ASE, pp. 349–360. ACM, New York (2014). https://doi.org/10.1145/2642937.2642987
14. Godlin, B., Strichman, O.: Regression verification. In: Proceedings of DAC, pp. 466–471. ACM, New York (2009). https://doi.org/10.1145/1629911.1630034
15. Goncalves, R., Amaris, M., Okada, T.K., Bruel, P., Goldman, A.: OpenMP is not as easy as it appears. In: Proceedings of HICSS, pp. 5742–5751. IEEE (2016). https://doi.org/10.1109/HICSS.2016.710
16. Jakobs, M.C.: Replication package for article 'PatEC: pattern-based equivalence checking'. In: SPIN 2021, Zenodo (2021). https://doi.org/10.5281/zenodo.4841071

17. Jakobs, M.C.: PEQcheck: localized and context-aware checking of functional equivalence. In: Proceedings of FormaliSE, pp. 130–140. IEEE (2021). https://doi.org/10.1109/FormaliSE52586.2021.00019
18. Lahiri, S.K., Hawblitzel, C., Kawaguchi, M., Rebêlo, H.: SYMDIFF: A language-agnostic semantic diff tool for imperative programs. In: Proc. CAV. pp. 712–717. LNCS 7358, Springer, Berlin (2012), https://doi.org/10.1007/978-3-642-31424-7_54
19. Li, Z., Atre, R., Huda, Z.U., Jannesari, A., Wolf, F.: Unveiling parallelization opportunities in sequential programs. Journal of Systems and Software **117**, 282–295 (2016). https://doi.org/10.1016/j.jss.2016.03.045
20. Liao, C., Lin, P., Asplund, J., Schordan, M., Karlin, I.: DataRaceBench: a benchmark suite for systematic evaluation of data race detection tools. In: Proceedings of SC, pp. 11:1–11:14. ACM, New York (2017) https://doi.org/10.1145/3126908.3126958
21. Liao, C., Quinlan, D.J., Willcock, J., Panas, T.: Extending automatic parallelization to optimize high-level abstractions for multicore. In: Proc. IWOMP. pp. 28–41. LNCS 5568, Springer, Berlin (2009), https://doi.org/10.1007/978-3-642-02303-3_3
22. Lin, Y.: Static nonconcurrency analysis of OpenMP programs. In: Mueller, M.S., Chapman, B.M., de Supinski, B.R., Malony, A.D., Voss, M. (eds.) IWOMP -2005. LNCS, vol. 4315, pp. 36–50. Springer, Heidelberg (2008). https://doi.org/10.1007/978-3-540-68555-5_4
23. Ma, H., Diersen, S., Wang, L., Liao, C., Quinlan, D.J., Yang, Z.: Symbolic analysis of concurrency errors in OpenMP programs. In: Proceedings of ICPP, pp. 510–516. IEEE (2013). https://doi.org/10.1109/ICPP.2013.63
24. Mattson, T.G., Sanders, B.A., Massingill, B.L.: Patterns for Parallel Programming (4th print). Addison-Wesley, Boston (2008)
25. McCool, M., Robison, A., Reinders, J.: Structured Parallel Programming: Patterns for Efficient Computation. Elsevier, Morgan Kaufman, Amsterdam (2012)
26. Mendonca, G.S.D., Liao, C., Pereira, F.M.Q.: AutoParBench: a unified test framework for OpenMP-based parallelizers. In: Proceedings of ICS, pp. 28:1–28:10. ACM, New York (2020). https://doi.org/10.1145/3392717.3392744
27. de Moura, L.M., Bjørner, N.: Z3: an efficient SMT solver. In: Proc. TACAS. pp. 337–340. LNCS 4963, Springer, Berlin (2008), https://doi.org/10.1007/978-3-540-78800-3_24
28. Nielson, F., Nielson, H.R., Hankin, C.: Principles of Program Analysis. Springer, Berlin (1999). https://doi.org/10.1007/978-3-662-03811-6
29. OpenMP: OpenMP application programming interface (version 5.1). Technical report, OpenMP Architecture Review Board (2020). https://www.openmp.org/specifications/
30. Person, S., Dwyer, M.B., Elbaum, S.G., Pasareanu, C.S.: Differential symbolic execution. In: Proceedings of FSE, pp. 226–237. ACM, New York (2008). https://doi.org/10.1145/1453101.1453131
31. Pugh, W.: A practical algorithm for exact array dependence analysis. Commun. ACM **35**(8), 102–114 (1992) https://doi.org/10.1145/135226.135233
32. Pugh, W., Wonnacott, D.: Going beyond integer programming with the Omega test to eliminate false data dependences. IEEE Trans. Parallel Distrib. Syst. **6**(2), 204–211 (1995) https://doi.org/10.1109/71.342135
33. Quinlan, D., Liao, C.: The ROSE source-to-source compiler infrastructure. In: Cetus Users and Compiler Infrastructure Workshop, vol. 2011, pp. 1–3. Citeseer (2011)

34. Ramos, D.A., Engler, D.R.: Under-constrained symbolic execution: correctness checking for real code. In: USENIX Security Symposium, pp. 49–64. USENIX (2015). https://www.usenix.org/conference/usenixsecurity15/technical-sessions/presentation/ramos
35. Royuela, S., Ferrer, R., Caballero, D., Martorell, X.: Compiler analysis for OpenMP tasks correctness. In: Proceedings of CF, pp. 7:1–7:8. ACM, New York (2015). https://doi.org/10.1145/2742854.2742882
36. Saillard, E., Carribault, P., Barthou, D.: Static validation of barriers and work-sharing constructs in OpenMP applications. In: Proc. IWOMP. pp. 73–86. LNCS 8766, Springer, Cham (2014), https://doi.org/10.1007/978-3-319-11454-5_6
37. Siegel, S.F., et al.: CIVL: the concurrency intermediate verification language. In: Proceedings of SC, pp. 61:1–61:12. ACM, New York (2015). https://doi.org/10.1145/2807591.2807635
38. Siegel, S.F., Zirkel, T.K.: FEVS: A functional equivalence verification suite for high-performance scientific computing. Mathematics in Computer Science 5(4), 427–435 (2011). https://doi.org/10.1007/s11786-011-0101-6
39. Swain, B., Li, Y., Liu, P., Laguna, I., Georgakoudis, G., Huang, J.: OMPRacer: a scalable and precise static race detector for OpenMP programs. In: Proceedings of SC. IEEE (2020)
40. Verma, G., Shi, Y., Liao, C., Chapman, B.M., Yan, Y.: Enhancing DataRaceBench for evaluating data race detection tools. In: Proceedings of Correctness@SC, pp. 20–30. IEEE (2020). https://doi.org/10.1109/Correctness51934.2020.00008
41. Wiesner, M., Jakobs, M.C.: Verifying pipeline implementations in OpenMP. In: Laarman, A., Sokolova, A. (eds.) SPIN 2021. LNCS, vol. 12864, pp. 81–98. Springer, Charm (2021). https://doi.org/10.1007/978-3-030-84629-9_5
42. Yu, F., Yang, S., Wang, F., Chen, G., Chan, C.: Symbolic consistency checking of OpenMP parallel programs. In: Proceedings of LCTES, pp. 139–148. ACM, New York (2012). https://doi.org/10.1145/2248418.2248438
43. Zaks, A., Pnueli, A.: CoVaC: Compiler validation by program analysis of the cross-product. In: Proc. FM. pp. 35–51. LNCS 5014, Springer, Berlin (2008), https://doi.org/10.1007/978-3-540-68237-0_5
44. Zhang, Y., Duesterwald, E., Gao, G.R.: Concurrency analysis for shared memory programs with textually unaligned barriers. In: Proc. LCPC. pp. 95–109. LNCS 5234, Springer, Berlin (2007), https://doi.org/10.1007/978-3-540-85261-2_7

Go2Pins: A Framework for the LTL Verification of Go Programs

Alexandre Kirszenberg, Antoine Martin, Hugo Moreau,
and Etienne Renault(✉)

LRDE, EPITA, Kremlin-Bicêtre, France
{akirszenberg,amartin,hmoreau,renault}@lrde.epita.fr

Abstract. We introduce Go2Pins, a tool that takes a program written in Go and links it with two model-checkers: LTSMin [19] and Spot [7]. Go2Pins is an effort to promote the integration of both formal verification and testing inside industrial-size projects. With this goal in mind, we introduce *black-box transitions*, an efficient and scalable technique for handling the Go runtime. This approach, inspired by hardware verification techniques, allows easy, automatic and efficient abstractions. Go2Pins also handles basic concurrent programs through the use of a dedicated scheduler.

In this paper we demonstrate the usage of Go2Pins over benchmarks inspired by industrial problems and a set of LTL formulae. Even if Go2Pins is still at the early stages of development, our results are promising and show the benefits of using black-box transitions.

1 Introduction and Motivation

The Go programming language was designed at Google in 2009 [16] to improve programming productivity in an era of multicore, networked machines and large codebases. Inspired by the idea of *Communicating Sequential Processes* (CSP) [17], designers focused on two principles: (1) having lightweight and easy to create threads (called goroutines) and, (2) promoting communication across threads by explicit messaging (through channels) rather than by shared memory. Even if other languages have also been designed to tackle similar problems (OCCAM and ERLANG), Go is probably the first large scale, widely used, industrial language to integrate these distinctive CSP features.

Previously (and except for OCCAM and ERLANG), mainly academic formal languages, implementing variations around the notion of CSP, have been developed: PROMELA, UPPAAL, DVE, GAL, CSP_M, etc. These languages have been built as a support for developing verification tools and their associated theory but have seldom been used in the industry.

The main idea defended in this paper is to consider the Go language not only as a disruptive, efficient, industrial, statically typed, compiled programming language but also as a good candidate for the specification and verification of asynchronous systems. Indeed, most of the time formal languages are only used

© Springer Nature Switzerland AG 2021
A. Laarman and A. Sokolova (Eds.): SPIN 2021, LNCS 12864, pp. 140–156, 2021.
https://doi.org/10.1007/978-3-030-84629-9_8

for modeling and verification while the actual implementation of the system is done in another language for efficiency. This switch between languages is error-prone. Moreover, most formal languages do not have associated compilers or interpreters: this is annoying since the only way to test the validity of the model is to express the desired behaviors through a temporal logic[1].

This paper tackles these problems by introducing Go2Pins: a Go-based unified framework for testing, modeling, verification, and efficient implementation of systems. This paper also introduces black-box transitions (see Sect. 4), an efficient and scalable technique for handling the Go runtime. This approach, inspired by hardware verification techniques, allows easy, automatic and efficient abstractions. Even if this idea is not new (premises of this technique are available the SPIN model checker), we extend it to be automatic, and then well suited for verifying large software systems.

2   Go2Pins: Overview

This section describe our journey towards the verification of Go programs. Figure 1 describes an overview of Go2Pins: the program to verify is processed by Go2Pins which produces a binary called **go2pins-mc**. This binary can then be used to verify any LTL formula (over the input program) using one of the two supported backends: LTSMin [19] or Spot [7].

Figure 2 provides more details about this approach. At coarse grain, the input program is processed by the core of our tool and then translated into the Partitioned Next-State Interface (PINS) [19]. This interface exposes two functions: one for retrieving the initial state of the system, and one for computing the successors of a state. Any program that exposes this interface is thereby compatible with any (explicit or symbolic) model checking solution that supports it (for instance LTSmin or Spot). Then, Go2Pins produces a set of files that are compiled together to build the **go2pins-mc** binary. We opted for this workflow since (1) it provides more flexibility, (2) it can be easily extended and (3) our code remains in the Go realm (useful for black-box transitions, see Sect. 4).

At fine grained level, our approach behaves like a transpiler that translates the input Go program into an output Go program that respects the PINS interface. This transformation has many advantages. First, it benefits from both the reflexivity and the standard library of the Go language. The reflexivity lets us avoid the development of the classic toolchain of a transpiler (scanner, parser, AST, etc.), while the use of the standard library lets us avoid redeveloping concepts such as Control Flow Graph, Call Graph, etc. The second benefit of our approach is the ease of building abstractions (see Sect. 4).

Figure 2 shows that Go2Pins processes the input program in steps. Each one modifies the Abstract Syntax Tree (AST) in order to desugar a specific feature. For instance, the *Arith & Assign* step decomposes complex arithmetic operations into consecutive elementary ones. For instance $v1 := 3 * g(n) * h(n)$ is

---

[1] Notice that in the particular context of CSP, validity can also be checked using refinement.

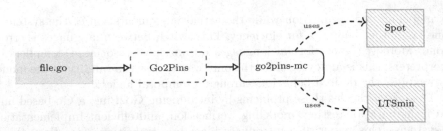

Fig. 1. Overview of Go2Pins. The input file is processed by Go2Pins which produces a binary called **go2pins-mc**. This binary can then be used to verify LTL formula using one of the two supported backends: Spot or LTSmin.

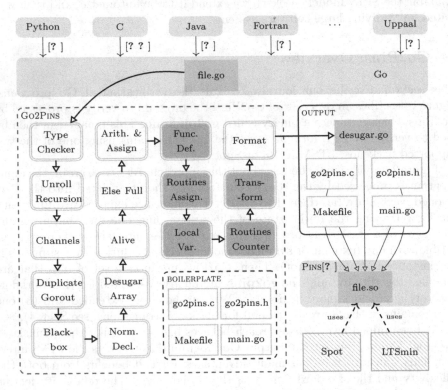

Fig. 2. Contributions of this paper (all except gray boxes). The dashed boxes represent the Go2Pins tool while the blue plain box represents the output directory produced by Go2Pins. The transformation steps are denoted by double shaped red boxes. Files grouped under the name *boilerplate* are copied as-is into the output directory. These files are generic and handle communication between the desugared program and the mandatory functions to respect the PINS interface. (Color figure online)

translated into three instructions: $v1 := 3$, then $v1 \mathrel{*}= g(n)$ and finally $v1 \mathrel{*}= h(n)$. Thus, this step does not change the semantics of the original program but simplifies it in order to be used by model-checkers.

With this workflow, it is easy to test each step. For almost all steps presented in Fig. 2, we can just apply the step on some input, run the modified program and check that the behavior stay unchanged.

Among the various steps in Go2Pins, some are of special interest:

1. **TypeChecker.** Ensures, via type deduction, that the current limitations of Go2Pins are respected. Currently Go2Pins is limited to unbuffered channels, Integer variables and static number of goroutines (i.e. no dynamic goroutine creation is yet supported). Notice that these kind of restrictions are common to most verification tools. Section 4 details how these restrictions can be by-passed.
2. **Core (*Func. Def.* to *Transform*).** This is the core of Go2Pins: it trans-lates the program into a structure that can easily be adapted to match the PINS interface (more details in Sect. 3.1).
3. **Recursion.** Since Go2Pins work only with finite state space (with possibly infinite behaviours), a specific attention must be paid to recursion. This step unrolls each function up to a limit fixed by the user. Since the depth of re-cursion is fixed, only bounded verification can be done on recursive programs.
4. **DuplicateGoroutines.** This step adds the support for goroutines, i.e. multi-threaded programs. This is achieved by the implementation of a scheduler that returns all the possible interleavings from a given state. More details can be found in Sect. 3.2.
5. **Black-Box.** This module reduces the state space explosion problem by fusing consecutive transitions into a single one (more details Sect. 4).

Fortuitous Behaviour of Our Approach. During the conception of our tool, we were advised that a lot of transpilers targeting Go exist. Some of these tools were developed by the Go Team in order to translate some parts of the Go com-piler (originally written in C) into Go. Thus, our workflow transitively supports model-checking these mainstream languages (details in Fig. 2 and Sect. 6).

3 Implementation Details

3.1 Core Translation: *Func. Def.* to *Transform*

The core of Go2Pins (steps *Func. Def.* to *Transform* of Fig. 2) translates the input program into a structure that can be easily adapted to match the PINS interface. This interface exposes two functions: one for retrieving the initial state of the system (represented by a vector of N integer variables), and one for computing the successors of a state[2]. The illustration of this transformation is given in Listing 1.1 for an original program and Listing 1.2 and 1.3 for the transformed program.

---

[2] Model checkers represent the model as a Kripke structure. These two functions are enough to provide a Kripke view of a Go program.

```
1  func fibo(n int) int {
2    n0 := 0
3    n1 := 1
4    for i := 0; i < n; i++ {
5      n2 := n0 + n1
6      n0 = n1
7      n1 = n2
8    }
9    return n1
10 }
11
12 func main() {
13   fibo(5)
14 }
```

Listing 1.1. Fibonacci computation in Go

```
1  type state [15]int
2
3  func G2PF_fibo(s state) state{
4    switch s.LabelCounter {
5      case 0: goto label0
6      //...
7      case 12: goto label12
8    }
9    label0: // n0 := 0
10     s.fibo.n0 = 0
11     s.LabelCounter = 1
12     s.fibo.isalive = 1
13     return s
14     //...
15   label12: // return n1
16     s.fibo.res0 = s.fibo.n1
17     s.fibo.FunctionCounter =
18         s.fibo.caller
19     s.fibo.LabelCounter =
20         s.fibo.callerLabel
21     return s
22 }
```

Listing 1.2. Fibonacci translation (1/2)

```
23 func G2PF_main(s state) state {
24   switch s.LabelCounter {
25     case 0: goto label0
26     //...
27     case 2: goto label2
28   }
29   label0:
30     s.fibo.n = 5
31     s.fibo.caller =
32         s.FunctionCounter
33     s.fibo.callerLabel = 2
34     s.FunctionCounter = 1
35     s.LabelCounter = 0
36     return s
37     //...
38 }
```

Listing 1.3. Fibonacci translation (2/2)

```
39 func G2PEntry(src state) []state {
40   r := make([]state, 0)
41   r := append(res, G2PF_main(src))
42   // From here it's the scheduler
43   // detailed Section 3.2
44   // Build all valid successors
45   for _, g := range goroutines {
46     r = append(r, g.Fun(src))
47   }
48   // See Listing 1.6
49   return r
50 }
```

Listing 1.4. Dispatch in Go2Pins

```
51 func get_successors(src state,
52       cb CB /*Callback*/) int {
53
54   // Compute all successors
55   dsts := G2PEntry(src)
56
57   // Call the model checker
58   // callback for each succ
59   for _, dst := range dsts {
60     CB(cb, dst)
61   }
62 }
```

Listing 1.5. Successor computation

The first step of this translation is to build a (finite) state vector for the program given in Listing 1.1. To build this vector, we must compute the total number of variables that are used. Here, four variables n, n0, n1 and i are displayed but Go2Pins requires extra-variables:

1. The *program counter* indicating the line currently executed. This information is hidden in Listing 1.1 since it is generally handled directly by the microprocessor. For the sake of clarity we opted for a two variables representation of this counter: a variable *FunctionCounter* that indicates the current function, and a variable *LabelCounter* that indicates the current instruction.

2. Another piece of information that is usually tracked at the assembly level is the *return address*, i.e., the position where the execution should continue after a **return** statement (or the end of the function). As previously two variables per function are used: ⟨*fun-name*⟩.*caller* that indicates the return function and ⟨*fun-name*⟩.*callerLabel* that specifies the instruction in this function.
3. When a function returns one or multiple values, a placeholder for these values should be available. Indeed, since these values may be used in various contexts (assignments, comparisons, etc.), the placeholder will represent them until their final use is detected. As a consequence, Go2Pins uses X placeholder variables ⟨*fun-name*⟩.*resX*, where X denotes the Xth return value.
4. Finally, each variable in the original program must be associated to an extra variable *isalive_*⟨*var-name*⟩. This is required in order to handle complex initialization such as $a := f()$. In this assignment the value of a is only known after the evaluation of $f()$. Since the PINS interface represents the program as a vector of integers, a default value must be fixed for all variables (here 0). As a consequence, a model-checking procedure may fail by considering this default value. Thus, the extra variable indicates whether or not the variable a has already been initialized. Due to lack of space, this transformation is not depicted here but would appear in line 14.

To respect the PINS interface, the previous variables are collapsed into a vector of integers (line 1, Listing 1.2). Since this vector handles all values of all variables at a given time, it can be see as a snapshot of the system. Listings 1.2 and 1.3 also detail the other modifications performed during the **core translation** (for the sake of clarity names are explicit, while our translation manipulates indexes: for instance, *s.fibo.res0* is then translated into *s[2]*):

- Each name has been changed to *G2PF_*⟨*fun-name*⟩ and its parameters have been replaced by a single parameter: the state vector representing the actual status of the execution (line 3 and 23).
- Each instruction of the original program has been extracted into a dedicated block of code (see lines 9–12 or 14–20 for an example). This block is accessible from a switch statement at the beginning of the function (lines 4–8 or 24–28). This switch uses the *LabelCounter* to detect the instruction to execute and then jump to the corresponding block.
  This transformation in blocks relies on the computation of *Basic Blocks* and *Control Flow Graph* (CFG). *Basic Blocks* are sequences of instructions without jumps (conditional or not) while the *Control Flow Graph* is a graph that represents all of the execution paths of the function and links each basic block to its potential successors. For the purpose of our tool we restrict basic blocks to contain only one instruction of the original program. As a consequence, the CFG represents the successors of each instruction. With this CFG, each basic block can now be augmented to update *FunctionCounter* and *Label-Counter*. In particular, moving inside a function modifies the *LabelCounter*

(line 11) while a call to another function modifies both variables (line 16–19
and 24–35) . For instance, line 9 details the modification of the *LabelCounter*
while lines 14 to 17 modifies both counters since they represents the original
return statement.

The last step of the translation aggregates all the previous transformations in
order to fit the PINS interface. With this architecture, the PINS *get_successors*
(Listing 1.5) delegates the processing to *GP2Entry* (Listings 1.4) which transitively[3] delegates to the current function *G2PF_⟨fun-name⟩*. This strategy preserves (with a minimal overhead) the structure of the original program which is
helpful for debugging or producing traces during the verification procedure.

3.2 Handling Concurrency: Goroutines and Unbuffered Channels

The previous section presents the core translation for sequential programs.
Nonetheless the main application of model checking is the verification of concurrent programs where bugs are hard to find and reproduce. The concurrency in
Go is provided through two elements: *goroutines* and *channels*. Goroutines are
triggered by the **go** instruction and spawn lightweight threads. Channels are a
communication features that avoid data races contrarily to shared variables.

In order to support goroutines, Go2Pins implements a scheduler. Indeed, at
any moment, the main thread can progress as well as any active goroutine. An
active goroutine is a goroutine that (1) has been spawned by the **go** keyword and,
(2) that is not yet finished. Consequently, this status is stored in the state vector
(so that the scheduler can arrange the various goroutines). Additionally, since
each goroutine needs its own recursive stack, a preprocessing phase is required
to reserve slots for each function that could be called by each goroutine. This
processing is similar to the one done for unrolling recursive functions.

Support for channels also requires to have dedicated slots in the state vector. These slots catch goroutines that are about to perform a synchronization
operation through the channel. As soon as our scheduler detects two of these
goroutines, a synchronization is triggered. In other words the scheduler ensures
a simultaneous progress of the two goroutines. Listing 1.6 details this part of the
scheduler (and finalize the code of Listing 1.4, line 48). It can be observed that
the set of successor is only composed of a set of PINS vectors.

4   Abstraction with Black-Box Transitions

4.1 Overview of Black-Box Transitions

The main problem that arises when verifying large (concurrent) software systems
is the state-space explosion problem since all of the details must be represented

---

[3] This is achieved by building one last extra function: *G2PMain* (see line 42). This
function takes a state vector as a parameter and returns an initialized state vector
during the first call. Then, this function dispatches the processing of the computation
to the function under execution.

```
final := []
for _, s := range r { // walk all successors and keep only valid ones
  if ∃ one channel with (at least) a pending read and a pending write {
    tmp := generate all read/write synchronizations on this channel
    final = append(final, tmp)
  } else if s has no pending operations on channels {
    final = append(final, s)
  }
}
r = final
```

Listing 1.6. Scheduler that synchronize operations on channels

to catch all possible behaviors. One way to tackle this problem is to use approximations that remove some irrelevant details in order to reduce the size of the state space. Two kind of approximations exist:

– **over-approximations** contain more behaviors than the full system. Thus, if there is no error in an over-approximation, then there is no error in the full system. On the other hand if an error is found in an over-approximation it can be spurious. Over-approximations cannot prove presence of errors. detection of errors.

– **under-approximations** contain less behaviors than the full system. Thus if there is an error in an under-approximation, then this error is real error in the full system. On the other hand, absence of errors in an under-approximation does not imply absence of errors in the full systems. Under-approximations cannot prove absence of errors. correctness of properties.

```
1  package main
2
3  import "fmt"
4  import "math"
5
6  func foo(n int) int {
7    return n * 2
8  }
9
10 func main() {
11   a := int(math.Sqrt(42))
12   a = a + foo(a)
13   fmt.Println(a)
14 }
```

Listing 1.7. Simple computations

In this paper, we introduce the **black-box transitions** technique in order to overcome limitations of both over and under-approximations. The underlying idea is to *automatically* build a representation of the program that abstracts away all behaviors irrelevant for the verification procedure while keeping effectiveness for proving correctness of properties or finding errors.

In order to illustrate the black-box transition technique, let us consider the example depicted in Listing 1.7. This example only performs arithmetical operations: it first calls *math.Sqrt* (line 11) which is part of the Go standard library and then calls *foo* (line 12) which is a local function. The result is then printed line 13. Suppose now that we want to check the (correct) LTL property FG '$a > 1$', which express that a will end to be strictly greater than 1.

Trying to verify this property over this program is hard due to lines 11 and 13. Indeed since both of these lines are calls to functions that belong to the Go standard library, the source code of these functions is not available[4]. Consequently the translation depicted in Sect. 3.1 will not work. More generally this problem occurs with any Go program that links with an external library. This problem is annoying since this is a common situation in a large software.

Fortunately, when checking FG '$a > 1$', we are only interested in (1) the value of the variable a and (2) the value returned by the $math.Sqrt$ function. All the details of the $math.Sqrt$ functions are irrelevant for the verification procedure.

Black-box transitions technique exploits this particularity by calling directly $math.Sqrt$. The returned value is then set in the slot corresponding to a in the PINS vector. More generally, black-box transitions technique automatically identifies external function calls, and directly insert these calls during the core translation described Sect. 3.1[5]. To achieved this some manipulation of the PINS vector are required to fill the parameters of the function.

Thus black-box helps to reduce significantly the state-space of the program. For instance, the state-space of the program in Listing 1.7 has only 12 states which is low considering that the definition of both $math.Sqrt$ and $fmt.Println$ function are complex and are several hundred lines of code long[6].

Discussion. Black-boxes address the state space explosion problem by fusing multiple transitions (here, external library function calls) into a single one. Thus, black-boxes assume the correctness of these external functions calls. The verification of these functions is then delegated to the writer of the external library who can opt to use testing or model-checking. Consequently, the developer can only focus on verifying its own code and on providing a high quality software. This strategy follows the idea of Godefroid [15] who states that some part of the software can be checked by model-checking while some part can be checked by testing. This strategy is interesting since it can progressively be integrated into all existing project in order to increase the quality of the project.

Remark on Go2Pins Limitations. Currently Go2Pins is limited to Integer variables. Nonetheless black-boxes transitions can check arbitrary complex code (for instance $math.Sqrt$ or $fmt.Prinln$. Consequently, Go2Pins restrictions only applies to user code and not imported code.

Blackbox and LTL Verification. One drawback of abstraction methods (such as Partial Order Reductions) is the compatibility with the LTL Next operator. Since blackbox transitions collapse successive transitions into one based only on the observed atomic propositions, the use of the Next operator is possible without altering the verification results. In other word this technique only removes the noise from the verification procedure.

A Word on Side Effects. Black-box transitions are not limited to pure functions and also work with functions containing side effects. For instance, call to

---

[4] The runtime of programming language is traditionally provided as a dynamic library.

[5] Notice that this technique is only possible since Go2Pins is developed in Go and produces Go files.

[6] The interested reader may look the definition of: https://golang.org/src/fmt/print.go, https://golang.org/src/math/sqrt.go.

fmt.Println is fully supported. The only drawback of our method is that we will observe the result of calling *fmt.Println* during the verification procedure.

4.2   User-Defined Black-Box Transitions

It is legitimate to ask whether the black-box transition technique could also be applied to user code. A closer look to Listing 1.7 shows that the *foo* function could also be black-boxed if we are only interested in the value of the variable *a*.

Go2Pins can automatically detect such functions. The computation of functions that can be black-boxed is more complex than we can think at first glance. A function can only be black-boxed if it respect the following rules:

1. None of its variable is referred during the verification process
2. It only calls functions that can be black-boxed
3. It does not manipulate global variables

A more precise definition could be stated but would require to compute all the possible executions paths. Since this may be costly we opted for this conservative approximation which is enough in most cases, and can be easily computed.

Once all black-boxed functions are detected, Go2Pins remove them from the original input and put them into a dedicated package. By achieving this, Go2Pins is back to the situation described in the previous section. Thus user defined functions can now be black-boxed. With this approach the state space of the program in Listing 1.7 can be reduced from 12 states to 9 states (25% reduction).

Thus, with this approach, an automatic abstraction, restricted to only behavior mandatory for the verification, is built.

Supporting Depth-1 Function Using Global Variables. There are some situations where the aforementioned rule (3) is too restrictive (more details in Sect. 6). Consider for example a simple function f that modifies a global variable v. Let us now suppose that we want f to be black-boxed. A simple rewriting system can be used to catch this situation. The function f is moved in the blackbox package and rewritten to accept one more argument: a reference to the actual PINS vector. Then every access to global variables is modified to reference the correct slot in the PINS vector. This technique works well but has a severe limitation[7]: we cannot have a black-box function g that will call f. In other words, g will never be considered as black-box. This is too restrictive and future work aims to investigate whether a solution to this problem exist.

---

[7] Another restriction concern the use of the LTL Next operator. Indeed, if the black-boxed function has multiple modification of one variable, only the later one will be visible.

5   Using Go2Pins on Go Programs

This section provides the necessary commands to run and play with Go2Pins[8]. To download Go2Pins you can either fetch it and compile it from the git repository using:

    git clone https://gitlab.lrde.epita.fr/spot/go2pins.git && make

or you can use the package manager of Go using the following command. In this case, the tool will be installed directly in your $GOBIN directory.

    go get gitlab.lrde.epita.fr/spot/go2pins

Notice that Go2Pins have two dependencies you have to install by your own: LTSmin[9] and Spot[10]. Once this have been done, you can run Go2Pins on the example of Listing 1.7 using   go2pins -f listing.1.7.go

The previous command produced an *out* directory containing the **go2pins-mc** binary. This binary can then be used for model-checking the original program.

- ./out/go2pins-mc -list-variables   lists all variables you can use for LTL model-checking. One can observe that each variable is prefixed by the package name and the function name.
- ./out/go2pins-mc -kripke-size   computes the state space of the program. You should obtain 12 states visited as aforementioned.
- ./out/go2pins-mc -ltl 'FG "main_main_a > 1"' -backend spot -nb-threads 1 runs the command of Sect. 4 with one thread using the Spot backend. You should observe an extra display 18, that corresponds to black-boxing *fmt.Println*.

Finally, if you want to blackbox the *foo* function, you have to regenerate the *out* directory and rerun the verification process. Go2Pins offers a shortcut to perform both actions simultaneously

    go2pins -f -blackbox-fn="auto" listing.1.7.go 'FG "main_main_a > 1"'

6   Benchmark

In order to test[11] Go2Pins we opted to translate industrial-inspired problems coming from the RERS challenge [28]. These reactive systems are represented through huge files written in C. To test the whole workflow of our approach, we first use C4Go [10] to translate them into Go, then apply the Go2Pins workflow.

The RERS challenge comes with a set of LTL formulae. Consequently, our benchmark is composed of 41 models (1 909 345 LOC) and 5 064 formulae. Among these 5 064 formulae 35% are verified and 65% are violated. Regarding the hierarchy of Manna and Pnueli [24], our benchmark is splitted in 25%

---

[8] Under GPL (v3), available at https://gitlab.lrde.epita.fr/spot/go2pins.
[9] https://ltsmin.utwente.nl.
[10] https://gitlab.lrde.epita.fr/spot/spot.
[11] Details of our benchmark and how to reproduce it are available at https://www.lrde.epita.fr/~renault/benchs/SPIN-2021/results.html.

pure guarantee, 44% pure safety, 2% pure obligation, 12% pure persistence, 12% pure recurrence, and 5% pure reactivity. Finally all experiments were run with a 4 min timeout and 200 Go memory limitation on a 24 cores Intel(R) Xeon(R) CPUX7460@ 2.66 GHz with 256 GB of RAM.

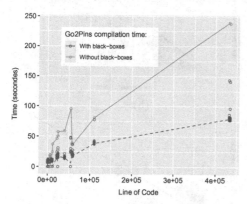

Fig. 3. Time required by Go2Pins to process and compile an input go program according to its number of line of code. Dots represent one computation in the benchmark (a pair model-formula), while lines join the mean of each series.

Figure 3 focuses on the scalability of Go2Pins. This figure details the time required by Go2Pins to translate and compile the files of the benchmark. For each pair model-formula a dot is displayed while lines join the mean of each series[12]. Two approaches are depicted: with or without the use of the black-box technique. Surprisingly, we can first observe that the use of black-boxes also reduce the processing time. Since our approach decomposes each statement in atomic operations, the use of black-box will produce smaller files that are easily processed by the go compiler. Thus, with the black-box technique, our tool process around 5000 line per second. A closer look to these results reveal that Go2Pins uses 60% of this time while the Go compiler uses 40% of it. Consequently, there is a room for improvement in our tool. Finally one can observe huge variation for some models. These models have low number of line of code, but each line has complex operation: Go2Pins spends time to reduce these operations to atomic operations.

Figure 4 display the time required to process the whole benchmark by both Spot and LTSmin. In (a) and (b) it can be observed that the use of black-boxes significantly improves both Spot and LTSmin. Figure 4(c) and (d) display the comparison between Spot and LTSmin on this benchmark. Without black-boxes, Spot outperform to find counterexamples while LTSmin seems better to find empty products (the hardest ones). These difference could come either from the type of Büchi automaton used (which differ between Spot and LTSmin default configurations) or from the default emptiness check algorithm used [3,8]. Further investigation could broaden the study of [2]. Finally, Fig. 4(d) show that the use of black-boxes help Spot to resolve empty products.

Figure 5(a) and (b) displays the number of states and the number of transitions with or without black-boxes when using Spot. Figure 5(c) and (d) depicts the same information for LTSmin. In explicit model checking these metrics are important: the runtime proportional to the number of transitions explored while

---

[12] In our benchmarks multiples programs have the same number of line of code (LOC). A serie is defined as all computations, i.e. one per formula, w.r.t. a specific LOC.

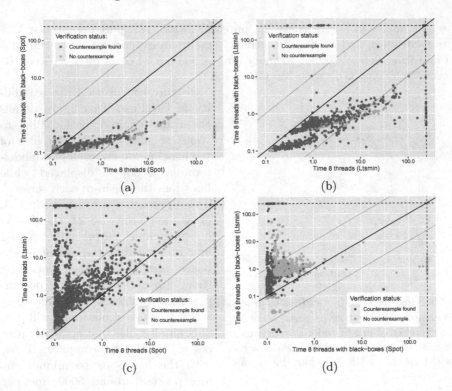

Fig. 4. Time comparison in $\log_{10}$ scale for each backend (Spot and LTSmin), with or without black-boxes. The dark line corresponds to identity while gray lines show the 10 factor speedup/slowdown. Dashed lines represent the 4 min timeout.

the memory consumption is proportional to the number of states. For both Spot and LTSmin, the number of states and transitions is divided by 10 to 100.

On conclusion, the black-box technique helps to reduce both preprocessing and verification runtime.

Correctness. We also opted to test our approach using the RERS benchmark in order to ensure correctness of our implementation. Indeed this benchmark fully specifies 10 models through exactly 964 LTL formulae. These pairs (models, formulae) describe all lines that are (or not) reachable in the input file. In addition to the tests developed during the conception of our tool, these specific models confirm the validity of our work-flow. One should note that most of this files are unprocessable within the 4 min timeout restriction. For black-box transitions, we compare all obtained results to the 5 064 original results. Also note that we plan to translate the BEEM database, used by Spin and DiVinE2.4 in order to increase the confidence in our tool[13].

---

[13] We also plan to translate the Promela database http://www.albertolluch.com/ research/promelamodels n Go in order to compare with other verification tools.

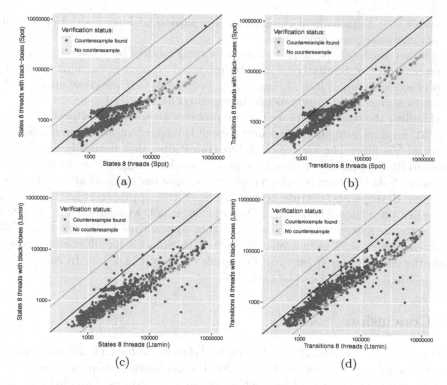

Fig. 5. States and transitions (with and without black-boxes) comparison for both Spot and LTSmin. The dark line corresponds to identity while gray lines show the 10 factor speedup/slowdown.

7 Related Work

The development of Go2Pins has been motivated by several empirical studies performed on the Go language [5, 27, 29]. Ray et al. [27] study the relation between types of bugs and multiple programming languages. Dilley and Lange [5] analyzed 865 Go projects in order to detect how channels are used in large Go projects. Tu et al. [29] study 171 real-world concurrency bugs in Go.

To our knowledge, the LTL-verification of full and unmodified Go programs has never been studied. Many studies [6, 21–23, 25] focus on a static analysis of operations on channels. Liu et al. [23] developed a tool that detect statically patterns of bugs and fix them according to some strategies. The other approaches [6, 21, 22, 25] focus on extracting channels operations. This extraction is then used to to build models that are then verified for correctness. These studies mainly focuses on concurrency problem by checking data-races, communication patterns or deadlocks. Focusing only on channels operation helps to build small models that are processable by verification tools. In this paper we developed a broader approach since (1) we are able to check all LTL properties, (2) we are not restricted to channels operations and (3) we developed a the black-box technique that helps to fight combinatorial explosion without restricting ourself to only channels communications.

Another approach [4] aims to execute formal models by converting Uppaal programs into Go. Similarly Giunti [14] proposed to map pi-calculus specifications of static channels into Go executable programs. Our workflow avoids such transformations, since programs can be executed and verified as-is.

Handling the standard library is a real problem for software verification tools. JPF [31] requires providing the source code of the standard library and relies on a Virtual Machine. The idea of black-box transitions, that naturally handle the standard library, has never been proposed to our knowledge. The closest idea is the one of Spin [18] that is able to execute multiple instructions atomically (see **atomics**, **d_steps** and **c_code** keywords). Since this approach is not automatic and relies on a model written in Promela, it is not well suited for verifying large software systems. One should note that approaches based on the LLVM bytecode also exist. The first one [32] links with Spin for handling concurrency while the second one [1] requires a program expressed in C++. In contrast to our approach, no model can be extracted.

8   Conclusion

This paper introduces Go2Pins, the first tool developed for LTL model-checking over Go programs. It relies on the idea that the Go language is a good candidate for specifying, verifying and building asynchronous systems. Go2Pins uses the PINS interface to link with an ecosystem of model-checkers and model-checking techniques. This paper also introduces black-box transitions to tackle the combinatorial explosion problem. Our benchmark has proven the efficiency of this technique by reducing by more than a factor the size of the state-spaces. Moreover, this technique provides an easy way to support features that are not yet supported by Go2Pins.

Future work aims to support more Go features in order to analyze the structure of the state space of industrial problems (following up the static empirical study of Dilley and Lange [5]). To handle industrial project we would like to support Partial Order Reductions (POR) [20, 26, 30]. Currently only LTSmin supports POR through the use of dependencies matrixes. We plan to compute these matrixes directly into Go2Pins and to integrate POR into Spot. We also would to like to study the relation between black-boxes and POR.

Additionally we would like to go deeper in the development of the black-box technique. For huge functions that cannot be black-boxed we could nonetheless find sequences of instructions that could be fused. Moreover we would like to investigate whether the black-box technique could be generalized to handle any-depth functions with global side-effects.

Finally, our tool only performs verification without fairness since both LTSmin and Spot require fairness to be expressed in the LTL-formula. Nonetheless, expressing fairness directly in Go2Pins could help to reduce state-space size.

References

1. Baranová, Z., et al.: Model checking of C and C++ with DIVINE 4. In: D'Souza, D., Narayan Kumar, K. (eds.) ATVA 2017. LNCS, vol. 10482, pp. 201–207. Springer, Cham (2017). https://doi.org/10.1007/978-3-319-68167-2_14
2. Blahoudek, F., Duret-Lutz, A., Rujbr, V., Strejček, J.: On refinement of Büchi automata for explicit model checking. In: Fischer, B., Geldenhuys, J. (eds.) SPIN 2015. LNCS, vol. 9232, pp. 66–83. Springer, Cham (2015). https://doi.org/10.1007/978-3-319-23404-5_6
3. Bloemen, V., van de Pol, J.: Multi-core SCC-based LTL model checking. In: Bloem, R., Arbel, E. (eds.) HVC 2016. LNCS, vol. 10028, pp. 18–33. Springer, Cham (2016). https://doi.org/10.1007/978-3-319-49052-6_2
4. Dekker, J., Vaandrager, F., Smetsers, R.: Generating a google go framework from an uppaal model. Master's thesis, Radboud University, August 2014
5. Dilley, N., Lange, J.: An empirical study of messaging passing concurrency in go projects. In: 2019 IEEE 26th International Conference on Software Analysis, Evolution and Reengineering (SANER 2019), pp. 377–387 (2019)
6. Dilley, N., Lange, J.: Bounded verification of message-passing concurrency in go using promela and spin. In: Electronic Proceedings in Theoretical Computer Science, pp. 314:34–45, April 2020. https://doi.org/10.4204/EPTCS.314.4
7. Duret-Lutz, A., Lewkowicz, A., Fauchille, A., Michaud, T., Renault, É., Xu, L.: Spot 2.0 — A framework for LTL and ω-automata manipulation. In: Artho, C., Legay, A., Peled, D. (eds.) ATVA 2016. LNCS, vol. 9938, pp. 122–129. Springer, Cham (2016). https://doi.org/10.1007/978-3-319-46520-3_8
8. Evangelista, S., Laarman, A., Petrucci, L., van de Pol, J.: Improved multi-core nested depth-first search. In: Chakraborty, S., Mukund, M. (eds.) ATVA 2012. LNCS, pp. 269–283. Springer, Heidelberg (2012). https://doi.org/10.1007/978-3-642-33386-6_22
9. GitHub repository. C2Go: Migrate from C to Go (2020). https://godoc.org/rsc.io/c2go
10. GitHub repository. C4Go: Transpiling C code to Go code (2020). https://github.com/Konstantin8105/c4go
11. GitHub repository. Transpiling fortran code to golang code (2020). https://github.com/Konstantin8105/f4go
12. GitHub repository. Grumpy: Go running Python (2020). https://github.com/google/grumpy
13. GitHub repository. Java2Go: Convert Java code to something like Go (2020). https://github.com/dglo/java2go
14. Giunti, M.: GoPi: compiling linear and static channels in go. In: Bliudze, S., Bocchi, L. (eds.) COORDINATION 2020. LNCS, vol. 12134, pp. 137–152. Springer, Cham (2020). https://doi.org/10.1007/978-3-030-50029-0_9
15. Godefroid, P.: Between testing and verification: dynamic software model checking. In: DSSE 2016, vol. 45, pp. 99–116, April 2016
16. Griesemer, R., et al.: Hey! ho! let's go! (2009). https://opensource.googleblog.com/2009/11/hey-ho-lets-go.html
17. Hoare, C.A.R.: Communicating Sequential Processes. Prentice-Hall Inc., Hoboken (1985)
18. Holzmann, G.J.: The Spin Model Checker: Primer and Reference Manual. Addison-Wesley, Boston (2003)

19. Kant, G., Laarman, A., Meijer, J., van de Pol, J., Blom, S., van Dijk, T.: Ltsmin: high-performance language-independent model checking. In: TACAS 2015, pp. 692–707, April 2015
20. Laarman, A., Pater, E., van de Pol, J., Hansen, H.: Guard-based partial-order reduction. Int. J. Softw. Tools Technol. Transfer 1–22 (2014)
21. Lange, J., Ng, N., Toninho, B., Yoshida, N.: Fencing off go: liveness and safety for channel-based programming. In: POPL 2017, pp. 748–761. ACM (2017)
22. Lange, J., Ng, n., Toninho, B., Yoshida, N.: A static verification framework for message passing in go using behavioural types. In: CSE 2018, pp. 1137–1148. ACM (2018)
23. Liu, Z., Zhu, S., Qin, B., Chen, H., Song, L.: Automatically detecting and fixing concurrency bugs in go software systems. In: International Conference on Architectural Support for Programming Languages and Operating Systems (ASPLOS), vol. 11, pp. 2227–2240 (2016)
24. Manna, Z., Pnueli, A.: A hierarchy of temporal properties. In: PODC 1990, pp. 377–410. ACM (1990)
25. Ng, N., Yoshida, N.: Static deadlock detection for concurrent go by global session graph synthesis. In CCC 2016, pp. 174–184. ACM (2016)
26. Peled, D.: Combining partial order reductions with on-the-fly model-checking. In: Dill, D.L. (ed.) CAV 1994. LNCS, vol. 818, pp. 377–390. Springer, Heidelberg (1994). https://doi.org/10.1007/3-540-58179-0_69
27. Ray, B., Posnett, D., Filkov, V., Devanbu, P.: A large scale study of programming languages and code quality in github. In: SIGSOFT 2014, pp. 155–165 (2014)
28. RERS challenge. Rigorous examination of reactive systems (RERS) (2019). http://rers-challenge.org/2019/
29. Tu, T., Liu, X., Song, L., Zhang, Y.: Understanding real-world concurrency bugs in go. In: ASPLOS 2019, pp. 865–878 (2019)
30. Valmari, A.: Stubborn sets for reduced state space generation. In: Rozenberg, G. (ed.) ICATPN 1989. LNCS, vol. 483, pp. 491–515. Springer, Heidelberg (1991). https://doi.org/10.1007/3-540-53863-1_36
31. Visser, W., Havelund, K., Brat, G., Park, S., Lerda, F.: Model checking programs. Autom. Softw. Eng. 10, 203–232 (2018). https://doi.org/10.1023/A:1022920129859
32. Zaks, A., Joshi, R.: Verifying multi-threaded C programs with SPIN. In: SPIN 2008, pp. 94–107 (2008)

Probabilistic Model Checking
of Randomized Java Code

Syyeda Zainab Fatmi[1], Xiang Chen[2], Yash Dhamija[1], Maeve Wildes[3],
Qiyi Tang[4], and Franck van Breugel[1(✉)]

[1] York University, Toronto, Canada
franck@eecs.yorku.ca
[2] University of Waterloo, Waterloo, Canada
[3] McGill University, Montreal, Canada
[4] University of Oxford, Oxford, UK

Abstract. Java PathFinder (JPF) and PRISM are the most popular
model checkers for Java code and systems that exhibit random behaviour,
respectively. Our tools make it possible to use JPF and PRISM together.
For the first time, probabilistic properties of randomized algorithms
implemented in a modern programming language can be checked. Furthermore, our tools are accompanied by a large collection of randomized
algorithms that we implemented in Java. From those Java applications
and with the help of our tools, we have generated the largest collection
of realistic labelled (discrete time) Markov chains.

Keywords: (Probabilistic) model checking · Java PathFinder ·
PRISM

1 Introduction

Java PathFinder (JPF) is the most popular model checker for Java code. It
takes as input Java bytecode and a configuration file. The latter includes which
properties to check. As output, JPF produces a report that tells us, among
other things, whether any of those properties have been violated. PRISM is
the most popular probabilistic model checker. As input, it takes a model of a
system that exhibits random behaviour. The model can be expressed in a simple
language, but also as a labelled Markov chain (LMC). Furthermore, it takes a
probabilistic property specified in a logic as input. PRISM checks, among other
things, whether the model satisfies the property.

The popularity of these model checkers is reflected by the facts that JPF
has been downloaded hundreds of times every month for almost two decades
and PRISM has been downloaded more than 75,000 times[1]. The papers that
describe JPF [24] and PRISM [12] have each been cited more than 1,800 times.

---

[1] www.prismmodelchecker.org/download.php.

Supported by the Natural Sciences and Engineering Research Council of Canada.

A. Laarman and A. Sokolova (Eds.): SPIN 2021, LNCS 12864, pp. 157–174, 2021.
https://doi.org/10.1007/978-3-030-84629-9_9

JPF is an explicit state model checker. It builds a model of the Java bytecode on the fly. This model can be seen as a directed graph, which is known as the state space. The vertices correspond to the states of JPF's virtual machine and the edges, also called transitions, represent sequences of bytecode instructions.

We have developed two extensions of JPF, jpf-label and jpf-probabilistic, that decorate the state space in orthogonal ways. jpf-label provides an easy way to label the states. To capture simple known facts about the states of JPF's virtual machine, jpf-label decorates those states with a set of atomic propositions. Our extension supports a range of atomic propositions. For example, it allows us to identify those states that are initial or final, those states in which a specific boolean static field is true, those states in which a specific method returns, etc. These atomic propositions may be used to express properties of the code. Such properties can be formalized in logics such as linear temporal logic (LTL) [17] and computation tree logic (CTL) [3].

Our extension jpf-probabilistic assigns probabilities to the transitions. Those probabilities reflect the random choices in the Java code. To make it easy for programmers to express those in Java and for our extension to detect them, we have introduced three Java classes. The class `Choice` contains the method `make` which takes an array of `doubles`, say p, as argument. The method invocation `Choice.make(p)` returns i, where $0 \leq i < $ `p.length`, with probability $p[i]$, provided that $\sum_{0 \leq i < \texttt{p.length}} p[i] = 1.0$. For convenience, we also introduced the class `Coin` with the method `flip`. Furthermore, the method invocation `UniformChoice.make`(n) returns i, where $0 \leq i < n$, with probability $\frac{1}{n}$. By adding probabilities to the transitions, we turn the state space into a (discrete time) Markov chain (DTMC).

By default, JPF uses depth-first search (DFS) to traverse the state space. It also supports breadth-first search (BFS). jpf-probabilistic contains several search strategies that take the probabilities into account. In particular, it supports probability-first search [26], random search [26], softmax search [23], and ϵ-greedy search [23]. The latter two are inspired by reinforcement learning [22]. We discuss these new search strategies in more detail in Sect. 3. Note that the search strategies produce the same state space, provided that it can be explored in its entirety. Otherwise, search strategies may explore different portions of the state space. As we will see in Sect. 6, the new search strategies are much more effective than DFS when model checking randomized Java code.

Our extensions jpf-label and jpf-probabilistic together with a converter allow us to use JPF and PRISM in tandem. Given a randomized algorithm implemented in Java and a configuration file, JPF with the help of jpf-label and jpf-probabilistic produces an LMC, that is, a Markov chain the states of which are labelled with atomic propositions. This chain can be graphically represented as a directed graph where the edges are labelled with probabilities and the vertices are coloured (where colours represent atomic propositions), and it can also be converted into a format that can be fed into PRISM together with a probabilistic property. This provides the first model checking tool, depicted in Fig. 1, that can check probabilistic properties of randomized algorithms implemented in a modern programming language.

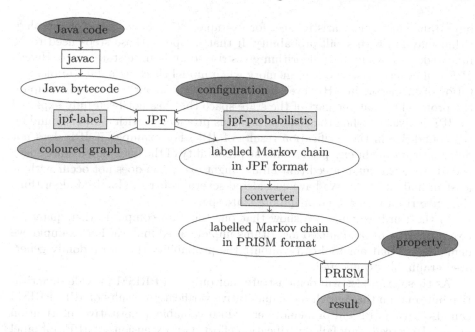

Fig. 1. The diagram provides an overview of the model checking tool. The ovals are data and the rectangles are tools. The blue ovals are input. The green ovals are output. The red rectangles are the parts that we developed. (Colour figure online)

Instead of using our tool, one could try to model randomized algorithms in PRISM's input language. However, numerous details of some algorithms cannot easily be handled directly by PRISM. Consider, for example, Frieze's randomized algorithm to find a Hamiltonian cycle in an undirected graph [8]. The algorithm uses lists which are rotated and reversed. Furthermore, the probabilities associated with the choices in the algorithm depend on the size of the lists and can be zero. Such features can easily be captured in Java but cannot be directly captured in PRISM's input language.

The Java implementations of sixty randomized algorithms are provided with our extension jpf-probabilistic. To illustrate how our tool can be used, we present three examples. In the first one, we consider the Miller-Rabin primality test [15,18]. This is a Monte Carlo algorithm as it may incorrectly report with small probability that the number provided as an argument is prime. This algorithm has been implemented in the method `isProbablePrime` of the class `java.math.BigInteger`. With our tool we can compute the probability of this algorithm erroneously reporting that a number is prime. We have applied our tool to several other Monte Carlo algorithms as well.

In the second example, we consider a variation of an algorithm due to Floyd and Rivest [7]. This is a Las Vegas algorithm as it always returns the correct result, however, the running time may vary. The algorithm selects the ith smallest of n numbers. Hence, it can be used to determine the median, which is an important clustering statistic (see, for example, [25]). Some steps of the algorithm may fail with small probability. If that happens, those steps need to be repeated. As a result, this algorithm gives rise to an infinite state space. Hence, JPF will eventually run out of memory when model checking a Java implementation of this algorithm. However, as we will show, with our tool we can compute the probability that the part of the state space that has not been fully explored by JPF is reached when the code is run. This provides us with a lower bound on the confidence in the verification results of JPF. For example, if JPF does not detect any uncaught exceptions and the probability of the unexplored state space is 0.01, then it is guaranteed that an uncaught exception does not occur with at least probability 0.99. We have considered several other randomized algorithms that give rise to very large or infinite state spaces.

In the third example, we show that our tool can compute other quantitative properties of randomized algorithms implemented in Java. For example, we demonstrate that our tool can compute the probability that a randomly generated graph [5] is connected.

As these examples will demonstrate, not only can PRISM provide quantitative information that enriches the qualitative verification results of JPF, PRISM can also turn a JPF out of memory error into valuable quantitative information about JPF's seemingly failed verification effort. Our extensions of JPF, jpf-label and jpf-probabilistic, as well as our converter are essential in both cases.

2   JPF-Label

As we already mentioned, to express properties of Java code in terms of logics such as LTL and CTL, we need a way to specify atomic propositions and to label those states that satisfy them. For example, we may want to label the final states or those states in which a specific static boolean field is true. Currently, there is no model checker for Java code that labels states.

In the past, several extensions of JPF, all named jpf-ltl, have been developed that supported the checking of properties expressed in LTL.[2] None of these extensions is compatible with the latest version of JPF. In [4], Cuong and Cheng describe a tool that given a property expressed in LTL generates an extension of JPF that checks the property. Unfortunately, an implementation of such a tool is not available [2].

In the literature, the following categories of atomic propositions in the context of Java code are distinguished:

- static boolean fields and local boolean variables (jpf-ltl),
- boolean expressions built from static integer fields and local integer variables (jpf-ltl and [11]),

---

[2] Only one version of jpf-ltl is still available. This version is based on the algorithms described in [9] and can be found at the URL code.google.com/archive/p/jpf-ltl/source. Most of the code is more than 15 years old. JPF has changed a lot in the last 15 years, thus, this extension is incompatible with the current version of JPF.

- method invocations (jpf-ltl and [4,11,21]),
- method returns and the values returned ([1,11]),
- thrown exceptions and the exception types ([11]), and
- AspectJ pointcuts ([21]).

Note that, apart from jpf-ltl and [4], all the above references describe verification tools that are not model checkers.

Our extension jpf-label[3] implements the following 12 different ways to label states, including instances of all the above mentioned categories apart from the last one.

- Initial: labels the initial state.
- End: labels the final states, also known as end states in JPF.
- BooleanStaticField: labels states with the value of a static boolean field.
- IntegerStaticField: labels states with the value of a static integer field.
- BooleanLocalVariable: labels states with the value of a local boolean variable.
- IntegerLocalVariable: labels states with the value of a local integer variable.
- InvokedMethod: labels those states in which a method is invoked.
- ReturnedBooleanMethod: labels those states in which a method has returned with the boolean return value.
- ReturnedIntegerMethod: labels those states in which a method has returned with the integer return value.
- ReturnedVoidMethod: labels those states in which a void method has returned.
- SynchronizedStaticMethod: labels those states in which a synchronized static method acquires or has released the lock.
- ThrownException: labels those states in which an exception has been thrown.

The field, variable, method, or exception of interest is specified in the JPF configuration file. Our tool also allows users to easily implement their own state labelling by simply extending an abstract class containing only five methods.

Any code that JPF can handle, can also be handled by jpf-label. When we run JPF extended with jpf-label on Java code, it can generate a file that contains the state labelling. An example is provided in Fig. 2. Furthermore, it can also produce a graphical representation of the labelled state space as a coloured directed graph, an example of which can be seen in Fig. 7. The probabilities on the edges of this figure are produced by the extension jpf-probabilistic which we discuss in detail in the next section.

Our extension jpf-label consists of 2,693 lines of Java code. More details about the design and implementation of jpf-label can be found in [6].

---

[3] jpf-label is available at github.com/javapathfinder/jpf-label.

```
1  O="init"  1="true__PrimalityTest_isPrime__II__Z"  2="end"
   ↪ 3="false__PrimalityTest_isPrime__II__Z"
2  -1: 0
3  2: 1
4  3: 2
5  4: 3
6  5: 2
7  6: 1
```

Fig. 2. The file `PrimalityTest.lab` contains the state labelling produced by JPF extended with our jpf-label from the Java app `PrimalityTest`. Line 1 lists the labels and their indices. The remaining lines provide the labelling for those states that have labels. For example, line 4 specifies that state 3 is labelled `"end"`, that is, it is a final state.

3 JPF-Probabilistic

Our extension jpf-probabilistic[4] decorates the transitions of the state space with probabilities, turning the state space into a DTMC. jpf-probabilistic can handle any Java code that can be model checked by JPF, which contains randomness, but does not contain any other sources of nondeterminism, such as concurrency. When we run JPF extended with jpf-probabilistic on randomized Java code, we can generate a file that contains the Markov chain corresponding to the code. An example can be found in Fig. 3. When using both jpf-label and jpf-probabilistic, JPF can produce a graphical representation of the LMC as a directed graph where the vertices are coloured and the edges are labelled with probabilities (see Fig. 7).

```
1  788962 1347606
2  -1 0 1.000000
3  0 1 0.200000
4  0 2 0.200000
5  0 3 0.200000
6  ...
```

Fig. 3. The file `LazySelect.tra` contains the Markov chain produced by JPF extended with our jpf-probabilistic from the Java app `LazySelect`. The first line specifies the number of states and the number of transitions. The transitions and their probabilities are described in the remaining lines. Here we only show four transitions. Each transition is captured by its source state, its target state, and its probability. For example, line 5 specifies the transition from state 0 to state 3 with probability 0.200000.

By default, JPF uses depth-first search to traverse the state space. It also supports breadth-first search. Since our extension jpf-probabilitic associates proba-

---

[4] jpf-probabilistic is available at github.com/javapathfinder/jpf-probabilistic.

bilities with the transitions, these probabilities can be used to drive the search of the state space. Our extension provides four such search strategies.

Probability-first search (PFS), which was introduced by Zhang in [26], uses the probabilities of the transitions to select the next state to explore. In particular, it always chooses a state whose path from the root in the search's spanning tree has the highest probability.

Random search (RS) [26] randomly selects a state among the states that have been discovered, but that have not yet been fully explored. The chance of choosing a state is proportional to the probability of the path from the root in the search's spanning tree. Let us make that precise. Assume that $\{s_0, \ldots, s_n\}$ is the set of states that have been discovered but their outgoing transitions have not all been explored yet. Then RS chooses state s_j, with $0 \leq j \leq n$, with probability

$$\frac{p(s_j)}{\sum_{0 \leq i \leq n} p(s_i)},$$

where $p(s_i)$ is the probability of the path from the root to s_i in the search's spanning tree.

In [23], Tang introduced two search strategies inspired by reinforcement learning [22]. The softmax search (SMS) selects the next state according to a Gibbs distribution. Assume again that $\{s_0, \ldots, s_n\}$ is the set of states that have been discovered but not yet fully explored. Then SMS chooses state s_j, with $0 \leq j \leq n$, with probability

$$\frac{e^{p(s_j)/\tau}}{\sum_{0 \leq i \leq n} e^{p(s_i)/\tau}},$$

where $p(s_i)$ is defined as above and the constant τ is called the temperature. This constant should be a positive real number. The ϵ-greedy search (EGS) relies on a parameter $\epsilon \in (0, 1)$. It combines RS and PFS in such a way that with probability $1 - \epsilon$ it behaves like PFS and with probability ϵ it behaves like RS. These different search strategies often visit the states in a different order and, as a result, may visit different parts of the state space and, hence, detect bugs in different parts of the code (see Sect. 6).

An earlier version of jpf-probabilistic has been discussed in [27]. Since then, a lot has changed. For example, the search strategies SMS and EGS have been added and the search strategies PFS and RS have been implemented more efficiently. Also, the ability of jpf-probabilistic to generate a file that contains the Markov chain and to produce a graphical representation of the LMC are both new. Furthermore, numerous examples have been added. The current version of jpf-probabilistic contains 14,224 lines of Java code. Only 996 lines of Java code of the original version of jpf-probabilistic have remained and the other 573 lines of Java code have been deleted or replaced.

4   Our Converter

The format of the transition and labelling files generated by JPF differs slightly from PRISM's input format. Whereas JPF numbers its states starting from -1,

PRISM starts at zero. JPF may produce multiple transitions between a given pair of states, while PRISM allows at most one transition between any pair of states. Furthermore, in PRISM a label may only consist of letters, digits and the underscore character, and it can neither begin with a digit nor contain any whitespace. Additionally, a label should not be a reserved keyword in PRISM. PRISM also requires that the initial states of the model are labelled as such.

Therefore, we have implemented a simple converter, named JPFtoPRISM, that renumbers the states in the transition and label files. The converter also checks if all labels satisfy the above mentioned restrictions. Furthermore, if the initial state of the model is not labelled, the converter adds the label "init" to the initial state. If JPF has produced multiple transitions from a given source state to a given target state, then the converter collapses those transitions into a single transition between the source and target state by adding up the transition probabilities. Moreover, if the probabilities of the outgoing transitions of each state do not sum to one, the converter adds a labelled sink state for the remaining probability. This ensures that if JPF has not traversed the state space completely, for example, because it ran out of memory, then the resulting LMC's transition matrix is a right stochastic matrix, preventing a deadlock warning in PRISM.

Consider the labelled Markov chain represented by the labelling file and the transition file shown in Fig. 4.

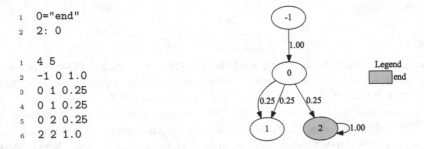

Fig. 4. The labelling file is shown on the top left. Line 1 lists the labels and their indices. In this case, there is only one label, namely "end", with index 0. Line 2 specifies that state 2 is labelled "end", that is, it is a final state. The transition file is shown on the bottom left. The first line specifies that there are four states and five transitions. The five transitions and their probabilities are described in the remaining lines. Each transition is captured by its source state, its target state, and its probability. A graphical representation of the state space is displayed on the right.

Using our converter, the LMC described above is transformed into an LMC in PRISM's format, represented by the labelling file and the transition file shown in Fig. 5. The converter renumbers the states such that the numbering begins at 0. Since the initial state of the model is not labelled, the converter adds the label "init" to the initial state. The converter also collapses multiple transitions from a given source state to a given target state into a single transition by adding up the transition probabilities. Finally, the converter adds a sink state for the remaining probability of those states of which the probabilities of their outgoing transitions do not sum to one.

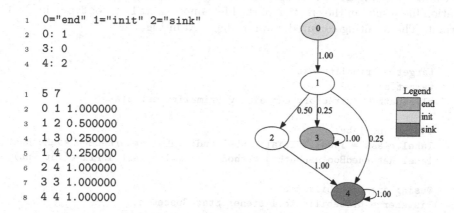

```
1   0="end" 1="init" 2="sink"
2   0: 1
3   3: 0
4   4: 2
```

```
1   5 7
2   0 1 1.000000
3   1 2 0.500000
4   1 3 0.250000
5   1 4 0.250000
6   2 4 1.000000
7   3 3 1.000000
8   4 4 1.000000
```

Fig. 5. The labelling file is shown on the top left. Line 1 lists the labels and their indices. Two labels have been added, namely "init" and "sink", to label the initial state 0 and sink state 4, respectively. The states have been renumbered. Note that line 3 specifies that the final state is now state 3. The transition file is shown on the bottom left. The first line specifies that there are five states and seven transitions. The states have been renumbered. The two transitions from state 0 to state 1 in Fig. 4 have been combined into one transition from state 1 to state 2. Transitions to the sink state, state 4, have been added from those states that have not yet been fully explored (state 1 and 2 in the transformed system). Note that the sink state transitions to itself with probability 1.0. A graphical representation of the state space is displayed on the right. (Colour figure online)

5   Monte Carlo Algorithms

Monte Carlo algorithms are randomized algorithms that may produce incorrect results with a small probability. As we will show, JPF and our extensions jpf-label and jpf-probabilistic together with our converter and PRISM can compute the probability that a Monte Carlo algorithm implemented in Java gets it wrong.

A number of algorithms provided with jpf-probabilistic are Monte Carlo algorithms, including the primality tests due to (1) Fermat [14], (2) Lucas, (3) Miller and Rabin [15,18], and (4) Solovay and Strassen [20]. These algorithms determine whether a number given as input is prime. The algorithms may erroneously report that the input number is prime. As most Monte Carlo algorithms, the algorithms contain a main loop. The more iterations of this loop, also known as trials, are executed, the lower the probability that the algorithms return an incorrect result.

We have implemented the Miller-Rabin primality test in Java in a class called `MillerRabinPrimalityTest`, abbreviated to `PrimalityTest` below. The randomization in the code is captured by jpf-probabilistic's `UniformChoice.make` method. We configure JPF as specified in Fig. 6. Running JPF with this configuration file results in the creation of the file named `PrimalityTest.dot` in DOT format. The resulting coloured graph is depicted in Fig. 7.

```
1   target = PrimalityTest
2   target.args = 9,2
3   classpath = <directory containing PrimalityTest.class>
4
5   @using jpf-label
6   label.class = label.Initial; label.End; label.ReturnedBooleanMethod
7   label.ReturnedBooleanMethod.method = PrimalityTest.isPrime(int,int)
8
9   @using jpf-probabilistic
10  listener = probabilistic.listener.StateSpaceDot,
        ↪ probabilistic.listener.StateLabelVisitor
11  probabilistic.listener.StateSpaceDot.precision = 3
```

Fig. 6. This JPF configuration file specifies that the Java app named `PrimalityTest` with the command line arguments 9 (the number to be tested for primality) and 2 (the number of trials) is to be model checked by JPF. The `classpath` tells JPF where to find the bytecode of the app. Line 5 and 9 specify that our extensions jpf-label and jpf-probabilistic are used. Line 6 specifies that the initial state and the final states (also known as end states in JPF) should be labelled, as well as those states in which the method `isPrime` of the class `PrimalityTest` that takes two `int`s as arguments (as specified in line 7) returns. Finally, line 10 specifies that JPF should generate a graphical representation of the state space (which forms an LMC) and line 11 captures that the probabilities of the transitions should be depicted with three digits precision.

The Miller-Rabin primality test returns true when a prime number is provided as input. We compute the probability that the algorithm returns the wrong result when a composite number is provided as input. We first run JPF as described above, but using this time `probabilistic.listener.StateSpaceText` and `label.StateLabelText` in line 10 of Fig. 6 instead. As a result, JPF creates the file `PrimalityTest.tra` that contains the transitions and their probabilities, and the file `PrimalityTest.lab` that contains the state labelling. Together they specify an LMC. The label `"true__PrimalityTest_isPrime__II__Z"`, abbreviated below as `"incorrect"`, captures that the method `isPrime` of the class `PrimalityTest`, which takes two arguments of type `int` and returns a value of type `boolean`, returns the value `true`. This label captures the scenario in which the method returns true but the input is not a prime. Note that we use name mangling similar to that used in the Java native interface [13].

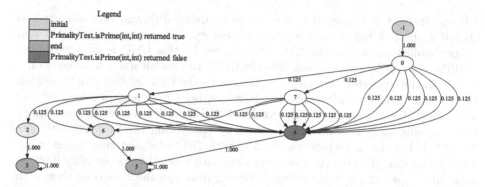

Fig. 7. This coloured graph has been generated by JPF extended with jpf-label and jpf-probabilistic. It represents the state space for the Miller-Rabin primality test run for two trials for the input number 9. The initial state (state -1) and the final states (states 3 and 5) are labelled, as well as those states in which the static method that determines whether the number is prime returns true (states 2 and 6) and false (state 4). (Colour figure online)

Subsequently, we use our converter to transform the LMC into PRISM's format. Finally, we use PRISM's explicit engine to compute for this LMC the property P=? [F "incorrect"]. That is, PRISM computes the probability that the LTL property F "incorrect" holds. This property specifies that eventually a state labelled "incorrect", that is, a state in which the method isPrime of the class PrimalityTest returns true, is reached. PRISM returns the probability 0.0625, which corresponds to reaching either state 2 or state 6 in Fig. 7.

6 Very Large and Infinite State Spaces

The size of the underlying LMC is often too large for JPF to explore entirely, before running out of time or memory. In such a case, we can measure the amount of progress made by JPF, using our extension jpf-probabilistic and our converter together with PRISM, as we will show below.

The lazy select algorithm [7] selects the ith smallest of n numbers. Some steps of the algorithm may fail with small probability. If that happens, those steps need to be repeated. As a result, this algorithm gives rise to an infinite state space. We implemented the algorithm in Java, again using jpf-probabilistic's UniformChoice.make method to capture randomization.

When we use JPF in combination with our extension jpf-probabilistic, to model check the Java code to select the third smallest of five elements, JPF runs out of its 10 GB of memory after 2 min and 9 s. In that time, JPF visits 788,962 states and does not detect any violations of properties such as uncaught exceptions. However, since JPF does not completely traverse the infinite state space, its verification effort provides very little, if any, useful information.

By using PRISM in combination with JPF, we can extract useful quantitative information from a seemingly failed verification effort. This is accomplished as follows. Instead of letting JPF run out of memory, JPF can be configured so that it stops just before running out of memory. Our extensions jpf-label and jpf-probabilistic generate the LMC. Subsequently, this LMC is converted into PRISM's format by means of our `JPFtoPRISM`. Since not all states have been fully explored, the converter also adds a sink state to the LMC as well as a transition to this sink state from all states that have not been fully explored by JPF and also labels the sink state. Finally, we use PRISM to determine the probability that the sink state is eventually reached by computing the property `P=?` [`F` `"sink"`]. For the above mentioned LMC with 788,962 states, this property has a value less than 0.00004. As a consequence, with more than probability 0.99996 only fully explored states are reached. Hence, if we run the Java code then with at least probability 0.99996 we will not encounter any violation of the properties checked by JPF. This number represents the progress made by JPF [28].

JPF provides two search strategies: DFS and BFS. As mentioned in Sect. 3, jpf-probabilistic provides a number of other search strategies that take the probabilities into account. Since different search strategies may visit states in different orders, they may make progress at different rates. As shown in Fig. 8, this is indeed the case for the Java implementation of lazy select. Some of the search strategies that take the probabilities into account make more progress than BFS. DFS, JPF's default search strategy, makes no progress for this particular example. Note that one can run multiple instances of JPF in parallel each using a different search strategy and combine the results.

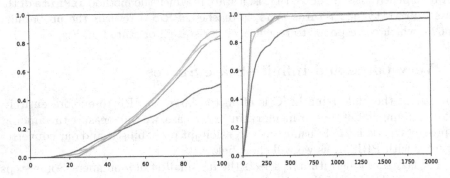

Fig. 8. This graph depicts results of the model checking tool applied to the Java code implementing lazy select that selects the third smallest of five elements. The x-axis represents time in milliseconds. The y-axis represents the progress made by JPF. The colours represent the different search strategies: • = depth-first search, • = breadth-first search, • = ε-greedy search, • = probability-first search, • = random search, • = softmax search. The graph on the left zooms in on the first 100 ms. The progress of depth-first search is zero and, therefore, coincides with the x-axis. (Colour figure online)

```
1   target = ErdosRenyiUndirectedModel
2   target.args = 5,0.6
3   classpath = <directory containing ErdosRenyiUndirectedModel.class>
4
5   @using jpf-label
6   label.class = label.ReturnedBooleanMethod
7   label.ReturnedBooleanMethod.method =
        ↪ ErdosRenyiUndirectedModel.isConnected()
8
9   @using jpf-probabilistic
10  listener = probabilistic.listener.StateSpaceText,label.StateLabelText
```

Fig. 9. This JPF configuration file specifies that the Java app named
ErdosRenyiUndirectedModel with the command line arguments 5 (the number of vertices in the graph) and 0.6 (the probability of adding an edge between two vertices)
is to be model checked by JPF. Line 5 and 9 specify that our extensions jpf-label
and jpf-probabilistic are used. Line 6 and 7 specify that those states in which the
boolean method isConnected of the class ErdosRenyiUndirectedModel returns should
be labelled. Line 10 specifies that JPF should generate a textual representation of the
state space.

7 Other Quantitative Properties

In addition to determining the probability that a Monte Carlo algorithm returns
an incorrect result and the progress made by JPF on a large or infinite state
space, our tool can check a wide range of other quantitative properties of randomized algorithms implemented in Java. The Erdös-Rényi model [5] is a model
for generating random graphs. In this model, a graph with a given number of
vertices is constructed by placing an edge between each pair of vertices with a
given probability, independent from every other edge. We implemented a version of the algorithm to generate random undirected graphs in Java in the class
ErdosRenyiUndirectedModel. We use jpf-probabilistic's Choice.make method
to express the random choices in the code.

Assume that we would like to determine the probability that the graph generated by the algorithm is connected. We add a boolean method to our class,
called isConnected, that returns true if the graph is connected and false otherwise. We run JPF with the configurations specified in Fig. 9, which results in the
creation of a transition and labelling file that represent the underlying LMC.

Using our converter JPFtoPRISM, we transform the LMC produced by
JPF into PRISM's format. We then run PRISM to compute the property
P=? [F "true__ErdosRenyiUndirectedModel_isConnected____Z"], which
captures the probability that eventually a state is reached in which the boolean
method isConnected of the class ErdosRenyiUndirectedModel returns true.
By varying the number of vertices in the random graph and the probability
of placing an edge between any two vertices, we construct the graph shown in
Fig. 10.

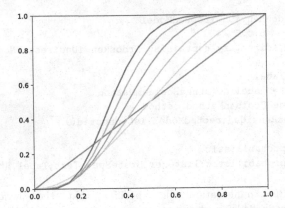

Fig. 10. This diagram depicts results of the model checking tool applied to the Java code implementing the Erdös-Rényi model. The x-axis represents the probability of adding an edge between two vertices. The y-axis represents the probability that the generated graph is connected. The colours represent the number of vertices in the generated graph: • = 2, • = 3, • = 4, • = 5, • = 6, • = 7 (Colour figure online)

8 Overhead

We monitored the memory and time usage of our tool on the examples provided with our extension jpf-probabilistic. In all cases we have observed so far, the overhead of jpf-label and jpf-probabilistic is very limited.

Consider the algorithm to determine whether an integer array given as input has a majority element [16]. The algorithm is a Monte Carlo algorithm and may erroneously report that the given array does not have a majority element. The algorithm contains a main loop. The more iterations of this loop, also known as trials, are executed the lower the probability that the algorithm returns an incorrect result.

We have implemented this algorithm in Java in a class called `HasMajorityElement`. We provide as input an integer array of size eleven. By increasing the number of trials we can increase the size of the state space linearly.

The amount of time (in seconds) used by JPF without and with jpf-label and jpf-probabilistic are shown in Fig. 11. jpf-probabilistic has virtually no overhead and jpf-label increases the time used by JPF by a factor of approximately 1.2. The amount of heap memory (in MB) used by JPF without and with jpf-label and jpf-probabilistic are shown in Fig. 12. For both jpf-label and jpf-probabilistic, the difference is only a few MB.

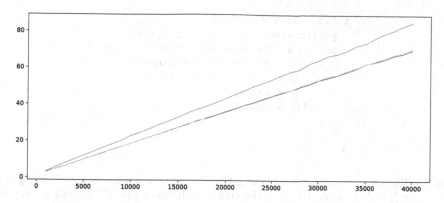

Fig. 11. This graph depicts the time used by JPF applied to the Java code implementing the majority element algorithm. The x-axis represents the number of iterations of the main loop. The y-axis represents the amount of time in seconds. The colours represent the following configurations: • = JPF run without jpf-label and jpf-probabilistic, • = JPF run with jpf-label, • = JPF run with jpf-probabilistic. (Colour figure online)

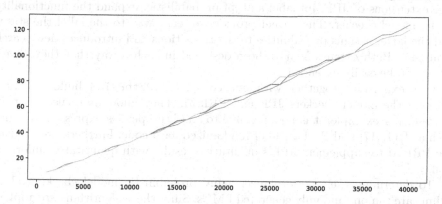

Fig. 12. This graph depicts the memory usage of JPF applied to the Java code implementing the majority element algorithm. The x-axis represents the number of iterations of the main loop. The y-axis represents the amount of heap memory in MB. The colours represent the following configurations: • = JPF run without jpf-label and jpf-probabilistic, • = JPF run with jpf-label, • = JPF run with jpf-probabilistic. (Colour figure online)

It should be mentioned that one can easily write a Java application for which the memory overhead caused by jpf-label is arbitrarily large (for example, see Fig. 13). However, one does not encounter such Java applications in practice.

```
1   public class Example {
2     public static boolean flip = true;
3     public static void main(String[] args) {
4       int n = Integer.parseInt(args[0]);
5       for (int i = 0; i < n; i++) {
6         flip = false;
7         flip = true;
8       }
9     }
10  }
```

Fig. 13. Running this example without jpf-label results in a single state. Running the code with jpf-label, while labelling the states with the value of the field `flip`, and passing the value n as command-line argument results in 2n+2 states.

9   Conclusion

Our extensions of JPF, jpf-label and jpf-probabilistic, expand the functionality of the model checker. The former provides an easy way to the label the states and the latter assigns probabilities to the transitions and introduces new search strategies. Both extensions have been designed in such a way that they themselves can be easily extended.

Our extensions together with our converter `JPFtoPRISM` build a bridge between the model checkers JPF and PRISM. They allow us to use them in tandem. For example, it is now possible to check properties expressed in logics such as LTL [17] and PCTL [10] of randomized Java code. Furthermore, we can use PRISM to supplement JPF's qualitative results with quantitative information.

To determine their performance, many probabilistic model checking algorithms are run on randomly generated LMCs. Since these algorithms are applied in practice to LMCs that are far from random, there is a pressing need for realistic LMCs. From the Java implementations of randomized algorithms that accompany jpf-probabilistic we can generate a large collection of LMCs. It almost doubles the number of available realistic LMCs in PRISM's collection. For all of these examples, the overhead of jpf-label and jpf-probabilistic is very limited, as discussed in Sect. 8.

Our tool handles any Java (byte)code acceptable by JPF (currently JPF fully supports Java 8 and most features of Java 11) that does not contain other forms of nondeterminism, such as concurrency, because such Java (byte)code gives rise to a probabilistic automaton [19] instead of a DTMC. Extending the tool so that it can handle other forms of nondeterminism is left for future research.

References

1. Arcaini, P., Gargantini, A., Riccobene, E.: Online testing of LTL properties for Java Code. In: Bertacco, V., Legay, A. (eds.) HVC 2013. LNCS, vol. 8244, pp. 95–111. Springer, Cham (2013). https://doi.org/10.1007/978-3-319-03077-7_7
2. Cheng, K.S.: Personal communication, October 2019
3. Clarke, E.M., Emerson, E.A.: Design and synthesis of synchronization skeletons using branching time temporal logic. In: Kozen, D. (ed.) Logic of Programs 1981. LNCS, vol. 131, pp. 52–71. Springer, Heidelberg (1982). https://doi.org/10.1007/BFb0025774
4. Cuong, N.A., Cheng, K.S.: Towards automation of LTL verification for Java Pathfinder. In: Proceedings of the 15th National Undergraduate Reseach Opportunities Programme Congress, Singapore, March 2010. National University of Singapore (2010)
5. Erdös, P., Rényi, A.: On random graphs I. Publ. Math. **6**, 290–297 (1959)
6. Fatmi, S.Z.: Probabilistic model checking of randomized Java code. Master's thesis, York University, Toronto, Canada, 2020
7. Floyd, R., Rivest, R.: Expected time bounds for selection. Commun. ACM **18**(3), 165–172 (1975)
8. Frieze, A.M.: Finding Hamilton cycles in sparse random graphs. J. Comb. Theor. Ser. B **44**(2), 230–250 (1988)
9. Giannakopoulou, D., Lerda, F.: From states to transitions: improving translation of LTL formulae to Büchi automata. In: Peled, D.A., Vardi, M.Y. (eds.) FORTE 2002. LNCS, vol. 2529, pp. 308–326. Springer, Heidelberg (2002). https://doi.org/10.1007/3-540-36135-9_20
10. Hansson, H., Jonsson, B.: A framework for reasoning about time and reliability. In: Proceedings of the 10th Real-Time Systems Symposium, pp. 102–111. IEEE, Santa Monica, CA, USA (1989)
11. Kähkönen, K., Lampinen, J., Heljanko, K., Niemelä, I.: The LIME interface specification language and runtime monitoring tool. In: Bensalem, S., Peled, D.A. (eds.) RV 2009. LNCS, vol. 5779, pp. 93–100. Springer, Heidelberg (2009). https://doi.org/10.1007/978-3-642-04694-0_7
12. Kwiatkowska, M., Norman, G., Parker, D.: PRISM 4.0: verification of probabilistic real-time systems. In: Gopalakrishnan, G., Qadeer, S. (eds.) CAV 2011. LNCS, vol. 6806, pp. 585–591. Springer, Heidelberg (2011). https://doi.org/10.1007/978-3-642-22110-1_47
13. Liang, S.: The Java Native Interface: Programmer's Guide and Specification. Addison-Wesley, Reading (1999)
14. Menezes, A.J., van Oorschot, P.C., Vanstone, S.A.: Handbook of Applied Cryptography. CRC Press, Baco Raton (1997)
15. Miller, G.L.: Riemann's hypothesis and tests for primality. In: Rounds, W.C., Martin, N., Carlyle, J.W., Harrison, M.A. (eds.) Proceedings of the 7th Annual ACM Symposium on Theory of Computing, pp. 234–239. ACM, Albuquerque, NM, USA, 1975
16. Motwani, R., Raghavan, P.: Randomized Algorithms. Cambridge University Press, New York (1995)
17. Pnueli, A.: The temporal logic of programs. In: Proceedings of the 18th Annual Symposium on Foundations of Computer Science, pp. 46–57. IEEE, Providence, RI, USA (1977)

18. Rabin, M.O.: Probabilistic algorithm for testing primality. J. Num. Theory **12**(1), 128–138 (1980)
19. Segala, R.: Modeling and verification of randomized distributed real-time systems. Ph.D. thesis, Massachusetts Institute of Technology, Cambridge, MA, USA (1995)
20. Solovay, R.M., Strassen, V.: A fast Monte-Carlo test for primality. SIAM J. Comput. **6**(1), 84–85 (1977)
21. Stolz, V., Bodden, E.: Temporal assertions using AspectJ. In: Barringer, H., Finkbeiner, B., Gurevich, Y., Sipma, H. (eds.) Proceedings of the 5th Workshop on Runtime Verification. ENTCS, vol. 144, pp. 109–124. Elsevier, Edinburgh, Scotland (2005)
22. Sutton, R., Barto, A.: Reinforcement Learning: An Introduction. MIT Press, Cambridge (2018)
23. Tang, Q.: Guiding probabilistic model checkers by reinforcement learning. Master's thesis, University of Oxford, Oxford, UK (2013)
24. Visser, W., Havelund, K., Brat, G., Park, S., Lerda, F.: Model checking programs. Autom. Softw. Eng. **10**(2), 203–232 (2003)
25. Dongkuan, X., Tian, Y.: A comprehensive survey of clustering algorithms. Ann. Data Sci. **2**(2), 165–193 (2015)
26. Zhang, X.: Checking progress of model checking randomized algorithms. Master's thesis, York University, Toronto, Canada (2010)
27. Zhang, X., van Breugel, F.: Model checking randomized algorithms with Java PathFinder. In: Proceedings of the 7th International Conference on the Quantitative Evaluation of Systems, pp. 157–158. IEEE, Williamsburg, VA, USA, September 2010
28. Zhang, X., van Breugel, F.: A progress measure for explicit-state probabilistic model-checkers. In: Aceto, L., Henzinger, M., Sgall, J. (eds.) ICALP 2011. LNCS, vol. 6756, pp. 283–294. Springer, Heidelberg (2011). https://doi.org/10.1007/978-3-642-22012-8_22

Case Studies

A Model-Checked I²C Specification

Lukas Humbel[✉], Daniel Schwyn, Nora Hossle, Roni Haecki, Melissa Licciardello, Jan Schaer, David Cock, Michael Giardino, and Timothy Roscoe

ETH Zurich, Zurich, Switzerland
{lukas.humbel,daniel.schwyn,nora.hossle,roni.haecki,
melissa.liccardello,jan.schaer,david.cock,michael.giardino,
timothy.roscoe}@inf.ethz.ch

Abstract. I²C is a pervasive bus protocol used for querying sensors and actuators, but it is plagued with incompatible devices, violating the specification at various levels.

Interacting with partially compliant devices poses several challenges. Compatibility of the controller interface, as well as the driver code, must be checked manually and potentially changed. This is a difficult process, as interactions with other bus devices must also be considered. We propose a model checking approach to quickly write high-assurance drivers and layers of the I²C stack. We do not propose a *single, true* formalization of I²C, but a framework that allows rapid modelling of non-compliant devices and verify the correct interaction with a host driver process.

Our contribution is twofold: First, we develop a framework that allows the specification of device and driver behavior together, and verification of their correct interaction. Second, we provide already verified, fine-grained building blocks, representing layers of the I²C stack that can be reused to interact with partially-compliant devices, as well as reducing model checking complexity.

Our specifications are stated in a machine-readable, executable, and layered DSL. From the DSL, we generate both Promela and C code. The Promela is used to apply model checking to ensure the layer implementations follow the abstract specifications. The C code is used to build and verify an EEPROM model and driver running on a Raspberry Pi.

Keywords: Model checking · Serial protocol · I2C · DSL · Layering

1 Introduction

We present a layered framework[1] for verifying implementations of the ubiquitous I²C protocol and provide initial layers of the I²C stack. Each layer has an executable implementation, formal specification, and the adherence of the implementation to the specification is model checked.

I²C is a low-speed bus that is a fundamental building block of almost all modern computer systems. It is used to network most integrated circuits and other

---

[1] Source code available http://github.com/lluki/filz.

© Springer Nature Switzerland AG 2021
A. Laarman and A. Sokolova (Eds.): SPIN 2021, LNCS 12864, pp. 177–193, 2021.
https://doi.org/10.1007/978-3-030-84629-9_10

devices in platforms ranging from mobile phone Systems-on-a-chip (SoCs) to server motherboards. It is also used as a sideband protocol in HDMI connections and memory DIMMs. While typically invisible to a machine's system software, I^2C is used by embedded *Baseboard Management Controllers* (BMCs) to control power and clock distribution to the rest of the computer system.

For this reason, I^2C is a critical (if often overlooked [1]) component. Incorrect programming of the I^2C network (e.g. misconfiguring a voltage regulator) can cause irrevocable hardware damage. Moreover, I^2C *controllers* (devices like the BMC, which initiate transactions on the network) have almost unrestricted visibility and authority over the hardware. To build a secure machine, board firmware (such as on the BMC) must be trusted. For systems as complex as modern computing platforms, real trust requires formal verification of the software stack. That, in turn, must be carried out in relation to a faithful model of the underlying hardware.

Unfortunately, I^2C is described in an ambiguous informal English-language document [13]. While almost all significant hardware components in a modern system talk I^2C, many interpret this standard differently, or only partially implement it.

Our I^2C specification is a first step in addressing this problem. Each logical layer in the I^2C protocol has a corresponding layer in the specification. At each layer, an abstract specification given as a single Promela process captures the correct behavior of the complete network (senders and receivers) at that layer. The lowest layer models electrical states on the bus and relies only on minimal timing assumptions.

In addition, deterministic, executable implementation specifications at each layer, written in a Domain Specific Language (DSL), describe end-point state machines, which are compiled into Promela. SPIN [9] is then used to verify that the abstract specification at each layer is correctly implemented by the composition of the implementations at all underlying layers. We generate C code from the executable specification which implements a complete, real-world I^2C stack. In Sect. 5.6 we show how to use this code to build a driver for an I^2C EEPROM.

Our specification can therefore serve as the basis for several applications and directions. Hardware designers can employ it as a rigorous, machine-checkable description of how compliant I^2C devices must behave, and generate high-coverage test suites for their designs. Firmware engineers can use it to generate functional, performant C code for parts of their stack, and build robust I^2C software implementations which can handle non-compliant devices in a robust and well-defined manner. Finally, for proof engineers seeking to do full-stack software verification of computer systems, we provide an abstract hardware model that captures the complexity of I^2C hardware on which to (partially) base refinement proofs of system software.

2   Background

I^2C is a de-facto standard [13] low-speed control bus used for connecting integrated circuits on a PCB and macrocells on an SoC. Board designers appreciate its efficiency since it uses only two shared wires, and allows much of the control sequencing of a computer system to be implemented in software by a BMC. In addition, the same bus can be used to both query sensors and control actuators, allowing for complex controller to be implemented efficiently. In this section, we describe the basic I^2C protocol stack and its implementation subtleties, which have motivated our specification.

An I²C bus has two wires, clock (SCL) and data (SDA), which are pulled up to the supply voltage. ICs may only drive the lines low, not high. I²C devices are either *controllers* or *responders*[2], and a bus can have multiple controllers and responders. Other devices (e.g. *multiplexers*), can connect different bus segments. Each responder has a bus-wide unique seven-bit address; some addresses are special and reserved. Communication is always initiated by a controller using the target responder's address.

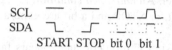

START STOP   bit 0   bit 1

Fig. 1. The four I²C bus symbols

The lowest level of the protocol uses the SCL and SDA wires to encode bits (0 or 1) and the start and end of a bus transaction as shown in Fig. 1. Outside of an I²C transaction, SCL is always high.

START/STOP conditions and the clock signal are generated by a controller. Responders signal a 0 bit by driving SDA low, a 1 bit by doing nothing. When a responder cannot provide the required data in a timely manner, it can perform *clock stretching* by driving SCL low during the clock low period, blocking the bus.

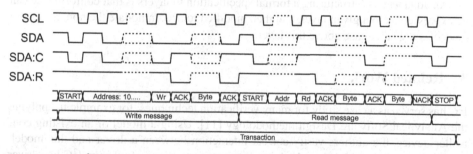

Fig. 2. Example I²C transaction with two messages: write one byte, then read two bytes. SDA:C and SDA:R are SDA signals asserted by controller and responder respectively. The address and byte transfers have been abbreviated.

Above the bit layer, I²C deals in *transactions* containing one or more *messages*, as shown in Fig. 2. Each message begins with a START condition, and the transaction ends with a STOP condition. After each START, the controller transmits the 7-bit responder address and a bit indicating READ or WRITE. If a responder with that address is present it acknowledges with a 0 bit (ACK), otherwise the controller sees a 1 bit (NACK). A message will not continue after a NACK. After an ACK, the message payload follows.

---

[2] In this paper, we will use the current, more precise terms 'controller' for 'master' and 'responder' for 'slave'.

If the controller sends a READ, the responder will respond to the controller with a sequence of bytes. Each byte is ACKed by the controller, otherwise the responder stops sending. Likewise, when the controller sends a WRITE, it is followed by zero or more bytes, each of which is ACKed by the responder.

The bus is only idle when both SDA and SCL are high. Collisions (two controllers starting to use the bus at the same time) are detected by a device seeing a 0 bit on the bus when it intended to transmit a 1 bit. In this case, the controllers stop transmitting and may retry the transaction later. An *undefined condition* [13, p. 12] occurs when START and STOP, START and a bit, or STOP and a bit are generated by different controllers simultaneously.

This is the complete, basic I²C protocol, and appears fairly straightforward. However, many devices deviate from this standard, making it hard to capture their behavior formally. For example, the hardware I²C controller in the *BCM2835* SoC (used in the Raspberry Pi 1) ignores *clock stretching* from responder devices [1], and cannot interoperate with devices that do so. The workaround is to ignore the hardware and implement the controller directly in software (known as "bit-banging"), a CPU-intensive technique. The *AS5011 Hall Sensor* [3] and the *CAT5259 Digital Potentiometer* [14] both ignore the READ/WRITE bit of a message and require every transaction to be a WRITE, while the *KS0127 video decoder* [2] ignores the STOP condition unless the controller can include it in a nonstandard position, and continues writing data on the bus. These examples are all violations of the informal protocol specification, but they occur at different layers (the bit, byte, and transaction layers).

An advantage of structuring a formal specification in layers is that conformance can be expressed up to a given layer, and then modified to accommodate the non-compliant device as a special-case above this layer.

3   Related Work

I²C has served as a case study for many verification techniques, for example in applying the Analytical Software Design methodology [11]. Using a model of an existing controller device, the authors verify correct interaction between a driver and this model. Similar, Bošnački *et al.* [6] study the concurrent interactions of a Linux I²C bus driver with hardware and syscalls. While our work overlaps in basic I²C properties, like adherence to the addressing mode, we specify and construct the controller itself. Finkbeiner *et al.* [7] study the information flow in an existing unverified I²C controller using Hyper-LTL, a logic that can reason about and quantify over the set of traces, and thus can correlate inputs and outputs. It is complementary to our work, since our specification could be verified against their information flow properties. In a simulation assisted verification approach [8] I²C is considered. The assumptions in this work differ from ours: The system under verification is treated as a black-box and simulation is used to reduce the state-space while our goal is to replace a black box with a specified, clear system. Bos *et al.* [5] proposes to express the I²C controller and devices in discrete time process algebra. Their work neither automatically verifies nor generates code. While they mention the ability to analyze deadlocks, they do not provide any conditions a higher-layer device must fulfill in order to guarantee deadlock freedom. In contrast our work's main focus is stating sufficient correctness properties for higher abstraction levels. *ACCESS.bus* is a standard that builds hotplug on top of I²C. Its handshake protocol has been model checked [4]. The I²C abstraction used is on a higher level (messages) than our model (down to level changes on the bus). Our work is complementary and could be used verify their assumptions. Other bus protocols that have been studied using model checking include the *CAN* bus [15] and the *AMBA* on chip bus [16]. These bus specification ensure more guarantees than I²C such as fault confinement, liveness, priority-based fairness.

4 Approach and Tools

We will illustrate our approach with an example with three layers: *electrical*, *bus*, and *nibble* layer. The **BusController** receives a 4-bit *nibble* from the **NibbleController** and writes it bitwise on the electrical layer. The **BusResponder** receives these bits from the electrical layer and returns the nibble to the **NibbleResponder**. The responder either ACKs or NACKs the message.

An example exchange is given below, between *bus* and *nibble* layers. We denote x receiving value y on the lower layer with $x{\uparrow}y$, while $x{\downarrow}y$ is x sending value y on the lower layer. c is the **NibbleController** and r is the **NibbleResponder**.

$$\ldots, c{\uparrow}\text{ACK}, c{\downarrow}3, r{\uparrow}3, r{\downarrow}\text{NACK}, c{\uparrow}\text{NACK}, \ldots$$

We see c receiving an ACK (presumably from the address phase), sending a payload nibble 3, which is received and NACKed by r, ending with the NACK arriving at c. The correctness statement for this layer is that any datum written by **NibbleController** will be received by **NibbleResponder**. We do so by ensuring that the message sequence produced by the implementation and an abstract process are equal.

We implement **BusController** (Listing 1.1) and **BusResponder** (Listing 1.2) in our DSL, whose semantics are based on coroutines. Coroutines can **call** other coroutines, and the callee executes until **yield**ing to the caller. The coroutine resumes at the last **yield** when called, with the local state preserved.

We implement the bus logic in process **El**. This calls **BusController** and **BusResponder** to get their current outputs, then combines these to compute the bus state (i.e. wired-AND—the bus is 0 if *any* agent drives it low).

We verify the correctness of **BusController** and **BusResponder** (see Listing 1.3) against **BusSpec**, a nondeterministic process capturing permissible bus behavior, and **NibbleValid**, which captures allowable event sequences from the next-highest level (i.e. what the bus layer may assume). Figure 3 depicts this.

BusSpec prescribes how actions *from* the nibble layer translate into events *to* the nibble layer e.g. the number 3 in the above example. **NibbleValid** includes all possible actions at the Nibble layer. It non-deterministically transmits a 4-bit nibble, which is either ACKed or NACKed (again non-deterministically). Correct delivery is guaranteed by **BusSpec**.

The verifier is an additional process that polls the message channels and forwards messages to both **BusSpec** and **BusImpl**. If both produce the same result, execution

```
proc (int) BusController(int res) {
    int data; int data_pos; int nibble_res;
    nibble_res = RES_ACK;
start:
    data = NibbleController(nibble_res);
    data_pos = 0;
    while(data_pos < 4){
        yield ((data >> (3-data_pos)) & 1);   //MSB first
        data_pos = data_pos + 1;        }
    yield (1);     // this reads back the ACK bit
    if(res == 0) {
        nibble_res = RES_ACK; goto start;
    } else {
        nibble_res = RES_NACK; goto start;      }
}
```

Listing 1.1. Bus Controller

```
proc (int) BusResponder(int res) {
    int buf; int read; int ack;
start:
    buf = 0; read = 0;
    while(read < 4){
        yield (1);
        assert(res == 0 or res == 1);
        buf = (buf << 1) | res;
        read = read + 1;        }
    (ack) = NibbleResponder(buf);
    yield (ack); goto start;
}
```

Listing 1.2. Bus Responder

continues, otherwise the verifier stalls (no transition/deadlock). Implementation correctness is then checked by using SPIN to verify the absence of deadlock in the combined process.

4.1   Programming Model, DSL, and Backends

As discussed, our DSL is based on coroutines. The language is (semantically) an executable subset of Promela with messages restricted to the **call** and **yield** primitives, and an acyclic call graph. These restrictions also allow for the generation of compact C code. Unlike existing C-to-Promela converters [10], we describe stateful processes (coroutines). Implicit state makes it convenient to express stateful protocols such as I^{2}C. Processes have state variables of type int or intarr (fixed-size array). No global

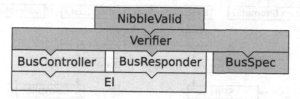

Fig. 3. Verification processes for verifying the Bus level. Gray processes are generated from the DSL; blue ones are expressed in Promela

```
1  proctype NibbleValid(chan ci, co, ri, ro) {
2      int c_res = RES_ACK; int dat;
3  start:
4      select(dat : 0..15);
5      ci?_; co!dat;
6      ri?_;
7      if
8      :: ro!ACT_ACK; c_res = RES_ACK; goto start;
9      :: ro!ACT_NACK; c_res = RES_NACK; goto start;
10     fi }
11
12 proctype BusControllerSpec(chan ci, co, ri, ro){
13     int dat; int res = RES_ACK;
14 start:
15     co!res; ci?dat;
16     ro!dat;
17     if
18     :: ri?ACT_ACK; res = RES_ACK; goto start;
19     :: ri?ACT_NACK; res = RES_NACK; goto start;
20     fi }
```

Listing 1.3. Bus example verification

variables are allowed. The size of `intarr` is implementation-defined, but guarded against overflow. The DSL supports `while`, `if` and `goto` as control flow.

The C backend translates a DSL process to a function and a process call into a function call. The backend assembles all state in a large static `struct`, kept intact between calls. To yield, a process is implemented as a large switch statement, with execution resuming at the most recent label.

From the language subset, Promela generation is straightforward. Each process has two channels: *input* and *output*. **Call**, sends arguments to the callee's input and blocks on the callee's output. Processes block on input until arguments arrive. **Yield** sends the result on the output channel.

Verification properties are specified directly in Promela, exploiting nondeterminism. The complete syntax of our DSL is expressed in Listing 1.4.

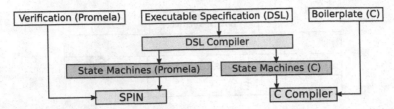

Fig. 4. Workflow of the user provided files (white), intermediary files (yellow), and tools (gray)

4.2   Calculus

We verify our layered system with the following calculus: Each layer has an implementation $LayerImpl_i$, a valid behavior $LayerValid_i$, and a specified behavior $LayerSpec_i$.

$LayerSpec_i$ is a state machine expressed as a function over its past result/action trace returning the next result symbol. $LayerSpec_i$ specifies the correct behavior at layer i.

$LayerValid_i$ is a predicate over the result/action trace that is true if the sequence is permissible at this layer and ends with an action symbol.

$LayerImpl_i$ has the same type as $LayerSpec_i$, except that it must be bound to a state machine of layer $i - 1$, which it can query to determine its next step. We denote the binding of this lower level state machine with $\circ$. $LayerImpl_0$ is the exception, which does not need to be bound.

As explained before, isolated specification is not possible, hence they operate on traces that include actions and results for both controller and responder.

In this calculus, our system is verified if it fulfills

$$\forall i. \forall \omega_i. LayerValid_{i+1}\omega_i \Rightarrow$$
$$LayerSpec_i\omega_i = (LayerImpl_i \circ LayerImpl_{i-1} \circ \ldots \circ LayerImpl_0)\omega_i$$

This verification procedure is depicted in Fig. 5 as an infinite sequence of directed messages $\omega = e_1, e_2, \ldots$. We denote the sequence of all messages as ω, and the sequence of messages exchanged between layer i and layer $i+1$ as ω_i. Examples of messages are the action to send an acknowledgement (represented by a down arrow $\downarrow$) or the receipt of an acknowledgment message (depicted as an up arrow $\uparrow$). Even though abstractly we deal simply with a trace of events, it is useful to denote if the message is destined for the controller or responder. We denote this with $c{\uparrow}x$ for a result with value x destined for the controller, and with $r{\uparrow}x$ a result x destined for the responder.

A $LayerImpl_i$ can not only be bound to other implementations, but also to a $LayerSpec_i$. We evaluate the verification time improvements of this in Sect. 6.

We verify this property by encoding it into Promela processes, such that a **verifier** process can not make progress when a violation has been found. Adherence to the protocol is shown by **verifier** always able to make progress. $LayerValid_i$ becomes a non-deterministic process, producing all valid actions. This action is sent to **verifier** which duplicates the action and sends it to both the $LayerSpec$ and the $LayerImpl$. If the $LayerSpec$ produces a result, the verifier ensures that the $LayerImpl$ produce the same result. If it differs, the verifier will not make progress. We also use this message

⟨*file*⟩   ::= (⟨*proc*⟩ | ⟨*procCopy*⟩)* 'EOF'

⟨*procCopy*⟩   ::= 'proccopy' ⟨*id*⟩ 'of' ⟨*id*⟩ ('where' (⟨*rename*⟩ (',' ⟨*rename*⟩)*)?)? ';'

⟨*proc*⟩   ::= 'proc' '(' (⟨*type*⟩ (',' ⟨*type*⟩)*)? ')' ⟨*id*⟩ '(' (⟨*varDecl*⟩ (',' ⟨*varDecl*⟩)*
)? ')' '{' (⟨*varDecl*⟩ ';')* ⟨*instr*⟩* '}'

⟨*rename*⟩   ::= ⟨*id*⟩ '=' ⟨*id*⟩

⟨*block*⟩   ::= '{' ⟨*instr*⟩* '}'

⟨*instr*⟩   ::= 'yield' (⟨*aEx*⟩ | '(' ⟨*aEx*⟩ (',' ⟨*aEx*⟩)+ ')') ';'
              | ⟨*varRef*⟩ '=' ⟨*aEx*⟩ ';'
              | ⟨*id*⟩ ':'
              | 'while' '(' ⟨*bEx*⟩ ')' ⟨*block*⟩
              | 'if' '(' ⟨*bEx*⟩ ')' ⟨*block*⟩ ('else' ⟨*block*⟩)?
              | 'goto' ⟨*id*⟩ ';'
              | 'assert' '(' ⟨*bEx*⟩ ')' ';'
              | (⟨*id*⟩ | '(' '(' ⟨*id*⟩ (',' ⟨*id*⟩)+ ')' ')') '=' ⟨*id*⟩ '(' (⟨*aEx*⟩ (',' ⟨*aEx*⟩)*)? ')' ';'

⟨*varDecl*⟩   ::= ⟨*type*⟩ ⟨*id*⟩

⟨*type*⟩   ::= 'intarr' | 'int'

⟨*cEx*⟩   ::= ⟨*aEx*⟩ ('>=' | '>' | '<=' | '<' | '==' | '!=') ⟨*aEx*⟩

⟨*bEx*⟩   ::= 'true' | 'false' | '(' ⟨*bEx*⟩ ')'
              | ⟨*bEx*⟩ ('and' | 'or') ⟨*bEx*⟩ | ⟨*cEx*⟩

⟨*aEx*⟩   ::= '(' ⟨*aEx*⟩ ')' | ⟨*varRef*⟩ | ('-'?['0'-'9']+) | ⟨*uOp*⟩ ⟨*aEx*⟩ | ⟨*aEx*⟩ ⟨*bOp*⟩ ⟨*aEx*⟩

⟨*bOp*⟩   ::= '&' | '|' | '*' | '/' | '+' | '-' | '<<' | '>>'

⟨*uOp*⟩   ::= '-' | '+'

⟨*varRef*⟩   ::= ⟨*id*⟩('[' ⟨*aEx*⟩ ']')?

⟨*id*⟩   ::= ⟨*char*⟩ (⟨*char*⟩ | ['0'-'9'] | '_')*

⟨*char*⟩   ::= ['a'-'z'] | ['A'-'Z']

Listing 1.4. Complete DSL syntax

dispatch to show liveness of the system, by marking it with a SPIN progress label and verifying the liveness check.

We currently do not verify that the layer implementation $LayerImpl_i$ adheres to $LayerValid_i$. Since we verify the full stack of implementations, we still do get the correctness guarantees, but it is possible, that in the middle of the implementation stack, the implementations rely on unspecified behavior.

5   The I^{2}C Model

5.1   Layering of I^{2}C

We divide our I^{2}C stack into the layers shown in Fig. 6, and we apply the verification principle from Sect. 4 at every layer.

The stack presented here includes two device-specific layers: World and Driver layer. We envision this process of device modelling and verification to be done for

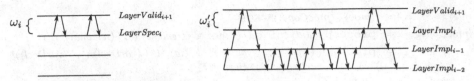

Fig. 5. Verification illustration, the system is verified if $\omega_i = \omega_i'$

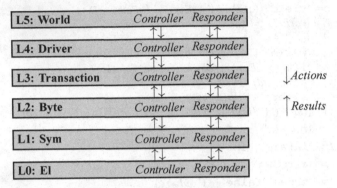

Fig. 6. Layering of the I^{2}C model.

each device that is connected to the bus. This also gives a high level of assurance for the device driver represented by Driver. But it is also feasible to directly interact in a system with, for example, the transaction layer and skip the verification of the higher layers.

5.2 Layer 0: Electrical Layer

The lowest layer, the electrical layer 0, is trusted. Hence it consists of only an *implementation*. It describes how two devices sending bus signals (a SCL/SDA pair, each 0 or 1) are combined into the next bus state, which is sent back to the devices. It does so by using the I^{2}C mandated AND combination of signals for each wire, which is a result of the active drive low logic.

We assume a reliable delivery of bits. Like prior work [5], we observe that I^{2}C bus events can be discretized. We assume sampling of the bus at the Nyquist frequency of the clock, such that two samples occur during a clock high period. This allows us to distinguish START and STOP conditions from BIT0 and BIT1.

5.3 Layer 1: Symbol Layer

Layer interface The symbol layer connects the electrical with the byte layer. It parses a sequence of bits into a symbol and vice-versa, turns a symbol into a bit sequence. The results and actions are depicted in Fig. 7. In addition to the I^{2}C symbols we define IDLE and STRETCH, which delay the next symbol.

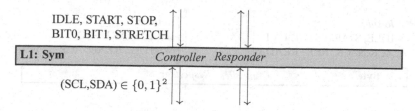

Fig. 7. Interface of the symbol layer. The label describes the datatype of all the channels in this layer.

The implementation differs for controller and responder, but they share a large part of the code (expressed as two sub-processes *SymbolReader* and *SdaDriver*) The controller is actively driving the clock (using a sub-process *SclDriver*). The responder is driving the clock only in one specfic case: When it is processing a STRETCH action, it will delay the clock rise by exactly one cycle. Both controller and responder are clock agnostic. For example the *SdaDriver* will wait until the clock rises and falls again, thus it is invariant against clock stretching. Both byte controller and byte responder are invoked in the same clock cycle. The exception again is during a STRETCH, which will produce an extra invocation in the next clock cycle.

The specification defines how two symbol actions are combined into a new one. In the initial, out-of-transaction state, two IDLE commands are combined into an IDLE result (i.e. $c{\downarrow}$IDLE, ..., $r{\downarrow}$IDLE will be followed by $c{\uparrow}$IDLE, ..., $r{\uparrow}$IDLE) as well as a START and a IDLE are combined into START (i.e. $c{\downarrow}$IDLE, ..., $r{\downarrow}$START will be followed by $c{\uparrow}$START, ..., $r{\uparrow}$START).

If a START result has been sent, the specification enters the in-transaction state. In this state, the following action combinations are valid. Note they are symmetrical, thus we skip the sender identifier as well as symmetrical cases.

- ${\downarrow}$BIT1, ${\downarrow}$BIT1 produces two ${\uparrow}$BIT1,
- ${\downarrow}$BIT0, ${\downarrow}$BIT1 produces two ${\uparrow}$BIT0,
- ${\downarrow}$BIT1, ${\downarrow}$START produces two ${\uparrow}$START,
- ${\downarrow}$BIT1, ${\downarrow}$STOP produces two ${\uparrow}$STOP, and enter out-of-transaction state.
- $r{\downarrow}$STRETCH is immediately followed by $r{\uparrow}$STRETCH, until r produces a non stretch action.

The valid actions of the next higher layer follow the same in- and out-transaction states as the specification. Outside a transaction, **ByteValid** either generates an IDLE pair to remain outside a transaction or initiates a transaction by allowing the controller to generate a START. In-transaction it generates a zero or more sequence of STRETCH, followed by all the valid symbol combinations.

5.4   L2: Byte Layer

Layer Interface I^{2}C is a byte-oriented protocol, where each byte is acknowledged. This layer reads and writes symbols, turning them into bytes. START and STOP conditions

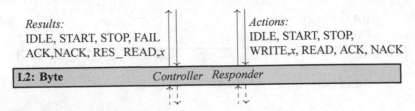

Fig. 8. Interface of the Byte layer. Both controller and responder have the same signature for *actions* and *results*.

are passed through: The higher layer must send START and STOP explicitly. The interface is depicted in Fig. 8.

The implementation does not distinguish between controller and responder. START and STOP actions are passed to the symbol layer directly, WRITE,x and READ operate bitwise (MSB first transmitted). If a written bit is not correctly transmitted, the layer will report FAIL and remain silent for the rest of the byte.

The specification describes how actions are combined into results. Controller and responder are not equal anymore; the controller must initiate the transaction. As in the symbol layer specification, an IDLE pair remains outside transaction and a START/IDLE is used to enter the in-transaction state. Within a transaction the following combinations hold

- $c{\downarrow}$ACT_WRITE, x and $r{\downarrow}$ACT_READ is followed by $r{\uparrow}$RES_READ, x, $r{\downarrow}$ACT_(N)ACK and $c{\uparrow}$RES_(N)ACK. Note that the variable x is bound, the written value must be the same as the read value.
- The symmetrical case of the above item where the controller reads and the responder writes.
- ACT_READ can also be combined with ACT_START and ACT_STOP. This is important for the responder, who can not predict the action of the controller, then ACT_READ is a safe choice.

The valid actions follow directly from the specification. All specified combinations are verified, with the caveat that the value of the written byte is constrained to a predefined set of 10 choices. In Sect. 6 we show the trade-offs to verify all values (0 to 255).

5.5 L3: Transaction Layer

I^2C defines the transaction format, such that a START condition must be followed by a 7-bit address and a direction bit. Then, depending on the direction bit, the controller reads or writes a sequence of bytes. This introduces an asymmetry: It is the controller that initiates a transaction, and the responder acts accordingly. Figure 9 shows all the actions and events processed at this layer. Starting from this layer, controller and responder have not only distinct specifications as before, but also distinct implementations. The responder also decodes a (currently fixed) I^2C address and ignores via NACKs all other addresses.

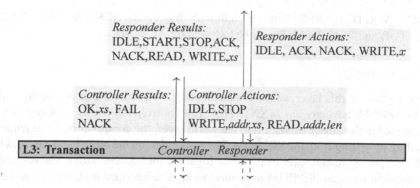

Fig. 9. Interface of the Transaction layer.

The implementation of the controller is fairly straightforward: Each higher level action is turned into a sequence of START and address byte with correct direction bit. If a write is requested, it continues to write the data. If a read is requested, it reads the desired number of bytes, sending an ACK for all except the last byte (per I^{2}C standard) which is answered with NACK that tells the responder to stop sending. If the responder receives a NACK, it is forwarded to the next higher layer.

The responder waits for a START, which is propagated to the driver. We propagate STARTs to the next higher layer to distinguish between two consecutive writes and a write – restart – write sequence. After a START, the responder reads the address byte, checks that the addresses match, and depending on the direction bit propagates either a RES_READ or a RES_WRITE. Since the responder cannot know how many bytes are read, we propagate each byte read request individually to the next level. Writes on the other hand can be buffered, until the controller is done. Then the whole array of written data is passed on.

The specification describes the interaction of driver layer actions. The sequence is determined solely by the controller: If it requests a WRITE of x bytes, we expect a RES_START from the responder, followed by x times a RES_READ. The responder either ACKs $x - 1$ times and then the controller will receive a RES_ACK, or if the responder decides to NACK before, the controller will receive a NACK.

The valid action sequences become conceptually simple but increasingly challenging to verify. The controller produces after a sequence of ACT_IDLE any combination of ACT_READ and ACT_WRITE until finally an ACT_STOP brings it back to the initial, out-of-transaction state. However the data that is either read or written is potentially infinite in length. Since we focused on the correct delivery of data at the lower layer, the verification cases for this layer focus on increasing the length of the transaction. Hence we show that for sequentially increasing payload of any length between 1 and 4 bytes our implementation conforms to the specification.

Conversely, the responder is completely driven by the result it receives. After a RES_START only ACT_IDLE is valid. After receiving START but before a STOP, the following combinations are valid: RES_READ followed by ACT_WRITE,x, RES_WRITE followed by ACT_ACK or ACT_NACK, RES_STOP, and RES_START must be followed by ACT_IDLE.

5.6   L4: Driver

Layer interface At this layer we start implementing the protocol that is specific to our model EEPROM, a Microchip 24XX16 [12]. The controller contains what typically is implemented in the device driver. From the world layer, the controller receives requests for reading or writing from the EEPROM. The responder, on the other hand, encodes the EEPROM-specific features, for example the logic for the address buffer. The responder forwards requests to an EEPROM implementation. The interface is shown in Fig. 10.

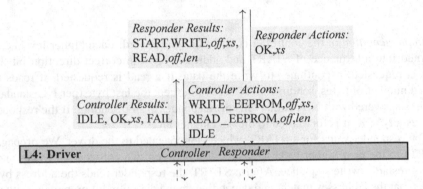

Fig. 10. Interface of the Driver layer.

The implementation of the controller turns an ACT_WRITE_EEPROM, parametrized by an *offset* and a data array, into a long write transaction. The first two bytes determine the EEPROM write offset followed by the data to be written. The data length is not communicated explicitly; if the data is written, the controller sends a STOP condition, signaling to the responder that the transaction is over. Reading works similarly: The controller issues two-byte write transaction followed by a *len*-long read transaction.

The responder behaves similarly. It waits for a START, then expects a write of at least two bytes. If more bytes follow, they are interpreted as a write transaction. It assembles the written data into a buffer and once the STOP condition arrives, passes it on (as RES_WRITE,xs) to the world layer. Read is more difficult, because by the time the first read byte must be supplied, the read length is unknown. Hence we assume there is a maximum read length, which we query from World (by issuing a RES_READ) then sending from this buffer.

The specification becomes fairly simple at this point. A controller ACT_WRITE,*off*,xs is turned into a responder RES_WRITE,*off*,xs. A controller ACT_READ,*off*,*len* becomes a RES_READ,*off*,*maxlen*, followed by a responder ACT_OK,xs, and a controller RES_OK,xs', where xs' is a prefix of xs with length *len*.

The valid action sequence is unconstrained at this point. The controller can choose between ACT_WRITE and ACT_WRITE, while the responder must subsequently receive RES_READ and RES_WRITE and reply with ACT_OK. However, we severely restrict the payload that is transmitted at this level by choosing one of 4 predefined datasets, to keep the full implementation verification time manageable.

5.7 L5: World

Since this is the highest layer, we can not verify the behavior given a higher layer behavior. We still provide a dummy implementation that performs a defined sequence of actions which is what we evaluate on our hardware platform.

6 Evaluation

6.1 Verification Runtime

The verification runtimes are evaluated on an AMD Ryzen 9 3900X with 32 GB of RAM running Ubuntu 20.04 with SPIN version 6.4.9.

Verification of the Symbol layer performs a complete state space search and finishes in 0.4 s. As mentioned in subsection 5.4, the byte layer is verified only on a small set of payload values, hence we would like to speed up the verification time. We can do so by replacing lower *LayerImpl* with *LayerSpec* (e.g. $LayerSpec_{byte} = LayerImpl_{byte} \circ LayerSpec_{sym}$ instead of $LayerSpec_{byte} = LayerImpl_{byte} \circ \ldots \circ LayerImpl_0$).

Table 1 shows the verification times using this method. The speedup factor depends on the layer complexity. Replacing the rather complex **Symbol** with **SymbolSpec** leads to a speedup of $10\times$, replacing **Byte** with **ByteSpec** leads to $5\times$ speedup.

Table 1. Verification time in seconds using different layers of abstraction.

	Full Implementation	SymbolSpec	ByteSpec	TransactionSpec
Symbol	0.1			
Byte	9.0	0.7		
Transaction	69.4	8.7	1.8	
Hl	62.9	6.7	1.0	0.3

Instead of decreasing verification time, this technique can be used to increase the search space size. For example the **Byte** layer can be completely verified (i.e. checking all 256 values for a byte write as well as for a byte read) using **SymbolSpec** in about 70 s.

6.2   Execution on a Raspberry Pi

Our DSL can generate C code for the deterministic state machines. Conceptually, the C code can interact with any layer directly. For example, it could get output from the transaction layer and translate it into Linux I^2C API calls. However to profit most from the verification, the whole stack (excluding the electrical layer) can be executed. This leads to an interface that only writes and reads SDA/SCL as high/low states from the bus. We demonstrate this using the Linux GPIO interface connected to an I^2C EEP-ROM. The boilerplate code runs in an infinite loop: reading the bus state, forwarding it to the controller state machine, reading back the command, and outputting it on the GPIOs. In conformance with the I^2C specification we actively drive the data and clock line low on zero. If a one is to be written, we set the pin to a high impedance state. The process repeats after an appropriate delay accounting for the required setup and hold time.

We currently hardcode the testcase in the World implementation. To expose an interface, we would also replace the highest layer with boilerplate C code that would e.g. do non-blocking reads from a UNIX pipe do receive the commands to be sent.

The total required boilerplate code consists of 128 lines of code; most of it implements interfacing with Linux's file-based `sysfs` GPIO interface. The generated I^2C state machine code consists of 2678 lines and compiles to a binary of 32 KB.

7   Conclusion and Future Work

We have successfully demonstrated that our approach of creating and verifying layered specifications for I^2C is feasible, and that it can be used to express bus interactions on a high level, to specify the expected behavior, and to verify that the specification fulfills this property. Furthermore, the executable specification can be used to generate code, which interacts with real physical devices.

While this work has already proven to verify desirable properties in a specific scenario, we cannot yet claim full generalization. We have empirically considered partially-conforming devices, but we did not formally model them at this stage. We expect the specification to be extended, but no change in the methodology nor the lower layers should be necessary. I^2C features we do not yet handle include broadcast, variable length read transactions and multi controller.

So far, we generate C code. In future work, we plan to generate synthesizable hardware descriptions, producing verified FPGA or even ASIC implementations. While we do not expect any problems with the state machine generation itself, we will also need to generate and verify the corresponding hardware-software interface.

From a theoretical perspective, we so far assumed that our layer calculus itself is correct, i.e. we assumed that a layer that follows the specification can be combined with any (lower and higher) layer that also fulfills the layer contract. Given the higher order nature of this, we think that either an embedding in an existing process calculus or a from-scratch formalization in an interactive theorem prover would be interesting. The second option would also open the possibility to reason about the system not only in a model checker, but in a theorem prover. This could lift the restriction that we verify only on a small set of payloads, at the cost of some manual proof engineering.

References

1. Raspberry Pi I2C clock-stretching bug. https://www.advamation.com/knowhow/raspberrypi/rpi-i2c-bug.html. Accessed 01 Apr 2021
2. Video capture driver (video for linux 1/2). https://git.kernel.org/pub/scm/linux/kernel/git/stable/linux.git/tree/drivers/media/i2c/ks0127.c?h=v5.8.3. Accessed 01 Apr 2021. Unfortunately the datasheet is not public
3. AMS AG. AS5011 Low power Integrated Hall IC for human interface applications, Rev. 3.6 (2009)
4. Boigelot, B., Godefroid, P.: Model checking in practice: an analysis of the ACCESS.bus^{TM} protocol using SPIN. In: Gaudel, M.-C., Woodcock, J. (eds.) FME 1996. LNCS, vol. 1051, pp. 465–478. Springer, Heidelberg (1996). https://doi.org/10.1007/3-540-60973-3_102
5. Bos, S.H.J., Reniers, M.A.: The I2C-bus in discrete-time process algebra. Sci. Comput. Program. **29**(1–2), 235–258 (1997)
6. Bošnački, D., Mathijssen, A., Usenko, Y.S.: Behavioural analysis of an I^{2}C linux driver. In: Alpuente, M., Cook, B., Joubert, C. (eds.) FMICS 2009. LNCS, vol. 5825, pp. 205–206. Springer, Heidelberg (2009). https://doi.org/10.1007/978-3-642-04570-7_18
7. Finkbeiner, B., Rabe, M.N., Sánchez, C.: Algorithms for model checking HyperLTL and HyperCTL*. In: Kroening, D., Păsăreanu, C.S. (eds.) CAV 2015. LNCS, vol. 9206, pp. 30–48. Springer, Cham (2015). https://doi.org/10.1007/978-3-319-21690-4_3
8. Gorai, S., Biswas, S., Bhatia, L., Tiwari, P., Mitra, R.S.: Directed-simulation assisted formal verification of serial protocol and bridge. In: Proceedings of the 43rd Annual Design Automation Conference, DAC 2006, pp. 731–736. Association for Computing Machinery, New York, NY, USA (2006)
9. Holzmann , G.J., Lieberman, W.S.: Design and Validation of Computer Protocols, vol. 512. Prentice hall Englewood Cliffs (1991)
10. Jiang, K., Jonsson, B.: Using spin to model check concurrent algorithms, using a translation from C to promela. In: MCC 2009, pp. 67–69. Department of Information Technology, Uppsala University (2009)
11. Klomp, A., Roebbers, H.W., Derwig, R., Bouwmeester, L.: Designing a mathematically verified I2C device driver using ASD. In: CPA, pp. 105–116 (2009)
12. Microchip. 24XX16: 16K I2C Serial EEPROM (2019)
13. NXP Semiconductors. I2C-bus specification and user manual, Rev. 6 (2014)
14. ON Semiconductor. CAT5259 Quad DigitalPotentiometer (POT) with 256 Tapsand I2C Interface, Rev. 11 (2013)
15. Pan, C., Guo, J., Zhu, L., Shi, J., Zhu, H., Zhou, X.: Modeling and Verification of CAN Bus with Application Layer using UPPAAL. Electr. Not. Theoret. Comput. Sci. **309**, 31–49 (2014)
16. Roychoudhury, A., Mitra, T., Karri, S.R.: Using formal techniques to debug the amba system-on-chip bus protocol. In: 2003 Design, Automation and Test in Europe Conference and Exhibition, pp. 828–833 (2003)

Author Index

Printed in the United States
by Baker & Taylor Publisher Services